Acclaim for *Provocations*

Richard Mouw, Fuller Theological Seminary
Kierkegaard's writings seem to get more "contemporary" every year. This well-selected collection of writings should be read and re-read by everyone who is attempting to minister to our present generation.

William Willimon, Duke University Chapel
Moore has done us a great service in sifting through Kierkegaard and giving us his essential writings. Here is a book to be savored, enjoyed, and yes, provoked by.

Donald Bloesch, author, *The Crisis of Piety*
An important and helpful guide to Kierkegaard's spirituality.

Gregory A. Clark, North Park University
Since Kierkegaard scholarship has become a cottage industry, it is has become possible to exchange Kierkegaard's passion for a passion for Kierkegaard's works. Moore's introduction and collection retrieve the passion that animates Kierkegaard himself. That passion, with all its force, still addresses the reflective reader.

Vernon Grounds, Chancellor, Denver Seminary
The editor needs to be congratulated on discerning in the overwhelming task of choosing the best when everything is of the highest quality. This book is an outstanding addition to Kierkegaard publications. It will influence readers to become enthusiastic students of his Christ-centered thought.

Daniel Taylor, author, *The Myth of Certainty*
I discover in Kierkegaard an honesty, passion, and insight into the human condition and the life of faith that speaks to my deepest needs. Kierkegaard is one of a small handful of thinkers with whom every reflective Christian must come to terms.

Clark H. Pinnock, author, *Flame of Love*
Provocations brings Søren Kierkegaard, a fountain of deep wisdom and radical faith, to readers who might otherwise have difficulty understanding him. Here one finds many solid and well-chosen excerpts from across the entire literary corpus of this most paradoxical prophet and insightful philosopher.

Arthur F. Holmes, author, *Fact, Value, and God*
...Provides a helpful overview of Kierkegaard's thinking that cannot be gained from reading just one or two of his books. *Provocations* captures his spirit and core concerns without neglecting lesser themes, while preserving his style and readying the reader for his major works.

Diogenes Allen, author, *Spiritual Theology*
A comprehensive selection from Kierkegaard's massive output, arranged so as to give the reader an appreciation of the main themes and preoccupations of Kierkegaard's thought.

Colin Brown, Fuller Theological Seminary
Moore has provided enough introductory material to enable the reader to understand Kierkegaard's thought in the context of his life and times. Otherwise, his judicious selection lets the texts speak for themselves. Here is a book for meditation, for quiet reading, for faith and for understanding.

Kelly James Clark, author, *When Faith Is Not Enough*
With its excellent introduction and astute selections of texts, this book unleashes the ferociously important Kierkegaard. This work admirably clarifies Kierkegaard's often opaque but passionate thoughts on faith, freedom, and the meaning of life.

PROVOCATIONS

PROVOCATIONS

Spiritual Writings of Kierkegaard

Compiled and Edited by
Charles E. Moore

THE PLOUGH PUBLISHING HOUSE

©1999 by The Plough Publishing House
of The Bruderhof Foundation
Farmington PA 15437 USA
Robertsbridge East Sussex TN32 5DR UK
All Rights Reserved

06 05 04 03 02 01 00 99   10 9 8 7 6 5 4 3

A catalog record for this book is available
from the British Library.

Library of Congress Cataloging-in-Publication Data

Kierkegaard, Søren, 1813–1855.
   [Selections. English. 1999]
   Provocations: spiritual writings of Kierkegaard/Søren
  Kierkegaard; compiled and edited by Charles E. Moore.--1st ed.
        p.   cm.
   Includes bibliographical references and index.
   ISBN 0-87486-981-1 (pbk.)
      1. Christian life--Lutheran authors. 2. Spiritual life-
 -Christianity. I. Moore, Charles E., 1956–. II. Title.
 BV4501.2.K4885213   1999
 248.4'841--dc21   99-28648
                                                        CIP

Printed in the USA

Table of Contents

Introduction

Søren Kierkegaard has been accused of being one of the most frustrating authors to read. He has also been praised as one of the most rewarding. Frustrating, because his style is so dense, his thought so complex, and his words so harsh. Rewarding, because embedded within his writings and journals are metaphors and truths so deep and vivid that they can overwhelm you with an almost blinding clarity. Kierkegaard is not one to be read lightly, lest you get burned.

The purpose of this collection is twofold. The first is to make Kierkegaard accessible. Even for the brightest, Kierkegaard is tough going. Walter Lowrie, Kierkegaard's most devoted biographer, writes: "Kierkegaard exacts of his reader a very great effort. He declines to make things easy for him by presenting a 'conclusion,' and he obliges him, therefore, to approach the goal by the same difficult path he himself has trod."

Even Kierkegaard's fellow Danes found him difficult. This is unfortunate. Contained within his writings are some of the richest, most illuminating passages on faith and commitment ever penned. To help unearth some of these treasures, I have taken the liberty to abridge lengthy pieces, paraphrase complex passages, and tighten and simplify convoluted constructions.

Secondly, this collection is meant to present in as concise a way as possible the "heart" of Kierkegaard. By heart I mean first those pieces that are concerned with the core themes of his prolific output, second, those that exemplify the essence of his thought, and last but not least, his passion.

Kierkegaard's Central Passion

Kierkegaard wrote industriously and rapidly, and under a variety of pen-names, presenting various esthetic, ethical, and religious viewpoints on life. His writings display such a wide range of genre and style, and his thought covers such a variety of subjects that even he himself felt compelled to write a book to explain his agenda. Despite this, Kierkegaard was single mindedly driven. He writes in his Journal: "The category for my undertaking is: to make people aware of what is essentially Christian." Two things are noteworthy. First, Kierkegaard aims to make us *aware*. "I have worked for a restlessness oriented toward inward deepening." "My whole life is an epigram calculated to make people aware." In short, Kierkegaard's task was not the introduction of new ideas, a theology or philosophy of life. Rather, he said "My task is in the service of truth; and its essential form is obedience." Kierkegaard was fundamentally existential: "to keep people awake, in order that religion may not again become an indolent habit…" His aim was to provoke the individual so as to become an individual in the truth. The last thing Kierkegaard wanted to do was to leave his reader the same – intellectually enlightened yet inwardly unchanged.

Early in his life, Kierkegaard made the discovery that one must "find a truth which is true *for me* – the idea for which I can live and die." Part of the human predicament was that we are all interested in far too many things and thus are not decidedly committed to any one thing. As he writes in his Journal:

> What I really lack is to be clear in my mind *what I am to do,* not what I am to know, except in so far as a certain understanding must precede every action. The thing is to understand myself, to see what

God really wishes *me* to do…What good would it do me if the truth stood before me, cold and naked, not caring whether I recognized her or not, and producing in me a shudder of fear rather than a trusting devotion? Must not the truth *be taken up into my life?* That is what I now recognize as the most important thing.

Kierkegaard's central task as an author, therefore, was to help the reader make the truth his own. He deliberately and carefully plotted his entire authorship to show his readers what it means to exist, and what inwardness and subjectivity signify. His strategy was to help them take a decisive stand: "I wish to make people aware so that they do not squander and dissipate their lives."

Secondly, Kierkegaard is concerned with what is essentially Christian: "Through my writings I hope to achieve the following: to leave behind me so accurate a characterization of Christianity and its relationships in the world that an enthusiastic, noble-minded young person will be able to find in it a map of relationships as accurate as any topographical map from the most famous institutes."

Of what does this map consist? In *Practice of Christianity*, Kierkegaard writes: "If anything is to be done, one must try to introduce Christianity into Christendom." The backdrop to his entire authorship was a Danish Lutheranism that had degenerated into a nominal state-religion. Three things, in particular, marred the church of his day: (1) Intellectualism – the "direct mental assent to a sum of doctrines"; (2) Formalism – "battalions upon battalions" of unbelieving believers; and (3) Pharisaism – a herd of hypocritical clergy that ignore the Christianity they were hired to preach. It was in this climate that Kierkegaard felt compelled to reintroduce Christianity. He sought to provide a kind of map that would, for the sake of Christian truth, steer people away from Christendom. "An apostle's task is to spread

Christianity, to win people to Christianity. My task is to disabuse people of the illusion that they are Christians – yet I am serving Christianity."

By Christianity Kierkegaard did not mean a system of correct doctrine or a set of behaviors: "The struggle is not between orthodoxy and heterodoxy. My struggle, much more inward, is about the *how* of the doctrine. I say that someone can accept the whole doctrine, but in presenting it he destroys it." Kierkegaard's contention was that despite sound doctrine, or the *what* of faith, "the lives people live demonstrate that there is really no Christianity – or very little." Genuine Christianity, according to Kierkegaard, is anything but doctrine. It is a way of being in the truth before God by following Jesus in self-denial, sacrifice, suffering, and by seeking a primitive relationship with God. Unfortunately, doctrine is what people want. And the reason for this is "because doctrine is the indolence of aping and mimicking for the learner, and doctrine is the way to power for the teacher, and doctrine collects people."

Kierkegaard's thinking originated in a violent revulsion for the spurious spirituality of his day. His difficulty was to find a way out of the confusion that consistently undermined anything truly Christian. How in the world are we to get out of the mess of Christendom, he wondered, when millions, due to the accident of geography, are Christians? How are we to get Christendom to drop its whole mass of nominal members when "it is the interest of the clergyman's trade that there be as many Christians as possible?" How, exactly, are we to *become* Christian, especially when "one is a Christian of a sort?"

Kierkegaard's strategy was to act as a corrective. He explains: "The person who is to provide the corrective must study the weak sides of the established order scrupulously and penetratingly and then one-sidedly present the opposite – with expert one-sidedness." This revelation is important to keep in mind while reading Kierkegaard. All the same he said, "a corrective made into the norm is by that very fact confusing." Therefore, one should not lift his thought up and turn it into a norm. He felt his situation to be desperate, so he sounded the alarm accordingly. Yet he did not do this as some self-proclaimed prophet. He wrote as one who was without authority and who himself needed reforming: "What I have said to myself about myself is true – I am a kind of secret agent in the highest service. The police use secret agents, too…But the police do not think of reforming their secret agents. God does."

Kierkegaard was adamant about his own Christian deficiency: "For my part I do not call myself a 'Christian' (thus keeping the ideal free), but I am able to make it evident that the others are still less than I." This is not meant as a judgment. Kierkegaard's hope was to arouse, to expose the deception he, as well as everyone else, was under. He never felt worthy of doing this. But he was compelled to strike out. "I want to make the crowd aware of their own ruin. Understand me – or do not misunderstand me. I do not intend to strike them (alas, one cannot strike the crowd) – no, I will constrain them to strike me."

Kierkegaard in Context

In reading Kierkegaard it would be a mistake to ignore the inner anguish of his own personal life. The currents of his thought spring forth from within, as much as they do from his broader cultural setting. Although a complete biography of Kierkegaard is beyond the scope of this introduction, it is important for our purposes to understand the four significant crisis relationships in his life. These relationships constitute Kierkegaard the man, and grasping them is paramount in understanding him as a writer.

The Earthquake

Kierkegaard's father, Michael Pedersen Kierkegaard, was 57, his mother, Ane Sørensdatter Kierkegaard, 45, when he was born in 1813. Outwardly his childhood was happy and calm. Morally and intellectually he was formed by his father, and he could afterwards say that "everything was done to develop his mind as richly as possible." Because he was his father's youngest child and his favorite, the intimacy between them was great. But Kierkegaard describes his upbringing as "an insane upbringing." His father was a pietistic, gloomy spirit, an old man whose melancholy sat like a weight on his children.

Kierkegaard's family was plagued by both physical and psychological instability. Only two of the children lived past age thirty-four. Three of his sisters, then two of his brothers, then his mother, had died in rapid succession. Kierkegaard's father was convinced that he would outlive all of his children, a conviction his son apparently shared. Kierkegaard's brother Peter was forced to resign his position as bishop because of emotional difficulties. Inwardly, Kierkegaard felt a gnawing sense of "silent despair." From childhood on he always felt under the power of "a monstrously brooding temperament." In an 1846 journal entry he reflects:

An old man who himself was extremely melancholy gets a son in his old age who inherits all this melancholy – but who also has a mental-spiritual elasticity enabling him to hide his melancholy. Furthermore, because he is essentially and eminently healthy of mind and spirit, his melancholy cannot dominate him, but neither is he able to throw it off; at best he manages to endure it.

Early on Kierkegaard realized that there was a strange inconsistency between his father's piety and his inner unrest. In another journal entry he writes:

The greatest danger for a child, where religion is concerned, is not that his father or teacher should be an unbeliever, not even his being a hypocrite. No, the danger lies in their being pious and God-fearing, and in the child being convinced thereof, but that he should nevertheless notice that deep within there lies hidden a terrible unrest. The danger is that the child is provoked to draw a conclusion about God, that God is not infinite love.

Eventually, a break occurred between Kierkegaard and his father (1835). It was no doubt related to his father's confession of his childhood cursing of God and of his sexual impropriety. (Kierkegaard's mother, his father's second wife, had been one of the family's maids. Kierkegaard's father had seduced her, discovered she was pregnant, and felt compelled to marry her.) On discovering the reality of his father's weaknesses – Kierkegaard had always admired his strict piety – he was shattered. As he described it later, the revelation was "a great earthquake, a terrible upheaval that suddenly forced on me a new and infallible interpretation of all phenomena." At first, the discovery disturbed Kierkegaard's entire moral outlook, throwing him into a period of dissipation and despair during which he completely neglected his theological studies at the University. Eventually, however, Kierkegaard began to suspect that his life was to be spent for some extraordinary purpose.

Prior to the death of Kierkegaard's father (1838), the two managed to reconcile. Kierkegaard realized that his father had left an indelible mark on his life. His call to a life of religious service, his intellectual gifts, his sense of absolute obedience, and even his melancholy were all part of an inheritance for which he came to be grateful. He saw that he had been mistaken concerning his family's curse and now felt under obligation to redeem his promise to his father and complete his university studies, which he did over the next two years.

Broken Engagement

At this time Kierkegaard became engaged to sixteen-year-old
Regine Olsen, whom he had felt attracted to for little over a
year. Next to his father, no aspect of Kierkegaard's life is as important as was his relationship to Regine. The day after his engagement, however, Kierkegaard felt he had made a mistake: He
saw that he could never conquer his melancholy and felt unable
to confide in Regine as to the causes of it. "I would have to keep
too much from her, base the whole marriage on a lie."

To break off an engagement was in those days a serious matter, and socially speaking, placed the woman in an unfavorable
light. To save Regine, therefore, Kierkegaard resolved to take all
the blame on himself for the broken engagement. This he did in
the most bizarre manner: for the next several months he posed
as an irresponsible philanderer, noisily showing off in public
and striving to turn appearances against himself by every
means in his power. Not surprisingly, he quickly aroused the in-
dignation of public opinion and the disapproval of friends.
Everyone was fooled, except Regine. When the break finally
came in 1841, he wrote: "When the bond broke, my feeling was
this: either to plunge into wild dissipation, or into absolute
religiousness – though of a different kind from that of the
parson's."

Kierkegaard chose the latter. But he also chose something
else: the writer's life. "From that moment, I dedicated my life
with every ounce of my poor ability to the service of an idea."
Less than a month after breaking off his engagement Kierkegaard sailed for Berlin, where he began to write. It came over
him like a torrent, driving him incessantly on during the next
ten years – a period in which he produced thirty-five books and
twenty volumes of journals (In 1843 he published no fewer than
six books, the first being his biggest, *Either/Or*).

The "Corsair" Affair

Kierkegaard's authorship proceeded along two lines, the aesthetic and the religious. The purpose of the first was "to represent the various life-views on existence." Using pen-names and an "indirect method," Kierkegaard sought to beguile his reader into the truth. His strategy was one of "entrapment" – to surround the reader with the alternatives before him, put them in contradiction to each other, and then help him see the many false ultimates by which people live their lives.

As for the second, Kierkegaard authored a string of discourses and works intended to enlighten readers by making them directly aware of what the Christian ideal really was. As far as Kierkegaard's writing went, he was able to realize this goal; as for his reception as a thinker with something serious to say, things took an unexpected twist: *The Corsair,* a gossipy tabloid weekly, reviewed *Either/Or* in such a way that Kierkegaard felt he had been made a laughingstock.

In actual fact, Goldschmidt, the publisher of *Corsair,* admired Kierkegaard's intellectual and writing gifts; after the publication of *Either/Or* he even hosted a banquet in Kierkegaard's honor. Yet Kierkegaard, offended by all the attention, tried to distance himself from the "scandalous" paper and did not attend. On top of that, he sought to retaliate by publishing a caustic pseudonymous article, which let loose a fire storm of fury that lasted well over a year. Week after week Kierkegaard was ridiculed, caricatured, parodied. His long nose, thin legs and the uneven length of his trousers became a standing joke. His wealth and his alms-giving, his drives and his walks were all over-exaggerated and discussed in detail.

Kierkegaard was deeply hurt. Publicly, he displayed indifference, but his journals refer to the incident for the next three years and show a deep hurt. He became an object of ridicule, with a nickname: "Either-or". Secretly, he complained that his little article created "more of a sensation...than all my writing put together." "I am positive that my whole life will never be as important as my trousers."

The *Corsair* affair embittered Kierkegaard and drove him once and for all to pen and paper. There could be no thought of retiring to a peaceful parsonage in the country. That would be fleeing from persecution. In fact, Kierkegaard felt that the event was providential, insofar as it clarified and affirmed his assertion that Christianity and "the public" are opposite terms. He now saw that God had entrusted him with a specific mission: to speak directly to his contemporaries about the colossal deception of Christendom. In the end, the incident only "put new strength into my instrument, forced me to publish even more."

Attack Upon Christendom

The event that brought Kierkegaard's attack upon Christendom to a head-on collision was the death of Bishop Mynster. Mynster, the Primate of the Danish Church, had been a family friend and pastor for many years, and Kierkegaard revered him highly. But after Kierkegaard published *Practice in Christianity*, which attacks clerical Christianity, Mynster was incensed, and the two became irreparably estranged.

In January, 1854, Mynster died. Martensen, Mynster's successor, declared Mynster to be "one of the holy chain of witnesses for the truth which extends through the centuries down from the time of the Apostles." The claim pushed Kierkegaard over the edge. It seemed like blasphemy, a corruption of all Christian values, to speak of Mynster in such a way. "Bishop Mynster a witness for the truth!" he exploded. "You who read this, you know well what in a Christian sense is a witness for the truth... It is absolutely essential to suffer for the teaching of Christianity. The truth is that Mynster was worldly-wise – weak, plea-sure-seeking, and was great only as a declaimer."

In a series of pamphlets entitled *The Instant*, Kierkegaard now turned agitator and addressed himself directly to the people. Little by little, Christianity had been weakened by removing all the difficulties of faith. "In the splendid palace chapel a stately court preacher, the cultivated public's elite, advances before an elite circle of fashionable and cultivated people and preaches emotionally on the text of the Apostle, 'God chose the lowly and despised' – and nobody laughs!" "This is the falsification of which official Christianity is guilty: it does not make known the Christian requirement – perhaps because it is afraid people would shudder to see at what a distance from it we are living." Here Kierkegaard broke with all that had gone before; he was now engaged "not in communication, but assault." "Strictly speaking, it is not I who am ringing the alarm bell; I am starting the fire in order to smoke out illusions and knavish tricks; it is a police raid, and a Christian police raid, for, according to the New Testament, Christianity is incendiarism."

The swiftness and mercilessness of his attack seem to have left his contemporaries without a defense. But the immense ex-ertions of the last months shattered him too. His strength, as well as his money, was gone. After fainting in the streets of Copenhagen on October 2, 1855, he was hospitalized.

Kierkegaard died on November 11, 1855. To the end, Kierke-gaard would not retract a word he wrote and refused commun-ion from a priest. He was at peace, he said, and felt his life's calling had been fulfilled. Dying was but a crown on his work.

Basic Themes

The story of Kierkegaard's life is actually the inward drama of a deeply religious thinker. His relationships with his father,

Regine, Goldschmidt, and Mynster were such that they turned his inner anguish into a kind of redemptive suffering on behalf of his contemporaries. In the crucible of his melancholy and in the chamber of his own relationship with God, there emerged a vision of faith and earnestness that influenced some of the greatest thinkers in the twentieth century.

Kierkegaard's thought, however, cannot be easily categorized. Some see him as the originator of Existentialism. Others identify him as a mystic. Still others argue that he was a quintessential ascetic. One thing is clear: Kierkegaard stands against every form of thinking that bypasses the individual or enables the individual to escape his responsibility before God. He also made an absolute demand that "idea" should be translated into existence (being and doing), which is exactly what his contemporaries, in his opinion, failed to do: "Most systematizers stand in the same relation to their systems as the man who builds a great castle and lives in an adjoining shack; they do not live in their great systematic structure. But in spiritual matters this will always be a crucial objection. Metaphorically speaking, a person's ideas must be the building he lives in – otherwise there is something terribly wrong."

This does not mean that Kierkegaard advocated a loose string of contradictory ideas. Far from it! His thought possesses an intricate pattern. He carefully weaves together numerous themes, and does so in such a way that the reader is left with clear options. But these options are not in terms of beliefs or theories. These would only rob life of its tension. Again, Kierkegaard's primary aim was to excite the reader to choose – to force the reader into self-examination. This has to be kept in the forefront whenever an attempt is made to summarize his thought.

In what follows I hope to place Kierkegaard in the context of certain recurring themes in his writings, and thus provide context for the selections of this book.

The Spheres of Existence

To become a genuine self, an individual in the truest sense, was of central concern to Kierkegaard. He often wrote of "stages on life's ways" or "spheres of existence" – different levels on which people live out their lives: the aesthetic, the ethical, and the religious. To become genuinely human, as a Christian individual, involves a movement toward the religious sphere of existence, a sphere that includes but also transcends the other two spheres.

The aesthetic life is life immediately lived – a life lived for "the moment." It is the lifestyle in which people are absorbed in satisfying their "natural" desires and impulses, whether physical, emotional, or intellectual. These people are solely concerned with their own happiness and believe that the key to happiness is found in externals – who they know, what they do, the roles they play, what they possess, where they live, and so on. They live for enjoyment, on the surface of life. They are observers, spectators, tasters, but not serious participants. They have no real inner life, no real self to offer to others. Their well-being is determined by the choices or moods of others and by forces that extend beyond their control. When they make decisions, they are not internalized. Thus, when things go wrong, aesthetic persons never accept responsibility or blame. Such people are apathetic, indifferent, and unintegrated. They are unable to commit themselves to any one thing. Something better might always come along, and so they split their energies in different directions.

The aesthetic life is certainly not restricted to the senses. Kierkegaard also criticizes the philosopher who is solely concerned

with ideas – intellectual systems that leave the thinker unchanged, with no reason to choose this or that. For Kierkegaard,
Hegel is the typical speculative thinker. Like all intellectualizers,
he confuses thought with existence. He assumes that truth can be
formulated into a system of ideas or a set of doctrines. In doing
this the philosopher becomes a mere observer of life. He forgets
that he exists, that he must choose and act and take responsibility
for what it is he knows. The speculative thinker makes Christianity into theology, instead of recognizing that a living relationship
to Christ involves passion, struggle, decision, personal appropriation, and inner transformation.

To move toward authentic personal existence, to become a
Christian, is to move beyond the aesthetic sphere and into the
ethical. The ethical life recognizes the significance of choice.
Here one accepts his duty as a moral actor. The person lays
aside his many desires or impulses, his careless "freedom," and
heeds his conscience, takes responsibility, and fulfills his moral
obligations. Aesthetic freedom is really enslavement to the passions and as such leads a person to the brink of despair. By contrast, ethical freedom is the enjoyment and fulfillment of doing
one's duty. The person who lives at this level tries to realize in
his life what is of eternal, universal value. Such a life recognizes
that within the soul there is something (i.e. the eternal) that
cannot be satisfied by a sensory life. Hence the realization of
enduring values – justice, freedom, peace, love – and respect
for the moral law within propel the ethical self forward into a
life of responsibility, of caring beyond one's own immediate interests. Herein lies true freedom: the ability to fulfill one's duty,
to move from what is to what ought to be.

The ethical involves both choice and resolution. It also involves struggle, because the realization of ethical values takes
effort and time. Therefore an authentic, fully realized indi-

vidual is one who is unified from within, whose actions are one, and who accepts responsibility for his commitments. Unlike someone who lives at the aesthetic level, the ethical individual is not swayed by his every emotion or by the opinions of others.

The key to the ethical sphere is freedom. A "bad choice," therefore, is better than no choice at all. The aesthetic person drifts along with the currents around him. The person who lives ethically, however, determines these very currents. It is not enough to just do one's duty. One must passionately choose the path. Life is an either/or, not just between good and evil, but between choosing and not choosing. The person who lives in the ethical sphere lives intentionally, intensively. Such a person possesses character and conviction, and is thus willing to sacrifice himself for something greater than oneself.

As admirable and as necessary as he finds the ethical sphere, however, Kierkegaard believes that life must ultimately be lived on yet another level: the religious sphere. This sphere has nothing to do with institutional religion per se. Rather, an individual lives religiously when he or she realizes that the ethical life is insufficient for solving life's riddles and choices. The ethical life fails to adequately deal with exceptional situations. Doing one's duty isn't always simple, especially when different duties conflict or when one's various obligations cannot all be fulfilled. Consequently, there is something higher than universal duty and this Kierkegaard calls the "Absolute."

A fully actualized person has to see himself "before God," to see himself as he really is. When this occurs, the wide chasm between oneself and God becomes apparent, both because of the sins one has committed but also because of one's failure to fulfill completely his moral duty. The ethical individual, if he is truly honest with himself, is one who lives in constant fear and dread precisely because of his inability to fulfill the moral law and his hesitation to give himself absolutely. In fact, the most ethical person is precisely the one who feels most inadequate. As the image of God, each person instinctively knows that God is higher than the moral law and greater than any set of values. His conscience tells him that the highest commitment one can make is to God – the very ground of every moral value. God's will, not some abstract law, is what finally matters. And because no human can measure the demands of God, one must ultimately surrender to God in a leap of faith.

To illustrate the difference between the ethical and religious spheres, Kierkegaard cites Abraham, the "father of all those who believe." Abraham, a righteous man, is the paragon of faith because instead of heeding the moral law – "Thou shall not kill" – he heeded God's command to sacrifice Isaac. Abraham acted as a true individual because his relationship to God, not to the moral law, was primary in his life. He did not merely perceive God through morality or reduce God to the moral law. As a man of faith, Abraham subjected everything, including his ethical actions, to God. He was willing to sacrifice Isaac for the sake of his own relationship to God. He acted because God commanded him to act. He stood before God, answering to no one but God.

When an individual stands before God he no longer sees himself as self-sufficient. He recognizes his own inability to transform himself. The religious person strives to allow himself to be transformed by God. Such transformation includes three things: (1) Infinite resignation – dying to the world, the willingness to sacrifice any finite good for the sake of God. (2) Suffering – undergoing a transformation of the self, though not by the self. It is the process of undergoing "self-annihilation" so that God, not self, can do his transforming work. (3) Guilt – the feeling of one's inability to give oneself completely, unreservedly, to God.

The religious person, though committed to many of the same ethical ideals as the ethical person, believes that those ideals are ultimately incapable of fulfillment, not because of external barriers but because of his own inner condition. He recognizes his sinful state. The person of faith relates himself to God not in self-confident action, but in repentance. He knows that he not only fails to fulfill his chosen ideals, but that he fails to have ideals of sufficient worth. To put it differently, he knows that his chosen "ideals" are themselves insufficient and incomplete. Thus Kierkegaard says: "An ethic which ignores sin is an absolutely idle science." Allowing oneself to be transformed by God is, in short, more important than fulfilling one's duty.

Herein lies the significance of Christianity and the gospel. Genuine Christian existence is different from religious existence in general. The religious person believes that the key to finding God is to recognize and realize his own guilt and need. The true Christian, however, recognizes that he, by himself, cannot do even this. He realizes that even his understanding of God, let alone of himself, is incomplete and thus defective. He acknowledges that there is an abyss between him and God, an "infinite qualitative difference between man and God." True awareness of sin comes not from within but only through God's revelation to the individual. Sin's corruption is total, and one's ability to choose is itself a gift. The distinguishing mark of a truly Christian existence is, according to Kierkegaard, the central paradox of the Gospel – the fact that God, the Eternal, becomes a human being. This, unlike the truths of the ethical life or religious insight, cannot be known by means of intuition only. It comes in revelation and is received by faith: the highest passion of inwardness.

Subjectivity and Truth

Kierkegaard expends great efforts contrasting objective think-ing and subjective truth. For him, faith is not a belief but a cer-tain way of being in the truth that extends beyond reason's ability to grasp. By "subjectivity" Kierkegaard does not mean subjectivism: a belief is true because one believes it to be true. He is concerned with the degree to which a person "lives within" the truth he confesses. To him subjectivity means turn-ing away from the objective realm of facts – that can be learned by detached observation and abstract thinking – and immers-ing oneself in the subjective, inward activity of discovering truth for oneself. At its highest pitch, subjectivity culminates in faith – an infinite passion that is both rationally uncertain and paradoxical. Faith requires risk, which objective certainty ab-hors. But this is the distinctive mark of Christian faith. Faith means to wager everything and to suffer for the truth, despite the offenses of the Incarnation and the Cross.

Faith, therefore, requires a leap. It is not a matter of galvaniz-ing the will to believe something there is no evidence for, but a leap of commitment. "The leap is the category of decision" – the decision to commit one's being totally to a God whose exist-ence is rationally uncertain and whose redemption is utterly an offense. This is why, according to Kierkegaard, all proofs for the existence of God and the deity of Christ fail. To try and prove God's existence by means of a purely neutral, objective stand-point is completely backwards. It is to go back to the aesthetic sphere. To the contrary, God is known by way of passionate, undivided commitment. Besides, Christianity is not a doctrine to be taught, but rather a life to be lived. "Proofs" are thus not only unconvincing but irrelevant. God is spirit and therefore can only be known in a spiritual (i.e., subjective, inward) way.

The how of one's existence is what is decisive. Herein lies the importance of commitment; an act of the will that transcends reason's requirement.

Again, we may refer to Abraham. Here was a man willing to commit infanticide in the name of God. "How then did Abraham exist? He believed. This is the paradox which keeps him upon the sheer edge and which he cannot make clear to any other person, for the paradox is that he as the individual puts himself in an absolute relation to the Absolute." God requires of each of us this degree of commitment: an absolute relation to the Absolute. Such commitment can be terrifying as God leads us "out upon the deep, over seventy thousand fathoms of water." And just as Jesus Christ produced certain effects on his contemporaries, to be his in faith one must be a contemporary of his and have vital, decisive contact with him now. There is no such thing as a second-string disciple.

The Single Individual

Kierkegaard understood that the key to the inwardness of faith was the individual. The "single individual" is paramount in his thought and contains several meanings. First, it means to stand alone before God and come to an awareness of God. The sooner I realize that I stand naked before God, the more authentic I will become. Second, an individual is a unified, integrated self ordered by a single purpose. "Purity of heart," Kierkegaard explains, "is to will one thing." Third, an individual is a responsible self, who in freedom gives account for one's decisions or failures to decide. One's true self is constituted by the decisions one makes. Lastly, to be an individual is to exist as a unique self that possesses a dignity above the race, the crowd.

In each of the above senses, Kierkegaard is careful to point out that before God the individual stands over and against the crowd. In his mind, "It is impossible to edify or be edified en masse." Being an individual resists the conformity-ideals of the crowd and its ideologies. "A crowd in its very concept is the untruth, by reason of the fact that it renders the individual completely impenitent and irresponsible, or at least weakens his sense of responsibility by reducing it to a fraction." Inauthenticity lies precisely in the attempt to live "as a numeral within a crowd, a fraction within the earthly conglomeration." For Kierkegaard, where there is the crowd, "there is externality, and comparison, and indulgence, and evasion."

Wherein lies salvation? There is salvation in only one thing, in becoming a single individual. The truly spiritual person is able to endure isolation, to pause "to deepen oneself in inwardness" before God and his Word. Although in this life one may find solace in the crowd from God's radical demands, "In eternity you will look in vain for the crowd. You will listen in vain to find where the noise and the gathering is, so that you can run to it." In actual fact, "For the Infinite One, there is no place, the individual is himself the place."

Passion and Existence

The backdrop of the above themes provides the framework for Kierkegaard's insistence that the modern age, including the church, lacks passion: "Our age is without passion. Everyone knows a great deal, we all know which way we ought to go and all the different ways we can go, but nobody is really willing to move." Kierkegaard understood present society as a mass of spectators who live vicariously at second and third hand. His own image of society is of a drunken peasant who lies asleep in the wagon and lets the horses take care of themselves: "When you listen to what he says in a cold and awful dread, you scarcely know whether it is a human being, or a cunningly contrived walking stick in which a talking machine has been concealed."

The malady of our age is mediocrity. It is easy to think that with all the busyness of modern life people are actually living engaged lives. In actual fact, however, very few live with passion, or on the basis of conscience. Everything is calculated in a way that whatever we do is reduced to the reasonable or unreasonable, or worse yet, to the law of least resistance. Suffering is to be avoided at all costs. In the name of unconditional freedom options remain open, but in the process, people drift along. "There are many people who arrive at conclusions in life much the way schoolboys do; they cheat their teachers by copying the answer book without having worked the problem themselves."

This cheating one's way through life is perhaps exemplified in today's preoccupation with the external and with one's temporal circumstances. Kierkegaard reminds us that "in the world of spirit, to change place is to be changed oneself." This, however, is precisely what scientific man abhors. We believe the key to happiness lies outside ourselves. We are thus obsessed with material benefits and results. We make our happiness dependent on situations outside ourselves and blame others in the process if things don't turn out well. "In all our 'freedom,' we seek one thing: to be able to live without responsibility."

Kierkegaard is convinced that Christendom is nothing but a lifeless outer shell of mediocrity. "Think of a very long railway train – but long ago the locomotive ran away from it. Christendom is like this…Christendom is tranquillity – how charming, the tranquillity of not moving from the spot." Kierkegaard argues that true Christianity is first and foremost a demand. "It is the deepest wound that can be dealt to a person designed to collide with everything on the most appalling scale." In short, faith is the passion of sacrifice and self-denial, a way of being in the world that suffers ridicule and persecution from the established order with its religious hypocrisy. For this reason, "The will of Christ is this: an examination in which one cannot cheat."

With these thoughts as a backdrop, the reader will note several things in the selections that follow. First, since Kierkegaard's primary concern is with Christian existence, the selections that follow are explicitly oriented in that direction. Kierkegaard is not interested in a general theory of human existence, religious or otherwise. His aim is to compel the reader to live contemporaneously with Christ. Second, some of Kierkegaard's terminology is technical. You may find it helpful, therefore, to turn to the final section where the selections are shorter and often easier to understand. But as you read, keep in mind the overarching thrust behind his thought. It is less important to grasp every nuance of his thought than to respond inwardly to his appeal. Lastly, read slowly. Allow yourself to undergo self-examination. As Kierkegaard reminds us: "It is true that a mirror has the quality of enabling a person to see his image in it, but to do this he must stand still."

Charles E. Moore
February 1999

I | TO WILL ONE THING

1 | Dare to Decide

Can there be something in life that has power over us which little by little causes us to forget all that is good? And can this ever happen to anyone who has heard the call of eternity quite clearly and strongly?

If this can ever be, then one must look for a cure against it. Praise be to God that such a cure exists – to quietly make a decision. A decision joins us to the eternal. It brings what is eternal into time. A decision raises us with a shock from the slumber of monotony. A decision breaks the magic spell of custom. A decision breaks the long row of weary thoughts. A decision pronounces its blessing upon even the weakest beginning, as long as it is a real beginning. Decision is the awakening to the eternal.

One could say that all this is very simple. It is just a matter of moments, make a decision and all is well. Dare like a bold swimmer to plunge into the sea, and dare to believe that the weight of the swimmer will go to the goal against all opposing currents.

Yet, our approach must begin differently from this. First, we must reject the devil's web of deception. Making decisions is often dangerous, or rather, talking about them is. Before you learn to walk you have to crawl on all fours; to try to fly right before walking is a dangerous set-up. Certainly there must be great decisions, but even in connection with them the important thing is to get under way with *your* decision. Do not fly so high with your decisions that you forget that a decision is but a beginning.

How wretched and miserable it is to find in a person many good intentions but few good deeds. And there are other dangers too, dangers of sin. With all your good intentions, you must not forget your duty, neither should you forget to do it with joy. And strive to carry your burdens and responsibilities in a surrendered way. If you don't, there is a danger of losing your decisiveness; of going through life without courage and fading away in death.

So what about the decision, which was after all meant so very well? A road well begun is the battle half won. The important thing is to make a beginning and get under way. There is nothing more harmful for your soul than to hold back and not get moving.

The path of an honest fighter is a difficult one. And when the fighter grows cool in the evening of his life this is still no excuse to retire into games and amusement. Whoever remains faithful to his decision will realize that his whole life is a struggle. Such a person does not fall into the temptation of proudly telling others of what he has done with his life. Nor will he talk about the "great decisions" he has made. He knows full well that at decisive moments you have to renew your resolve again and again and that this alone makes good the decision and the decision good.

In the end, the archenemy of decision is cowardice. Cowardice is constantly at work trying to break off the good agreement of decision with eternity. When the minister preaches a sermon against pride, he has many listeners. But if he wants to warn his listeners against cowardice, things look very different. His listeners look around to see if there is any such miserable fellow among them. A cowardly soul – after all, that is the most miserable thing one can imagine, that is something one simply can't endure. We can put up with one who is spoiled or decadent in some way or another, even if he is proud, but only if he is not a coward.

And yet the separation of cowardice and pride is a false one, for these two are really one and the same. The proud person always wants to do the right thing, the great thing. But because he wants to do it in his own strength, he is fighting not with man but with God. He wants to have a great task set before himself and to carry it through on his own accord. And then he is very pleased with his place. Many have taken the first leap of pride into life, many stop there. But the next leap is different.

How? The proud person, ironically, begins looking around for people of like mind who want to be sufficient unto themselves in their pride. This is because anyone who stands alone for any length of time soon discovers that there is a God. Such a realization is something no one can endure. And so one becomes cowardly. Of course, cowardice never shows itself as such. It won't make a great noise. No, it is quite hidden and quiet. And yet it joins all other passions to it, because cowardice is very comfortable and obliging in associating with other passions. It knows very well how to make friends with them.

Cowardice settles deep in our souls like the idle mists on stagnant waters. From it arise unhealthy vapors and deceiving phantoms. The thing that cowardice fears most is decision; for decision always scatters the mists, at least for a moment. Cowardice thus hides behind the thought it likes best of all: the crutch of time. Cowardice and time always find a reason for not hurrying, for saying, "Not today, but tomorrow", whereas God in heaven and the eternal say: "Do it today. Now is the day of salvation." The eternal refrain of decision is: "Today, today." But cowardice holds back, holds us up. If only cowardice would appear in all its baseness, one could recognize it for what it is and fight it immediately.

Cowardice wants to prevent the step of making a decision. To accomplish this it takes to itself a host of glorious names. In the name of caution cowardice abhors any over-hastiness. It is against doing anything before the time is ripe. Besides, "Is it not best to speak of a continued endeavor, which is by far the superior act, rather than of a sudden decision?" Ah, not decision, but continual striving, continuous endeavor; what a glorious expression. What a glorious deception!

Whereas decision reminds us of the end to come, cowardice turns us away from finality. Hence, cowardice is adaptable and takes pride in being able to meet various opinions in different ways. If, for example, someone's ideas are first-rate, then cowardice will argue: "Well if such a one as you is so well equipped, then why hurry? Why limit yourself so?" What pride! And the thing of it is that for such a person it is not that the task is too easy but that it is too difficult.

Or consider the person whose advantages are few. Cowardice is now quick to sing a different tune: "What you've got is far too little to make a good beginning." This, of course, is particularly stupid. If we always need more to begin with we would never begin. But "God does not give us the spirit of cowardice, but the spirit of power, and of love and of self-control" (1 Tm. 1:7). Cowardice does not come from God. One who wants to build a tower sits down and makes an estimate as to how high he can build it. But if no decision is ever made then no tower is ever built. A good decision is our will to do everything we can within our power. It means to serve God with all we've got, be it little or much. Every person can do that.

In the end, failure to decide prevents one from doing what is good. It keeps us from doing that great thing to which each of us is bound by virtue of the eternal. This does not mean that everything is decided once a decision is made, nor does it mean that only in great decisions is one lifted to a higher plane – a place where one now no longer needs to bother about little things, petty things. Such thinking amounts to nothing more than a fine show.

We must not support high and important things while ignoring the practical, daily stuff of life. Indeed, decision is something truly great; the life of eternity shines over decision. But the light of eternity does not shine on every decision. Decision may be once and for all; but decision itself is only the first thing. Genuine decision is always eager to change its clothes and get down to practical matters. The real significance of decision is that it gives us an inner connection. Decision gets us on our way, and here there are no longer little things. Decision lays its demanding hand on us from start to finish. Cowardice, on the other hand, wants only to concern itself with the really important, big things, not in order to carry something out wholeheartedly but to be flattered by doing something that is noble and great. Yet hiding behind the exalted is nothing but an excuse for not conquering all the little things one has omitted, simply because they were little.

Therefore, don't be fooled. It may well be that with great decisions others will marvel at you. All the same, you miss the one thing that is needful. You may be honored in this life, remembered by monuments set up in your honor, but God will say to you: "You unhappy person. Why did you not choose the better path? Confess your weakness and face it."

Perhaps just in this weakness God will meet you and come to your aid. This much is certain: the greatest thing each person can do is to give himself to God utterly and unconditionally – weaknesses, fears, and all. For God loves obedience more than good intentions or second-best offerings, which are all too often made under the guise of weakness.

Therefore, dare to renew your decision. It will lift you up again to have trust in God. For God is a spirit of power and love and self-control, and it is before God and for him that every decision is to be made. Dare to act on the good that lies buried within your heart. Confess your decision and do not go ashamed with downcast eyes as if you were treading on forbidden ground. If you are ashamed of your own imperfections, then cast your eyes down before God, not man. Better yet, in weakness decide and go forth!

2 | Either/Or

A choice! Do you, my listener, know how to express in a single word anything more magnificent? Do you realize, even if you were to discuss year in and year out how you could mention nothing more awesome than a choice, what it is to have choice! For though it is certainly true that the ultimate blessing is to choose rightly, yet the faculty of choice itself is still the glorious prerequisite. What does it matter to the young lover to take inventory of all the outstanding qualities of her fiancé if she herself cannot choose? And, on the other hand, whether others praise her beloved's many perfections or enumerate his faults, what more magnificent thing could she say than when she says, He is my heart's choice!

A choice! Yes, this is the pearl of great price, yet it is not intended to be buried and hidden away. A choice that is not used is worse than nothing; it is a snare in which a person has trapped himself as a slave who did not become free – by choosing. It is a good thing that you can never be rid of it. It remains with you, and if you do not use it, it becomes a curse. A choice – not between red and green, not between silver and gold – no, a choice between God and the world! Do you know anything in comparison to choice? Do you know of any more overwhelming and humbling expression for God's condescension and extravagance towards us human beings than that he places himself, so to say, on the same level of choice with the world, just so that we may be able to choose; that God, if language dare speak thus, woos humankind – that he, the eternally strong one, woos sapless humanity? Yet, how insignificant is the young lover's choice between her pursuers by comparison with this choice between God and the world!

A choice! Or is it perhaps an imperfection in the choice under discussion here that a human being not only *can* choose but that he *must* choose? Would it not be to the young lover's advantage if she had a zealous father who said, "My dear girl, you have your freedom, you yourself may choose, but you must choose." Or would it be better that she had the choice but coyly picked and picked and never really chose?

No, a person must choose, for in this way God retains his honor while at the same time has a fatherly concern for humankind. Though God has lowered himself to being that which can be chosen, yet each person must on his part choose. God is not mocked. Therefore the matter stands thus: If a person avoids choosing, this is the same as the presumption of choosing the world.

Each person must choose *between God and the world, God and mammon.* This is the eternal, unchangeable condition of choice that can never be evaded – no, never in all eternity. No one can say, "God and world, they are not, after all, so absolutely different. One can combine them both in one choice." This is to refrain from choosing. When there is a choice between two, then to want to choose both is just to shrink from the choice "to one's own destruction" (Heb. 10:39). No one can say, "One can choose a little mammon and also God as well." No, it is presumptuous ridicule of God if someone thinks that only the person who desires great wealth chooses mammon. Alas, the person who insists on having a penny without God, wants to have a penny all for himself. He thereby chooses mammon. A penny is enough, the choice is made, he has chosen mammon; that it is little makes not the slightest difference.

The love of God is hatred of the world and love of the world hatred of God. This is the colossal point of contention, either love or hate. This is the place where the most terrible fight must be fought. And where is this place? In a person's innermost being. Whether the struggle is over millions or over a penny, it is a matter of loving and preferring God – the most terrible fight is the struggle for the highest. What immeasurable happiness is promised to the one who rightly chooses. If anyone is unable to understand this, the reason is that he is unwilling to accept that God is present in the moment of choice, not in order to watch but in order to be chosen. Therefore, each person must choose. Terrible is the battle, in a person's innermost being, between God and the world. The crowning risk involved lies in the possession of choice.

Whatsoever a person chooses, when he does not choose God he has missed the either/or, or rather he is in perdition with his either/or. So then: either God/...What does this either/or signify? What does God demand by this either/or? He demands obedience, unconditional obedience. If you are not obedient in everything unconditionally, without qualification, you don't love him, and if you don't love him – then you hate him. If you are not obedient in everything unconditionally, then you are not bound to him, and if you are not bound to him then you despise him.

If you can become absolutely obedient, then when you pray, "Lead us not into temptation" there will be no ambiguity in you, you will be undivided and single before God. And there is one thing that all Satan's cunning and all the snares of temptation cannot take by surprise – an undivided will. What Satan spies with keenness of sight as his prey, what all temptation aims at certain of its prey, is the ambiguous. When unclarity resides, there is temptation, and there it proves only too easily the stronger. Wherever there is ambiguity, wherever there is wavering, there is disobedience down at the bottom.

Where there is no ambiguity, Satan and temptation are powerless. But with the merest glimpse of wavering, Satan is strong and temptation is enticing, and keen-sighted is the evil one whose trap is called temptation and whose prey is called the human soul. Of course, it is not really from Satan that temptation comes, but ambiguity cannot hide itself from him. If he discovers it, temptation is always at hand. But the person who surrenders absolutely to God, with no reservations, is absolutely safe. From this safe hiding-place he can see the devil, but the devil cannot see him. And if with absolute obedience he remains in his hiding-place, then he is "delivered from the evil one."

There is a tremendous danger in which we find ourselves by being human, a danger that consists in the fact that we are placed between two tremendous powers. The choice is left to us. We must either love or hate, and not to love is to hate. So hostile are these two powers that the slightest inclination towards the one side becomes absolute opposition to the other. Let us not forget this tremendous danger in which we exist. To forget is to have made your choice.

3 | Under the Spell of Good Intentions

There is a parable in the Scriptures that is seldom considered yet very instructive and inspiring. "There was a man who had two sons. The father went to the first and said, 'Son, go and work in the vineyard today.' And he answered, 'I will not'; but afterward he changed his mind and went. And the father went to the second son and said the same and he answered, 'I will go, sir,' but did not go. Which of the two did the will of his father?" (Mt. 21:28–31). We could also ask in another manner: which of these two was the prodigal son? I wonder if it was not the one who said "Yes," the one who not only said "Yes," but said, "I will go, sir," as if to show his unqualified, dutiful submission to his father's will.

Now, what is the point of this parable? Is it not meant to show us the danger of saying "Yes" in too great a hurry, even if it is well meant? Though the yes-brother was not a deceiver when he said "Yes," he nevertheless became a deceiver when he failed to keep his promise. In his very eagerness in promising he became a deceiver. When you say "Yes" or promise something, you can very easily deceive yourself and others also, as if you had already done what you promised. It is easy to think that by making a promise you have at least done part of what you promised to do, as if the promise itself were something of value. Not at all!

In fact, when you do not do what you promise, it is a long way back to the truth.

Beware! The "Yes" of promise keeping is sleep-inducing. An honest "No" possesses much more promise. It can stimulate; repentance may not be far away. He who says "No," becomes almost afraid of himself. But he who says "Yes, I will," is all too pleased with himself. The world is quite inclined – even eager – to make promises, for a promise appears very fine at the *moment* – it inspires! Yet for this very reason the eternal is suspicious of promises.

Now suppose that neither of the brothers did his father's will. Then the one who said "No" was surely closer to realizing that he did not do his father's will. A "no" does not hide anything, but a *yes* can very easily become a deception, a self-deception; which of all difficulties is the most difficult to conquer. Ah, it is all too true that, "The road to hell is paved with good intentions."

It is the most dangerous thing for a person to go backwards with the help of good intentions, especially with the help of promises; for it is almost impossible to discover that one is really going backwards. When a person turns his back on someone and walks away, it is easy to see which way he is going. That is that! But when a person finds a way of turning his face towards him who he is walking away from, and in so doing walks backwards while appearing to greet the person, giving assurances again and again that he is coming, or incessantly saying "Here I am" – though he gets farther and farther away by walking backwards – then it is not so easy to become aware. And so it is with the one who, rich in good intentions and quick to promise, retreats backwards farther and farther from the good. With the help of intentions and promises, he maintains the honest impression that he is moving towards the good, yet all the while he moves farther and farther away from it. With every renewed intention and promise it seems as if he is taking a new step forward but in reality he is only standing still, no, he is really taking another step backward.

The good intention, the "Yes," taken in vain, the unfulfilled promise leaves a residue of despair, of dejection. Beware! Good intention can very soon flare up again in more passionate declarations of intention, but only to leave behind even greater desperation. As an alcoholic constantly requires stronger and stronger drink, so the one who has fallen under the spell of good intentions and smooth-sounding declaration constantly requires more and more good intentions. And so he keeps himself from seeing that he is walking backwards.

We do not praise the son who said "No," but we need to learn from the gospel how dangerous it is to say, "Lord, I will." A promise with respect to action is somewhat like a changeling (an infant secretly changed for another) – one needs to be very watchful. In the very moment a child is born the mother's joy is greatest, because her pain is gone. When because of her joy she is less watchful – so says the superstition – evil powers come and put a changeling in the child's place. In the crucial initial moment when one sets out and begins, a dangerous time indeed, enemy forces come and slip in a changeling promise, thus hindering one from making a genuine beginning. Alas, how many have been deceived in this manner, yes, as if cast under a spell!

4 | The Greatest Danger

Imagine a kind of medicine that possesses in full dosage a laxative effect but in a half dose a constipating effect. Suppose someone is suffering from constipation. But – for some reason or other, perhaps because there is not enough for a full dose or because it is feared that such a large amount might be too much – in order to do something, he is given, with the best of intentions, a half dose: "After all, it is at least something." What a tragedy!

So it is with today's Christianity. As with everything qualified by an either/or – the half has the very opposite effect from the whole. But we Christians go right on practicing this well-intentioned half-hearted act from generation to generation. We produce Christians by the millions, are proud of it – yet have no inkling that we are doing just exactly the opposite of what we intend to do.

It takes a physician to understand that a half dose can have the opposite effect to that of a full dose. Common sense, cool-minded mediocrity never catches on. It undeviatingly continues to say of the half-dosage: "After all, it is something; even if it doesn't work very well, it is still something." But that it should have an opposite effect – no, mediocrity does not grasp that.

The greatest danger to Christianity is, I contend, not heresies, heterodoxies, not atheists, not profane secularism – no, but the kind of orthodoxy which is cordial drivel, mediocrity served up sweet. There is nothing that so insidiously displaces the majestic as cordiality. Perpetually polite, so small, so nice, tampering and meddling and tampering some more – the result is that majesty is completely defrauded – of course, only a little bit. And right here is the danger, for the infinite is more disposed to a violent attack than to becoming a little bit degraded – amid smiling, Christian politeness. And yet this politeness is what our Christianity amounts to. But the very essence of Christianity is utterly opposed to this mediocrity, in which it does not so much die as dwindle away.

Today's orthodoxy essentially has its abode in the cordial drivel of family life. This is utterly dangerous for Christianity. Christianity does not oppose debauchery and uncontrollable passions and the like as much as it is opposes this flat mediocrity, this nauseating atmosphere, this homey, civil togetherness, where admittedly great crimes, wild excesses, and powerful aberrations cannot easily occur – but where God's unconditional demand has even greater difficulty in accomplishing what it requires: the majestic obedience of submission. Nothing is further from obeying the either/or than this sweet family drivel.

Consider what Christ thinks about mediocrity! When the apostle Peter, for instance, with good intentions wanted to keep Christ from being crucified, Christ answered: "Get behind me, Satan! You are an offense to me" (Mk. 8:33).

In the world of mediocrity in which we live it is assumed that only crackpots, fanatics, and the like should be deplored as offensive, as inspired by Satan, and that the middle way is the right way, the way that alone is exempted from any such charge. What nonsense! Christ is of another mind: mediocrity is the worst offense, the most dangerous kind of demon possession, farthest removed from the possibility of being cured. To "have" religion on the level of mediocrity is the most unqualified form of perdition.

The advantages and benefits of earthly life are bound up in mediocrity. But genuine religion has an inverse relationship to the finite. Its aim is to raise human beings up so as to transcend what is earthly. It is a matter of either/or. Either prime quality, or no quality at all; either with all your heart, all your mind, and all your strength, or not at all. Either all of God and all of you, or nothing at all!

We clever humans, however, prefer to treat faith as if it were something finite, as if it were something for the betterment and enjoyment of temporal life. It is supposed to bring us meaning and fulfillment, happiness and direction. This kind of religion is nothing but a deception. If you were honest and if you would look at it more closely, you would see that this really is contempt for religion, a dangerous and culpable irreligion. True faith insists on being an either/or. To treat it as if it were like drink and food is fundamentally to scorn it. But this is precisely the way of mediocrity.

5 | The Task

Why is it that people prefer to be addressed in groups rather than individually? Is it because conscience is one of life's greatest inconveniences, a knife that cuts too deeply? We prefer to "be part of a group," and to "form a party," for if we are part of a group it means goodnight to conscience. We cannot be two or three, a "Miller Brothers and Company" around a conscience. No, no. The only thing the group secures is the abolition of conscience.

It is the same with busyness. A person can very well eat lettuce before it has formed a heart, yet the tender delicacy of the heart and its lovely coil are something quite different from the leaves. Likewise, in the world of spirit, busyness, keeping up with others, hustling hither and yon, makes it almost impossible for an individual to form a heart, to become a responsible, alive self. Every life that is preoccupied with being like others is a wasted life, a lost life.

A sparrow, a fly, a poisonous insect is an object of God's concern. It is not a wasted or lost life. But masses of mimickers, a crowd of copycats are wasted lives. God has been merciful to us, demonstrating his grace to the point of being willing to involve himself with every person. If we prefer to be like all the others, this amounts to high treason against God. We who simply go along are guilty, and our punishment is to be ignored by God.

By forming a party, by melting into some group, we avoid not only conscience, but martyrdom. This is why fear of others dominates this world. No one dares to be a genuine self; everyone is hiding in some kind of "togetherness." Sensitive organs are shielded and not in immediate contact with objects, so us ordinary people are afraid to come into personal, immediate contact with the eternal. Instead, we rely on traditions and the voice of others. We are content to be a specimen or a copy, living a life shielded against individual responsibility before the Truth.

True individuality is measured by this: how long or how far one can endure being alone without the understanding of others. The person who can endure being alone is poles apart from the social mixer. He is miles apart from the man-pleaser, the one who manages successfully with everyone – he who possesses no sharp edges. God never uses such people. The true individual, anyone who is going to be directly involved with God, will not and cannot avoid the human bite. He will be thoroughly misunderstood. God is no friend of cozy human gathering.

Yes, in the purely human world the rule is this: Seek out the help and opinion of others. Christ says: Beware of men! The majority of people are not only afraid of holding a wrong opinion, they are afraid of holding an opinion *alone*. In the physical world water puts out fire. So too in the spiritual world. The "many", the mass of people, put out the inner fire – beware of men!

According to the New Testament to be a Christian means to be salt. Christianity addresses this question to each individual: Are you willing to be salt? Are you willing to be sacrificed, instead of belonging to the crowd, which seeks to profit from the sacrifice of others? Here again is the distinction: to be salt or to melt into the mass; to let others be sacrificed for us on behalf of the Truth or to let ourselves be sacrificed – between these two lies an eternal qualitative difference.

The deep fault of the human race is that there are no individuals any more. We have become split in two. When a book has become old and shabby, the binding separates and the pages fall out. Similarly, in our time we are disintegrated. Our understanding, our imaginations do not bind us in character. We are spineless wimps who only flirt with the highest. How can we ever possibly avoid the dizziness that comes from fear of people in the midst of this whirlpool of millions where everything is either crowds or movements? What faith it takes to believe that one's life is noticed by God and that this is enough!

Wanting to hide in the crowd, to be a little fraction of the group instead of being an individual, is the most corrupt of all escapes. Granted, it will make life easier, but it will do so by making it more thoughtless. Yet the question is that of the responsibility of each single individual – that each of us is an authentic, answerable self. It is a cop-out to make a racket along with a few others for a so-called conviction. We ought, before God, to make up our own minds about our convictions, and then live them out regardless of the others. Eternity will single each person out as individually responsible – the busy one who thought he was safe in some group or some enterprise, and the poorest wretch who thought he was overlooked.

Every person must render account to God. No third person dares venture to intrude upon this accounting. God in heaven does not talk to us as to an assembly; he speaks to each individually. This is why the most ruinous evasion of all is to be hidden away in a herd in an attempt to escape God's personal address. Adam attempted this when his guilty conscience led him to imagine that he could hide himself among the trees. Similarly, it may be easier and more convenient, and more cowardly too, to hide yourself among the crowd in hope that God will not recognize you from the others. But in eternity each shall individually render an account. Eternity will examine each person for all that he has chosen and done as an individual before God.

It will be horrible on judgment day, when all souls come to life again, to stand utterly alone, alone and unknown by all, and yet candidly, exhaustively known by him who knows all. No one may ever pride himself at being more than an individual. Nor can anyone despondently think that he is not an individual. No, each one can and shall render account to God. Each one has the task of becoming an individual.

6 | Against the Crowd

We warn young people against going to dens of iniquity, even out of curiosity, because no one knows what might happen. Still more terrible, however, is the danger of going along with the crowd. In truth, there is no place, not even one most disgustingly dedicated to lust and vice, where a human being is more easily corrupted – than in the crowd.

Even though every individual possesses the truth, when he gets together in a crowd, untruth will be present at once, for the crowd *is* untruth. It either produces impenitence and irresponsibility or it weakens the individual's sense of responsibility by placing it in a fractional category. For instance, imagine an individual walking up to Christ and spitting on him. No human being would ever have the courage or the audacity to do that. But as part of a crowd, well then they somehow have the "courage" to do it – dreadful untruth!

The crowd is indeed untruth. Christ was crucified because he would have nothing to do with the crowd (even though he addressed himself to all). He did not want to form a party, an interest group, a mass movement, but wanted to be what he was, the truth, which is related to the single individual. Therefore everyone who will genuinely serve the truth is by that very fact a martyr. To win a crowd is no art; for that only untruth is needed, nonsense, and a little knowledge of human passions. But no witness to the truth dares to get involved with the crowd.

His work is to be involved with all people, if possible, but always individually, speaking with each and every person on the sidewalk and on the streets – in order to split apart. He avoids the crowd, especially when it is treated as authoritative in matters of the truth or when its applause, or hissing, or balloting are regarded as judges. He avoids the crowd with its herd mentality more than a decent young girl avoids the bars on the harbor. Those who speak to the crowd, coveting its approval, those who deferentially bow and scrape before it must be regarded as being worse than prostitutes. They are instruments of untruth.

For this reason, I could weep, even want to die, when I think about how the public, with its daily press and anonymity, make things so crazy. That an anonymous person, by means of the press, day in and day out can say whatever he wants to say, what he perhaps would never have the courage to say face-to-face as an individual to another individual, and can get thousands to repeat it, is nothing less than a crime – and no one has responsibility! What untruth! Such is the way of the crowd.

7 | Suspending the Ethical

The ethical dimension of existence has to do with the universal, of doing what is unconditionally right. The ethical applies to everyone and at every moment. It possesses its own validity. That is, it has nothing outside itself as its end or purpose. It has no further to go. By contrast, the single individual is the particular that has its purpose in the universal. The individual's task is always to express himself within the confines of duty, to limit his particularity and to forgo his own interests so as to fulfill his universal duty. Thus, as soon as an individual wants to assert himself in his particularity, in direct opposition to the universal, he sins. Only by recognizing this can he again reconcile himself with the universal. He can free himself only by surrendering to the universal in repentance.

If this is the highest that can be said of our existence, then the ethical and a person's happiness are identical. The philosopher is proved right. The ethical is the universal and, in turn, the divine. The whole of human existence is entirely self-enclosed, and the ethical is at once the limit and completion of our lives. Doing one's duty becomes sufficient, with the result that God becomes an invisible, vanishing point, an impotent thought unrelated to my life. His being is no more than the ethical itself, which fills all existence.

But what about the question of faith? Is the ethical the final reality? No. The philosopher goes wrong when it comes to this question. Actually, he fails to protest loudly and clearly enough against the honor and glory given to Abraham as the father of faith. If the ethical is final, if it is the ultimate determination of life's meaning, then Abraham should really be remitted to some lower court for trial and exposed as the murderer he is.

Now faith is just this paradox, that the single individual, though under the demands of the universal, is higher than the universal. If that is not faith, then Abraham is done for and faith has never existed in the world. If the ethical life is the highest and nothing incommensurable is left over, except in the sense of what is evil, then one needs no other categories than those of the philosophers. Goodbye to Abraham! But faith is just this paradox, that the single individual, though bound by the universal, is higher than the universal. As a single individual, as the particular, he stands in an absolute relation to the Absolute. The ethical is thus suspended. Faith *is* this paradox.

The story of Abraham contains just such a suspension of the ethical. Abraham acts on the strength of the absurd. As a single individual before God he found himself to be higher than the universal. This paradox cannot be mediated – there is no middle-term to explain it. If Abraham had tried to find an explanation, he would have been in a state of temptation, and in that case he would have never sacrificed Isaac, or if he had done so he would have had to return as a murderer repentant before the universal.

In his action Abraham overstepped the ethical altogether. He had a higher aim outside it in relation to which he suspended it. How else could one ever justify Abraham's action? Not in terms of the ethical. How could any point of contact ever be discovered between what Abraham did, or planned to do, and the universal other than that Abraham overstepped it? It was not to save a nation that Abraham went to sacrifice Isaac, nor to appease angry gods. Abraham's whole action stands above and apart from the universal. It is ultimately a private undertaking, an act of purely personal conscience. To judge Abraham's action according to the ethical – in the sense of the moral life – is therefore quite out of the question. In so far as the universal was there at all, it was latent in Isaac, concealed as it were in his loins, and it would have to cry out from Isaac's mouth: "Don't do it, you are destroying everything."

Then why does Abraham do it? For God's sake, and what is exactly the same, for his own. He does it for the sake of God because God demands this proof of his faith. He does it for his own sake in order to be able to produce the proof.

Abraham's situation is a kind of trial, a temptation. But what does that mean? What we usually call a temptation is something that keeps a person from carrying out a duty, but here the temptation is the ethical itself ("Thou shalt not kill") which would keep him from doing God's will. But what then is duty? In Abraham's case, duty is found in the doing of God's will, which is itself higher than the universal. His duty transcends the ethical.

Now when the ethical is suspended, as in Abraham's case, how or in what way, does the individual in whom it is suspended exist? Does this mean he sins? Not necessarily. Take a child for example. In one sense a child's bad behavior is not sin because the child is not yet fully conscious of its own existence. Looked at ideally, however, the child sins; he falls short from the demands of the ethical. Does this mean Abraham also sinned? No. Then how did Abraham exist? He had faith. He lived by and in faith. That is the paradox that kept him at the summit and which he could not explain or justify to himself or to anyone else. His faith was grounded in the paradox that as the single individual he was higher that the universal. He had an absolute relation to the Absolute. Was he justified? His justification is, once again, the paradox. He was not justified by being virtuous, but by being an individual submitted to God in faith.

This doesn't mean that the ethical is to be done away with. No. Only that it receives an entirely different expression, so that for example, love of God can cause the knight of faith to love his neighbor in a way that is quite opposite from what is usually demanded by the ethical. Unless this is how it is, faith has no place in existence. Faith becomes a temptation, and Abraham, since he gave into it, is done for.

But faith's paradox is precisely this, that the single individual is higher than the universal, that the individual determines his relationship to the universal through his relation to the Absolute (i.e. God), not his relation to the Absolute through his relation to the universal. That is, to live by faith means that one has an absolute duty to God and to God alone. In this tie of obligation the individual relates himself absolutely, as the single individual, to the Absolute – the God who commands. This duty alone is absolute and for this reason the ethical, for the person of faith, is relegated to the relative. In fear and trembling, this is faith's paradox – the suspension of the ethical.

Any way we look at it, Abraham's story contains a suspension of the ethical. He has, as the single individual, become higher than the universal. This is the paradox of faith that cannot be explained. How Abraham got himself into it is just as inexplicable as how he stayed in it. If this is not how it is with Abraham, then he is not even a tragic hero, but a murderer. To want to go on calling him the father of faith, to talk of this to those who are only concerned with words, is thoughtless. A tragic hero can become a human being by his own strength, but not the knight of faith. When a person sets out on the tragic hero's arduous path there are many who are ready to lend him advice.

But he who walks the narrow path of faith no one can advise, no one can understand. Faith is a miracle, and yet no human being is excluded from it.

8 | To Need God Is Perfection

With respect to physical existence, one needs little, and to the degree that one needs less, the more perfect one is. In a human being's relationship with God, however, it is inverted: the more one needs God the more perfect he is. To need God is nothing to be ashamed of but is perfection itself. It is the saddest thing in the world if a human being goes through life without discovering that he needs God!

For what is a human being after all? Is he just one more ornament in the vast array of creation? And what is his power? What is the highest he is able to will? Well, we do not want to defraud the highest of its price, but we cannot conceal the fact that the highest is realized only when a person is fully convinced that he himself is capable of nothing, nothing at all. What rare dominion – not rare in the sense that only one individual is born to be king, since everyone is born to it! What rare wisdom – not rare because it is offered to just a few who are educated, but because it is offered to all, and accessible to all! True, if a person turns outward, it will probably seem as if he were capable of accomplishing something amazing, something that satisfies him, something that draws enthusiastic admiration. From a human perspective, humankind may well be the most glorious creation, but all its glory is still only in the external and for the external. Does not the eye aim its arrow outward every time passion and desire tighten the bowstring? Does not the hand grasp outward, is not his arm outstretched, and is not his ingenuity all-conquering? Deception!

A human being is great and at his highest only when before God he recognizes that he is nothing in himself. Consider Moses or the so-called works of Moses. What is the deed of even the greatest hero; what are demolishing mountains and filling rivers compared with having darkness fall upon all Egypt! But these were not really Moses' works. Moses was capable of nothing at all, for the work was the Lord's. Do you see the difference? Moses – he did not make decisions and formulate plans while the council of the common sense listened attentively – Moses was capable of nothing at all. If the people had said to him, "Go to Pharaoh, because your word is powerful, your voice is triumphant, your eloquence irresistible," he would have answered, "Oh, you fools! I am capable of nothing, not even of giving my life for you if the Lord does not so will. I am capable only of submitting everything to the Lord." Or if the people who thirsted in the desert had appealed to Moses, saying, "Take your staff and order the rock to give water," would not Moses have answered, "What is my staff but a stick?"

A person who knows himself perceives that he, in and of himself, is actually capable of nothing. The same applies to the internal world. Are any of us capable of anything there, either? If a capability is actually to be a capability, it must have some kind of opposition. Without opposition, one is either all-powerful or one's capability is something entirely imaginary. In the internal world of spirit, opposition can come only from within. In this way, we struggle with ourselves. If a person does not discover this conflict, his understanding is faulty and consequently his life is imperfect; but if he does discover it, he will understand that he *himself* is capable of nothing at all.

Such self-knowledge we are referring to is really not complicated. But is one not able, then, to overcome oneself by oneself?

How can I be stronger than myself? When we speak of over-coming oneself by oneself, we really mean something external, so that the struggle is unequal. Take, for example, someone who has been tempted by worldly prestige but who conquers himself so that he no longer reaches out for it. If he is to guard his soul against a new vanity, he will have to admit that he is not really able to overcome himself. He understands that with will power alone he creates in his innermost being temptations of glory, fear, despondency, of pride and defiance, and sensuality greater than those he meets in the external world. For this reason he struggles with himself. Victory proves nothing with regard to this greater temptation. If he is victorious in facing the tempta-tion with which the surrounding world confronts him, this does not prove that he would be victorious if the temptation were as terrible as he is able to imagine it. He knows deep within himself that he is capable of nothing at all.

In one sense, to need God and to know that this is a human being's highest perfection, makes life more difficult. However, insofar as a person does not know himself, he does not actually become conscious in the deeper sense that God *is*. The person who realizes that he is capable of nothing cannot undertake the slightest thing without God's help, without becoming conscious that God is. We sometimes speak of learning to know God from the events of past history. We open up the chronicles and read and read. Well, that may be fine, but how much time it takes, and how dubious the outcome frequently is! But someone who is conscious that he is capable of nothing has every day and eve-ry moment the precious opportunity to experience that God lives. If he does not experience it often enough, he knows very well why that is. It is because his understanding is faulty and he believes that he himself is, after all, capable of something.

This does not mean that a person's life becomes easy simply because he learns to know God in this way. On the contrary, it can become that much more difficult. But in this difficulty his life acquires a deeper meaning. Should it mean nothing to him that he continually keeps his eyes on God, knowing that he himself is capable of nothing at all, yet with the help of God he is indeed capable? Should it mean nothing to him that he is learning to die to the world, to esteem less and less the things that fade away? Finally, should it not have meaning for him that he most vividly and confidently understands that God is love, that God's goodness passes all understanding?

We are not saying that to need God is to sink into a dreaming admiration and some visionary contemplation. No. God does not let himself be taken in vain in this way. Just as knowing ourselves in our own nothingness is the condition for knowing God, so knowing God is the condition for the sanctification of a human being by God's assistance and according to his intention. Wherever God is, there he is always creating. He does not want a person to be spiritually soft and to bathe in the contemplation of his glory. He wants to create a new human being. To need God is to become new. And to know God is the crucial thing. Without this knowledge a human being becomes nothing. Without this knowledge, he is scarcely able to grasp that he himself is nothing at all, and even less that to need God is his highest perfection.

9 | Purity of Heart

Purity of heart is to will one thing: "Draw near to God and he will draw near to you. Wash your hands, you sinners, and purify your hearts, you double-minded" (Jas. 4:8). Only the pure in heart can see God, and therefore, draw near to him. And only by God's drawing near to the pure in heart can they maintain this purity.

The person who in truth wills only one thing can will only the Good, and the person who wills only one thing when he wills the good can will only the Good in truth. Let your heart, therefore, will in truth only one thing, for therein is the heart's purity.

In a certain sense only a few words are needed to describe the Good. The Good, without condition, qualification, or compromise, is absolutely the only thing that a person can and should undividedly will. The person who tries to will anything else will discover that he does not truly will one thing. It is a delusion, an illusion, a deception to try and do so. For in his innermost being he is, and is bound to be, double-minded. The Good alone can be willed *as* one thing.

Although pleasure, honor, riches, and power and all that this world has to offer appear to be one thing, they are not. These can never in all circumstances remain the same. They are always subject to constant change. Each in its own way consists of a multitude of things, a dispersion, the sport of changeableness, and the prey of corruption! For example, in the pursuit of pleasure, look at how so many seek for one pleasure after another. In such a pursuit, variety is the watchword. But this is utterly futile. How can one will one thing that can never in itself remain the same thing? When a person wills in such a fashion he not only becomes double-minded, but self-divided; at complete odds with himself. He wills first one thing and then immediately another, and sometimes the opposite, and so and so on. What does such a person really will? New pleasures; something new! change! change! Ask him now if he really wills one thing. Ask him if he wills at all!

The fact is that the worldly ideal is not one thing at all. In essence it is unreal. Its so-called unity is actually nothing but emptiness concealed by a multiplicity. In the short-lived moment of experience the worldly goal is nothing but a vacuous diversion. For what else is desire in its boundless extreme but nausea? What else is earthly honor at its dizzy pinnacle but contempt for existence? What else is the overabundance of wealth but poverty? No matter how much all the earth's gold hidden in covetousness may amount to, it is infinitely less than the tiniest bit hidden in the contentment of the poor! What else is worldly power other than dependence? What slave in chains is as unfree as a tyrant!

Everyone who in truth wills one thing will eventually be led to will the Good. Though it may sometimes be that a person innocently begins by willing one thing that is not in the deepest sense the Good, he will, little by little, be transformed so as to will the Good. For example, romantic love has sometimes helped a person along the right road – he faithfully tries to will one thing, namely, the happiness of his love. In the deepest sense, however, falling in love is still not the Good. At best it is a formative educator that will lead to the willing of one thing and to the willing of the Good.

Only the Good is one thing. It alone is one in its essence and the same in each of its expressions. Take true love as an illustration. One who genuinely loves does not love but once. Nor does he offer part of his love, and then again another part. No, he loves with all of his love – not a bit here and a bit there. It is wholly present in each expression. He continues to give it away as a whole, and yet he keeps it intact as a whole, in his heart. Wonderful riches! When the miser has gathered all the world's gold in sordidness – then he has become poor. Yet when the lover gives away his whole love, he keeps it entire – in the purity of the heart.

If we in truth will one thing, then this one thing must be such that it remains unconditionally unaltered. In willing it we can win eternal constancy. If, however, what we will continually changes, then we become double-minded and unstable. This is nothing else than impurity. The one who wills anything other than the Good will become divided. And as the coveted object is, so becomes the coveter.

Let us not be deceived in this matter of willing one thing. The one who desires the Good, for instance, for the sake of some reward also fails to will one thing. He is double-minded. This is not difficult to see. The Good is one thing; the reward is something else. To will the Good for the sake of reward is not to will one thing but two. If a man loves a woman for the sake of her wealth, who will call him a lover? To will the Good for the sake of reward is hypocrisy – sheer duplicity! The person who in truth wills the Good thinks only of the Good, not of some resulting benefit. For the Good is its own reward. In fact, the pure in heart understands that here on earth the Good is often rewarded by ingratitude, by lack of appreciation, by poverty, by contempt, by many afflictions, and now and then by death. Of course, these are inconsequential for the one who in truth wills only one thing.

Neither can one who wills the Good do so out of fear of punishment. In essence, this is the same thing as willing the Good for the sake of a reward. The one who wills in truth one thing fears only doing wrong, not the punishment. In fact, he who does wrong, yet sincerely wills the Good, actually desires to face the consequences – so that the punishment, like medicine, may heal him. He understands that punishment only exists for the sake of the sinner. It is a helping hand. It goads one to press on further toward the Good, if one really wills it. On the other hand, the one who is divided considers punishment or hardship as a sickness. He fears all worldly setback for there is nothing eternal in him.

True, fear deceptively offers to help us. It too offers to keep us on the right track. Yet the one who strives in fear never becomes God's friend. Fear is a deceitful aid. It can sour your delight, make life arduous and miserable, make you old and decrepit; but it is never able to help you toward the Good. The Good will not tolerate any alien helper.

Those who live in fear may indeed desire heaven but not for itself. They anxiously do what they really would rather not do, or at least what they have no pleasure in doing. Their satisfaction consists solely in avoiding, never gaining, something. What emptiness! They are blinded to the fact that the Good wants only that they humbly and gladly follow its beckoning. For the Good there exists no limitation. It contains the impetus of eternity and possesses the Infinite's open road before it. Fear, on the other hand, is a dry nurse for the child – it has no milk. It is an anemic disciplinarian for the youth – it has no lasting beckoning power. Only one thing can help us to will the Good in truth: the Good itself.

As the Good itself is only one thing, so it alone wishes to be what helps us along. But the Good is not something external to us, like a slave who comes against his will when the master uses the whip. The place and the path are within each of us. And just as the place is the blessed state of the striving soul, so the path is the striving soul's continual transformation.

10 | Emissaries from Eternity

Providence watches over each one of us as we journey through life providing us with two guides: repentance and remorse. The one calls us forward. The other calls us back. Yet they do not contradict each other, these two guides, nor do they leave the traveler in doubt or confusion. Rather, these two guides eternally understand each other. For the one calls forward to the Good, the other back from the evil. This is precisely why there are two of them, because in order to make our journey secure we must look ahead as well as look back.

When a long procession is about to start, there is first a call from the person who is in the lead, but everyone waits until the last one has answered. The two guides call to a person early and late, and if he pays attention to their calls he finds the road and can know where he is. Likewise, Eternity's two guides call out to us early and late, and when we listen to their call, we know where we are and where we are going. Of these two, the call of remorse is perhaps the better. For the eager traveler who travels casually and quickly along the way does not get to know it as well as does the traveler with his burden. The eager traveler hurries forward to something new, away from experience, but the remorseful one, the one who comes along afterward, laboriously gathers up the experience.

These two guides call to us early and late. And yet, no, when remorse calls out it is always late. The call to find the road again by seeking God in the confession of sins is always at the eleventh hour. When remorse awakens guilt, whether it be in one's youth, or in the twilight of one's life, it does so always at the eleventh hour. It does not have much time at its disposal. It is not deceived by a false notion of a long life. For in the eleventh hour one understands life in a wholly different way than in the days of youth or in the busy time of adulthood or in the final days of old age. If we repent at any other hour of the day we fool ourselves – we fortify ourselves by a false and hasty conception of the insignificance of our guilt.

True repentance does not belong to a certain period of life, as fun and games belong to childhood, or as the excitement of romantic love belongs to youth. It does not come and disappear as a whim or as a surprise. No, no. There is a sense of reverence, a holy fear, a humility, a pure sincerity which insures that repentance does not become vain and overhasty.

From the point of view of the eternal, repentance must come "all at once," where in one's grief there is not even time to utter words. But the grieving of repentance and the heartfelt anxiety that floods the soul must not be confused with impatience or the momentary feeling of contrition. Experience teaches us that the right moment to repent is not always the one that is immediately present. Repentance can too easily be confused with a tormenting agonizing or with a worldly sorrow; with a desperate feeling of grief in itself. But by itself, sorrow never becomes repentance, no matter how long it continues to rage. However clouded the mind becomes, the sobs of contrition, no matter how violent they are, never become tears of repentance. They are like empty clouds that bear no water, or like convulsive puffs of wind. This kind of repentance is selfish. It is sensually powerful for the moment, excited in expression – and, for this very reason, is no real repentance at all. Sudden, quick repentance wants only to drink down the bitterness of sorrow in a single draught and then hurry on. It wants to get away from guilt, away from every reminder of it, and fortify itself by imagining that it does not want to be held back in the pursuit of the Good. What a delusion!

There is a story about a man who by his misdeeds deserved to be punished according to the law. After he had served his sentence he went back into ordinary society, reformed. He went to a foreign country, where he was unknown and where he became known for his upright conduct. All was forgotten. Then one day a fugitive appeared who recognized him from the past. The reformed man was terrified. A deathlike fear shook him each time the fugitive passed. Though silent, his fear shouted with a loud voice, until it became vocal in that dastardly fugitive's voice. Despair suddenly seized him and it seized him just because he had forgotten his repentance. His self-improvement had never led him to surrender to God so that in the humility of repentance he might remember what he had once been.

Yes, in the temporal and social sense, repentance may come and go. But in the eternal sense, it is a quiet daily commitment before God. In the light of eternity, one's guilt is never changed, even if a century passes by. To think anything of this sort is to confuse the eternal with what it is least like – human forgetfulness. One can tell the age of a tree by looking at its bark. One can also tell a person's age in the Good by the intensity and inwardness of his repentance. It may be said of a dancer that her time is past when her youth is gone, but not so with a penitent. Repentance, if it is forgotten, is nothing but immaturity. The longer and the more deeply one treasures it, however, the better it becomes.

Repentance must not only have its time, but also its time of preparation. And herein lies the need of confession, the holy act that ought to be preceded by preparation. Just as a person changes his clothes for a celebration, so a person preparing for confession is inwardly changed. But if in the hour of confession one has not truly made up his mind he is still only distracted. He sees his sin with only half an eye. When he speaks, it is just talk – not true confession.

We mustn't forget that the One who is present in confession is omniscient. God knows everything, remembers everything, all that we have ever confided to him, or what we have ever kept from his confidence. He is the One "who sees in secret," with whom we speak even in silence. No one can venture to deceive him either by talk or by silence. When we confess to God, therefore, we are not like a servant that gives account to his master for the administration entrusted to him because his master could not manage everything or be everywhere at once. Nor when we confess are we like one who confides in a friend to whom sooner or later he reveals things that his friend did not previously know. No, much of what you are able to keep hidden in darkness you only first get to know by revealing it to the all-knowing One. The all-knowing One does not get to know something about those who confess, rather those who confess find out something about themselves.

11 | God Has No Cause

There are those who talk about God's cause, and about wanting to serve that cause. This is all very fine, but how, exactly, is this to be interpreted? The common view thinks that God has a cause in the human sense of the word, that he is some kind of advocate, interested in having his cause win and therefore eager to help the person who would serve his cause, and so forth. If we follow this line of thinking God becomes a minor character who arrives at the embarrassing dilemma of needing human beings.

No, no! God has no cause, is no advocate in this sense. For God everything is infinitely nothing. Any second he wills it, everything, including all opposition to his cause, becomes nothing. Wanting to serve God's cause can never mean the same thing as coming to his aid. No, to serve God's cause is to face examination. If someone wants to serve his cause, it is not God who loses his balance and sublimity; no, he fixes his attention upon this volunteer – observantly – and sees how he conducts himself, whether he has integrity and resolve. Because God is not interested in temporal causes, because he is infinitely the conquering Lord, precisely for that reason he examines. He is quite able to accomplish his will alone.

This is why the more one is involved with God the more rigorous everything becomes. It is out of God's infinite love that he involves himself with every human being. The very fact that

God permits evil people to thrive in this world is a mark of his infinite majesty. Do you not understand this frightful punishment, that God overlooks them? God's punishment is upon those he chooses to have nothing more to do with. And yet he always accomplishes what he wills.

We usually think that when we honestly want to serve God's cause, God will also help us along. Well, how? In a material way? By a successful outcome, prosperity, earthly advantage, or the like? But in that case everything gets turned around and it no longer remains *God's* cause but a finite endeavor. Besides, maybe I am only a cunning fellow, who really does not want to serve God but in a deceptive, pious way to cheat God to my advantage. Perhaps I even think that God is in a bind and is made happy as soon as someone volunteers to serve his cause. Utter nonsense and blasphemy! No, God is spirit – and our task is to be transformed into spirit. But spirit is absolutely opposed to being related to God by way of temporal benefits. Such is God's sublimity – and yet this is the infinite love of God!

Yes, infinite love, so infinite that God desires to involve himself with every human being, with every weak, foolish, carnal heart who tries to make him into a nice uncle, a really fine grandfather whom we can make good use of.

God is infinite love and for this reason has no cause. He will not suddenly overpower a person and demand that he instantly become spirit. If that were the case we would all perish. No, he handles each person gently. His is a long operation, an upbringing in love. Yes, there are times when one gasps and God strengthens with material blessings. But there is one thing God requires unconditionally at every moment – integrity – that one does not reverse the relationship and try to prove his relationship to God or the truth of his cause by good fortune, prosperity, and the like. God wants us to understand that material blessings are a concession to our weakness and very likely something he will withdraw at some later date to help us make true progress, not in some finite endeavor but in passing the examination.

12 | An Eternity in Which to Repent

Let me tell a story. Somewhere in the Orient there lived a poor old couple. They possessed nothing but poverty. Naturally, anxiety about the future increased as they grew older. They did not assail heaven with their prayers, for they were too pious for that; but nevertheless they continually cried to heaven for help.

Then it happened one morning that the wife, going out to the oven, found a precious stone of great size upon the hearth. She immediately showed the stone to her husband, who saw at once that they were well supplied for the rest of their life. A bright future for this old couple – what joy! Yet, God-fearing as they were, and content with little, they resolved that since they had enough to live upon for another day, they would sell the jewel not that day, but the following. And then a new life would begin.

That night the woman dreamed that she was transported to paradise. An angel took her around and showed her all the glories an oriental imagination could invent. Then the angel led her into a hall where there were long rows of armchairs adorned with pearls and precious stones, which, the angel explained, were for the devout. Finally the angel showed her the chair that was intended for her. Looking more closely, the woman saw a large jewel was missing from the back of the seat. She asked the angel how that had come about.

Now be alert, here comes the story! The angel answered, "That was the precious stone you found on the hearth. You received it in advance, and so it cannot be inserted again."

In the morning the woman related the dream to her husband. She felt they should hold on to the stone for a few years longer rather than let the precious stone be absent throughout eternity. And her devout husband agreed. So, that evening they laid the stone back on the hearth and prayed to God that he would take it back. In the morning, sure enough, it was gone. Where it had gone the old couple knew: it was now in its right place.

Oh, remember this well! You may perhaps be cunning enough to avoid suffering and adversity in this life, you may perhaps be clever enough to evade ruin and ridicule and instead enjoy all the earth's goods, and you may perhaps be fooled into the vain delusion that you are on the right path just because you have won worldly benefits, but beware, you will have an eternity in which to repent! An eternity in which to repent, that you failed to invest your life upon that which lasts: to love God in truth, come what may, with the consequence that in this life you will suffer under the hands of men.

Therefore do not deceive yourself! Of all deceivers fear most yourself! Even if it were possible in relation to the eternal to take something in advance, you would yet be deceiving yourself by taking something in advance – and gain an eternity in which to repent.

II | TRUTH

AND

THE

PASSION

OF

INWARDNESS

13 | Truth Is the Way

Truth is not something you can appropriate easily and quickly. You certainly cannot sleep or dream yourself into the truth. No, you must be tried, do battle, and suffer if you are to acquire truth for yourself. It is a sheer illusion to think that in relation to truth there is an abridgment, a short cut that dispenses with the necessity of struggling for it. With respect to acquiring truth to live by, every generation and every individual must essentially begin from the beginning.

What is truth, and in what sense was Christ the truth? The first question, as is well known, was asked by Pilate (Jn. 18:38), and it is doubtful whether he ever really cared to have his question answered. Pilate asks Christ, "What is truth?" That it did not occur to Pilate that Christ was the truth demonstrates precisely that he had no eye at all for truth. Christ's life was the truth (Jn. 14:6). To this end was Christ born, and for this purpose did he come into the world, that he should bear witness to the truth. What, then, is the fundamental confusion in Pilate's question? It consists in this, that it occurred to him to question *Christ* in this way; for in questioning Christ he actually denounced himself; he revealed that Christ's life had not illumined him. How could Christ enlighten Pilate with words when Pilate could not see through Christ's own life what truth is!

Pilate's question is extremely foolish. Not that he asks, "What is truth?" but that he questions Christ, he whose life is expressly the truth and who at every moment demonstrates more power-fully by his life what truth is than all the most profound lectures of the cleverest thinkers. Though it makes perfect sense to ask any other person, a thinker, a teacher, or whoever, "What is truth?" to ask Christ this it is the greatest possible confusion. Obviously Pilate is of the opinion that Christ is just a man, like everyone else. Poor Pilate! Pilate's question is the most foolish and confusing question ever asked by man. It is as if I were to ask someone standing right before me, "Do you exist?" How can that person reply? So also with Christ in relation to Pilate. Christ is the truth. "If my life," he might say, "cannot open your eyes to what truth is, then what can I say? For I *am* the truth."

As with Pilate, in our day Christ as the truth has also been abolished: we take Christ's teaching – but abolish Christ. We want truth the easy way. This is to abolish truth, for Christ the teacher is more important than the teaching. Just as Christ's life, the fact that he lived here on earth, is vastly more important than all the results of his life, so also is Christ infinitely more important than his teaching.

Christ is the truth in the sense that to *be* the truth is the only true explanation of it; the only true way of acquiring it. Truth is not a sum of statements, not a definition, not a system of con-cepts, but a life. Truth is not a property of thought that guaran-tees validity to thinking. No, truth in its most essential character is the reduplication* of truth within yourself, within me, within him. Your life, my life, his life expresses the truth in the striving. Just as the truth was a life in Christ, so too, for us truth must be lived.

Reduplication is Kierkegaard's term meaning to exist in what one understands, to manifest the truth in one's life. It means to live out in life the challenges of thought, to be what one says.

Therefore, truth is not a matter of knowing this or that but of being in the truth. Despite all modern philosophy, there is an infinite difference here, best seen in Christ's response to Pilate. Christ did not know the truth but was the truth. Not as if he did not know what truth is, but when one is the truth and when the requirement is to be in the truth, to merely "know" the truth is insufficient – it is an untruth. For knowing the truth is something that follows as a matter of course from being in the truth, not the other way around. Nobody knows more of the truth than what he is of the truth. To properly know the truth is to be in the truth; it is to have the truth for one's life. This always costs a struggle. Any other kind of knowledge is a falsification. In short, the truth, if it is really there, is a being, a *life*. The Gospel says that this is eternal life, to know the only true God and the one whom he sent, the truth (Jn. 17:3). That is, I only know the truth when it becomes a life in me.

Truth is not a deposit of acquired knowledge, the yield. This might have been if Christ had been, for example, a teacher of truth, a thinker, one who made a discovery. But Christ is the way as well as the truth. His teaching is infinitely superior to all the inventions of any and every age, an eternity older and an eternity higher than all systems, even the very newest. His teaching is the truth – not in terms of knowledge, but in the sense that the truth is a way – and as the God-man he is and remains the way; something that no human being, however zealously he professes that the truth is the way, dare assert of himself without blasphemy.

Christ compares truth to food and appropriating it to eating it (Jn. 6:48–51). Just as food is appropriated (assimilated) and thereby becomes the sustenance of life, so also spiritually, truth is both the giver and the sustenance of life. It is life. Therefore one can see what a monstrous mistake it is to impart or represent

Christianity by lecturing. The truth is lived before it is understood. It must be fought for, tested, and appropriated. Truth is
the way. And when the truth is the way, then the way cannot be
shortened or drop out unless the truth itself is distorted or
drops out. Is this not too difficult to understand? Anyone will
easily understand it if he just gives himself to it.

14 | The Road Is *How*

There is a generally accepted metaphor that compares life to a road. To compare life to a road can indeed be fruitful in many ways, but we must consider how life is unlike a road. In a physical sense a road is an external actuality, no matter whether anyone is walking on it or not, no matter how the individual travels on it – the road is the road. But in the spiritual sense, the road comes into existence only when we walk on it. That is, the road *is* how it is walked.

It would be unreasonable to define a highway by how it is walked. Whether it is the young person who walks it with his head held high or the old decrepit person who struggles along with head bowed down, whether it is the happy person hurrying to reach a goal or the worrier who creeps slowly along, whether it is the poor traveler on foot or the rich traveler in his carriage – the road, in the physical sense, is the same for all. The road is and remains the same, the same highway. But not the road of virtue. We cannot point to the road of virtue and say: There runs the road of virtue. We can only show how the road of virtue is walked, and if anyone refuses to walk that way, he is walking another road.

The dissimilarity in the metaphor shows up most clearly when the discussion is simultaneously about a physical road and a road in the spiritual sense. For example, when we read in the Gospel about the good Samaritan, there is mention of the road between Jericho and Jerusalem. The story tells of five people who walked "along the same road." Spiritually speaking, however, each one walked his own road. The highway, alas, makes no difference; it is the spiritual that makes the difference and distinguishes the road. Let us consider more carefully how this is.

The first man was a peaceful traveler who walked along the road from Jericho to Jerusalem, along a lawful road. The second man was a robber who "walked along the same road" – and yet on an unlawful road. Then a priest came "along the same road"; he saw the poor unfortunate man who had been assaulted by the robber. Perhaps he was momentarily moved but went right on by. He walked the road of indifference. Next a Levite came "along the same road." He saw the poor unfortunate man; he too walked past unmoved, continuing his road. The Levite walked "along the same road" but was walking his way, the way of selfishness and callousness. Finally a Samaritan came "along the same road." He found the poor unfortunate man on the road of mercy. He showed by example how to walk the road of mercy; he demonstrated that the road, spiritually speaking, is precisely this; *how* one walks. This is why the Gospel says, "Go and do likewise." Yes, there were five travelers who walked "along the same road," and yet each one walked his own road.

The question "how one walks life's road" makes all the difference. In other words, when life is compared to a road, the metaphor simply expresses the universal, that which everyone who is alive has in common by being alive. To that extent we are all walking along the road of life and are all walking along the same road. But when living becomes a matter of truth, then the question becomes: How shall we walk in order to walk the right road on the road of life? The traveler who in truth walks life's road does not ask, "Where is the road?" but asks how one ought to walk along the road. Yet, because impatience does not mind be-ing deceived it merely asks where the road is, as if that decided everything as when the traveler finally has found the highway. Worldly wisdom is very willing to deceive by answering cor-rectly the question, "Where is the road?" while life's true task is omitted, that spiritually understood the road is: how it is walked.

Worldly sagacity teaches that the road goes over Gerizim, or over Moriah, or that it goes through some science or other, or that the road is certain doctrines, or certain behaviors. But all this is a deception, because the road is how it is walked. It is in-deed as Scripture says – two people can be sleeping in the same bed – the one is saved, the other is lost. Two people can go up to the same house of worship – the one goes home saved, the other is lost. Two people can recite the same creed – the one can be saved, the other is lost. How does this happen except for the fact that, spiritually speaking, it is a deception to know where the road is, because the road is: how it is walked?

15 | Two Ways of Reflection

There are two ways of reflection. For objective reflection, truth becomes an object, and the point is to disregard the knowing subject (the individual). By contrast, in subjective reflection truth becomes personal appropriation, a life, inwardness, and the point is to immerse oneself in this subjectivity. Now, then, which of the ways is the way of truth that matters for an existing person?

The way of objective reflection turns the individual into something accidental, and thus turns existence into an indifferent, vanishing something. The way of objective truth turns away from the knowing subject. The subject and subjectivity become unimportant, and correspondingly, the truth is a matter of indifference. Objective validity is paramount. Any personal interest is subjectivity. For this reason the objective way is convinced that it possesses a security that the subjective way does not have. It is of the opinion that it avoids the danger that lies in wait for the subjective way, and at its extreme this danger is madness. In its view, a solely subjective definition of truth make lunacy and truth indistinguishable. But by staying objective one avoids becoming a lunatic. However, is not the absence of inwardness also lunacy?

It is true that subjective reflection turns inward, but in this inward deepening there is truth. Lest we forget, the subject, the individual, is an *existing* self, and existing is a process of becoming. Therefore truth as the identity of thought and being is an illusion of the abstract. The knower is first and foremost an existing person. In other words, thinking and being are not automatically one and the same. If the existing person could actually be outside himself, the truth would then be something concluded for him. However, for the truly existing person, passion, not thought, is existence at its very highest: true knowing pertains essentially to existence, to a life of decision and responsibility. Only ethical and ethical-religious knowing is essential knowing. Only truth that matters to me, to you, is of significance.

Let me clarify the difference between objective and subjective reflection. True inwardness in an existing subject involves passion, and truth as a paradox corresponds to passion. In forgetting that one is an existing subject, one loses passion, and in turn, truth ceases to be a paradox. If truth is the comprehensible, the knowing subject shifts from being human to being an abstract thinker, and truth becomes an abstract, comprehensible object for his knowing. When the question about truth is asked objectively, what is reflected upon is not the relation but the *what* of the relation. As long as what one relates oneself to is the truth, the subject is supposedly in the truth. But when the question about truth is asked subjectively, the individual's *relation* to the truth is what matters. If only the *how* (not the *what*) of this relation is in truth, then the individual is in truth, even if he in this way were to relate himself to untruth.

When approached objectively, the question of truth is only about categories of thought. Approached subjectively, however, truth is about inwardness. At its maximum, the how of inwardness is the passion of the infinite, and the passion of the infinite is the essential truth. Decision exists only in subjectivity. Thus the passion of the infinite, not its content, is the deciding factor, for its content is precisely itself. In this way the subjective *how* and subjectivity, not the objective *what* and objectivity, are the truth.

Let us take the knowledge of God as an example. The way of objectivity concerns itself with what is reflected upon, of whether this is the true God. In the way of subjectivity, however, the individual relates to God in such a way that this relation is in truth a God-relation. Now, on which side is the truth? Is it on neither side? Or, better yet, does it lie somewhere in between? But how can this be? An existing person cannot be in two places at once. He cannot exist as a subject-object.

God is a subject to be related to, not an object to be studied or mediated on. He exists only for subjective inwardness. The person who chooses the subjective way immediately grasps the difficulty of trying to find God objectively. He understands that to know God means to resort to God, not by virtue of objective deliberation, but by virtue of the infinite passion of inwardness. Whereas objective knowledge goes along leisurely on the long road of deliberation, subjective knowledge considers every delay of decision a deadly peril. Knowing subjectively considers decision so important that it is immediately urgent, as if the delayed opportunity had already passed by unused.

Now, if the problem is to determine where there is more truth, whether on the side of the person who only objectively seeks the true God and the approximating truth of the God-idea or on the side of the person who is infinitely concerned that he in truth relate himself to God with the passion of his need, then there can be no doubt about the answer. If someone lives in the midst of Christianity and enters, with knowledge of the true idea of God, the house of God, the house of the true God, and prays, but prays in untruth, and if someone lives in an idolatrous land but prays with all the passion of infinity, although his eyes are resting upon the image of an idol – where, then, is there more truth? The one prays in truth to God although he is worshipping an idol; the other prays in untruth to the true God and is therefore in truth worshipping an idol. The distance between objective reflection and subjectivity is indeed an infinite one.

16 | The Weight of Inwardness

Truth is the work of freedom and in such a way that freedom constantly brings forth truth. What I am referring to is very plain and simple, namely, that truth exists for a particular individual only as he himself produces it in action. If the individual prevents the truth from being for him in that way, we have a phenomenon of the demonic. Truth has always had many loud proclaimers, but the question is whether a person will in the deepest sense acknowledge the truth, allow it to permeate his whole being, accept all its consequences, and not have an emergency hiding place for himself and a Judas kiss for the consequence.

There is a lot of talk about truth. But the task before us is to vindicate certitude and inwardness, not in abstraction but in an entirely concrete sense. Certitude and inwardness determine whether or not the individual is in the truth. It is not a lack of content that gives rise to arbitrariness, unbelief, mockery of religion, but lack of certitude. Whenever inwardness and appropriation are lacking, the individual is unfree in relation to the truth, even though he otherwise "possesses" the whole truth. He is unfree because there is something that makes him anxious, namely, the good.

It is not my desire to use big words in speaking about the Age as a whole. However, you can hardly deny that the reason for its anxiety and unrest is because in one direction, "truth" increases in scope and in quantity – via science and technology – while in the other, certainty and confidence steadily decline. Our age is a master in developing truths while being wholly indifferent to certitude. It lacks confidence in the good.

Take the thought of immortality, for example. The person who knows how to prove the immortality of the soul but who is not himself convinced by it, and does not live by it will always be anxious. Despite all his proofs, he shrinks from the truth of immortality. He deceives both himself and others by pretending that the proof is enough. In the process of trying to prove immortality he forgets immortality, since immortality is precisely what he fears. He remains anxious and is thus forced to seek yet a further understanding of what it means to believe in the soul's immortality.

Without inwardness, an adherent of the most rigid orthodoxy may be demonic. He knows it all. He genuflects before the holy. He is ceremoniously flawless. He speaks of meeting before the throne of God and knows how many times to bow. He knows everything, but only like the person who can prove a mathematical proposition when the letters are ABC, but not when the letters are DEF. He is nonetheless anxious, especially whenever he hears something that is not exactly the same as his belief. He resembles the philosopher who has discovered a new proof for the immortality of the soul and then, in peril of his life, cannot produce the proof because he has forgotten his notebooks! What is it that both of them lack? It is certitude.

With what industrious zeal, with what sacrifice of time, diligence, and writing materials the theologians and philosophers in our time have spent to prove God's existence! Yet to the same degree that the excellence of these proofs increase certainty declines. What is it that such individuals lack? Again, it is inwardness.

But inwardness may also be lacking in an opposite direction. So-called pious Christians are also unfree. They too lack the authentic certitude of inwardness. That is why they are so pious! And the world is surely justified in laughing at them. If, for example, a bowlegged man wants to be a dancing master but is not able to execute a single step, he is comical. So it is also with the multitudes who are so religious. Often you can hear the pious beating time, as it were, exactly like one who cannot dance but nevertheless knows enough to beat time, yet who are never fortunate enough to get in step. In order to reassure themselves, the pious seize upon grandiose ideas that the world hates. They battle ideas, but not with their lives. Such is the life of those who lack inwardness.

Eternity is a very radical thought, and thus a matter of inwardness. Whenever the reality of the eternal is affirmed, the present becomes something entirely different from what it was apart from it. This is precisely why human beings fear it (under the guise of fearing death). You often hear about particular governments that fear the restless elements of society. I prefer to say that the entire Age is a tyrant that lives in fear of the one restless element: the thought of eternity. It does not dare to think it. Why? Because it crumbles under – and avoids like anything – the weight of inwardness.

17 | **Christ Has No Doctrine**

A **true believer** is infinitely interested in what is real. For faith this is decisive, and this interestedness does not just involve a little curiosity but an absolute dependence on the object of faith.

The object of faith, understood Christianly, is not a doctrine, for then the relation is merely intellectual. Neither is the object of faith a teacher who has a doctrine, for when a teacher has a doctrine, then the doctrine is more important than the teacher. The object of faith is the actuality and authority of the teacher; that the teacher actually is. Therefore faith's answer is absolutely either yes or no. Faith's posture is not in relation to a teaching, whether it is true or not, but is the answer to the question about a fact: Do you accept as fact that he, the Teacher, actually exists? Please note that the answer to this is a matter of infinite concern. Of course, if the object of faith is only a human being, then the whole thing is a sham. But this is not the case for Christians. The object of Christian faith is God's historical existence, that is, that God at a certain point in time existed as an individual human being.

Christianity, therefore, is not a doctrine about the unity of the divine and the human, not to mention the rest of the logical paraphrases of typical religious thought. Christianity is not a doctrine but a fact: God came into existence through a particular human being at a particular point in history.

Christianity is not to be confused with objective or scientific truth. When Christ came into the world it was difficult to become a Christian, and for this reason one did not become preoccupied with trying to understand it. Now we have almost reached the parody that to become a Christian is nothing at all, but it is a difficult and very involved task to understand it. Everything is reversed. Christianity is transformed into a kind of worldview, a way of thinking about life, and the task of faith consists in understanding and articulating it. But faith essentially relates itself to existence, and *becoming* a Christian is what is important. Believing in Christ and wanting to "understand" his way by articulating it and elaborating on it is actually a cowardly evasion that wants to shirk the task. To become a Christian is the ultimate, to want to "understand" Christianity, as if it were some doctrine, is open to suspicion.

That one can know what Christianity is without being a Christian is one thing. But whether one can know what it is to *be* a Christian without being one is something else entirely. And this is the problem of faith. One can find no greater dubiousness than when, by the help of "Christianity," it is possible to find Christians who have not yet become Christians.

Faith, therefore, and the object of faith is not a lesson for slow learners in the sphere of knowledge, an asylum for the ignorant. Faith exists in a sphere of its own. The immediate identifying mark of every misunderstanding of Christianity is that faith is changed into a belief and drawn into the range of intellectuality – a matter of understanding, of knowledge. Infinite interestedness in the actuality and authority of the Teacher, absolute commitment, *becoming* Christian – that is the sole passion and object of faith.

18 | Faith: The Matchless Lack of Logic

Can one come to *know* anything about Christ from history? No. And why not? It is because Christ is the paradox, the object of faith, and exists only for faith. About him nothing can be known; he can only be believed. You cannot come to know anything about Christ from history. Whether one learns little or much about him, it will not represent who he is in reality. Obtaining historical facts makes Christ into someone other than who he in fact is.

Can't you at least demonstrate from history that Christ was God, even though we might know little else? Let me ask another question first: Can any more absurd contradiction be imagined than wishing to prove that an individual person is God? Now think of proving that! How can you make something that conflicts with reason into something reasonable? You can't, unless you wish to contradict yourself. The so-called proofs for the divinity of Christ that people claim Scripture sets forth – his miracles, his resurrection, his ascension – are not, when you think about it, in harmony with our reason. On the contrary, they demonstrate that believing in Christ's works is a matter of faith.

What can all the miracles really demonstrate anyway? At most that Jesus Christ was a great man, perhaps the greatest who ever lived. But that he was – God – no, stop; that conclusion will surely miscarry.

How is it possible to observe the gradually unfolding results of something and then arrive at, by some trick of deduction, a conclusion different in quality from what you began with? Is it not sheer insanity (providing humanity is sane) to let your judgment become so altogether confused as to land in the wrong category? A footprint is certainly the consequence of some creature having made it. I may mistake it for that of a bird, but on closer inspection, and by following the prints for some distance, I may determine that some other animal made it. Fine. But can I at some point reach the conclusion: ergo it is a spirit that has walked along this way, a spirit – which leaves no print? Precisely the same holds true whenever we try to infer from the results of a person's life that therefore he was God.

True, if God and humankind resemble each other so closely so as to essentially belong to the same category of being, the conclusion "therefore Christ was God" makes perfect sense. But this is nothing but humbug. If that is all there is to being God, then God does not exist at all! But if God belongs to a category infinitely different from the human, why, then neither I nor any one else can start with the assumption that Christ was human and then logically conclude that therefore he was God. Anyone with a bit of logical sense should be able to see this. The question of whether or not he was God lies on an entirely different plane: each person must decide for himself whether or not he will *believe* Christ to be what he himself claimed to be.

Faith protests against every attempt to approach Christ by means of historical facts. Faith's contention is that the historian's whole approach is – blasphemy. How strange! With the help of history, that is, by looking at the results of Christ's life, we think we can arrive at the conclusion that he was God. Yet faith makes the very opposite claim. Anyone who begins with this kind of logic is guilty of blasphemy. The blasphemy is not so much the hypothetical assumption that Christ was a human being, but in the thought that the results of his life can be separated from who he was. When you scrutinize the facts, you make Christ out to be just a man.

With regard to Christ we have only sacred history (which is qualitatively different from the historian's account). Christ is the divine-human paradox that history can never digest or convert into a proof. Even with what we know of Christ's life and of all his brilliant works, they will pale in comparison to his coming again in glory! Or perhaps you think that Christ's return will be nothing more than the progressive result of his life in history? No! Christ's return will be something entirely different, something that can only be believed. That Christ was God incarnate in his lowliness and that he will come again in glory, all this is far beyond the comprehension of history. This cannot be inferred from "facts" or from history, no matter how matchlessly you regard them, except through a matchless lack of logic.

It is infinitely beyond history's capacity to demonstrate that God, the omnipresent One, lived here on earth as an individual human being. History can indeed richly communicate knowledge, but such knowledge annihilates Jesus Christ. How strange, then, that anyone ever wanted to use history to demonstrate that Christ was God. Even if Christ's life had manifested no astonishing results, it makes no difference. Besides, what's so extraordinary about the fact that *God's* life had extraordinary results? To talk this way is sheer nonsense. No, God lived here on earth, in true lowliness, and that is what is infinitely extraordinary – extraordinary in itself. The fact that he lived among us is infinitely more important than all the extraordinary results ever recorded in history.

19 | Passion and Paradox

How shall we understand the truth in terms of subjectivity? Here is a definition: The truth is an objective uncertainty held fast through personal appropriation with the most passionate inwardness. This is the highest truth there can be for an existing person. At the point where the road divides, objective knowledge is suspended, and one has only uncertainty, but this is precisely what intensifies the infinite passion of inwardness. Subjective truth is precisely the daring venture of choosing the objective uncertainty with the passion of the infinite.

I observe nature in order to find God, and I do indeed see omnipotence and wisdom. However, I also see much that is troubling and unsettling. The sum total of this is that God's existence is an objective uncertainty, but the inwardness, the certainty of his existence, is still so very great, precisely because of this objective uncertainty. In a mathematical proposition absolute objectivity is given, but for that reason its truth is also an indifferent truth and concerns me very little.

Now the definition of truth stated above is actually a paraphrasing of faith. No uncertainty, no risk. No risk, no faith. Faith is the contradiction between the infinite passion of inwardness and objective uncertainty. In other words, if I apprehend God objectively, I do not have faith; but because I cannot do this, I must have faith. If I want to keep myself in faith, I must continually see to it that I hold fast the objective uncertainty. I must see to it that in the objective uncertainty I am "out on 70,000 fathoms of water" and still have faith.

This is not all. Truth as subjectivity, when it is in highest intensity, holds fast to more than objective uncertainty. When subjectivity or inwardness is truth, then truth, objectively defined, is a paradox. Paradox shows precisely that subjectivity is truth, for objectivity's repulsion, the paradox, is the resilience and barometer of inwardness.

Socrates' great merit is precisely in being an *existing* thinker, not a speculative thinker who forgets what it means to exist. And this is indeed admirable. But let us now go further; let us assume that the eternal, essential truth is itself the paradox. How does the paradox emerge? By placing the eternal, essential truth together with *existing*. The eternal truth itself has come into existence in time. That is the paradox, and the highest truth for an existing person.

Again, without risk, no faith; the more risk, the more faith. Therefore, the more objective reliability, the less inwardness (inwardness is subjectivity); the less objective reliability, the deeper the possible inwardness. Hence, when the paradox is the object of faith it thrusts away by virtue of the absurd, and the corresponding passion of inwardness is faith. What, then, is the absurd? The absurd is that the eternal truth has come into existence in time, that God has come into existence, has been born, has grown up, has come into existence exactly as an individual human being, indistinguishable from any other human being.

Subjectivity is truth and if subjectivity is in existing, then, if I may put it this way, Christianity is a perfect fit. Subjectivity culminates in passion; Christianity culminates in paradox (God in Christ; God on the Cross); paradox and passion fit each other perfectly, for paradox perfectly fits a person situated in the extremity of existence. Indeed, in the whole wide world there are not to be found two loves who fit each other as do paradox and passion, Christianity and faith.

Thus, if someone wants to have faith and reason too, well, let the comedy begin. He wants to have faith, but he wants to assure himself with the aid of objective deliberation. What happens? With the aid of reason, the absurd becomes something else; it becomes probable, it becomes more probable, it may become to a high degree exceedingly probable, even demonstrable. Now he is all set to believe it, and he dares to say of himself that he does not believe as shoemakers and tailors and simple folk do, but only after long and careful deliberation. Now he is all set to believe, but, lo and behold, now it has indeed become impossible to believe. The almost probable, the probable, the to-a-high-degree and exceedingly probable, that he can almost know, or as good as know, to a higher degree and exceedingly almost *know* – but *believe,* that cannot be done, for the absurd is precisely the object of faith and only that can be believed with the passion of inwardness.

Christianity claims to be the eternal, essential truth that has come into existence in time. It proclaims itself as *the* paradox and thus requires the inwardness of faith – that which is an offense to the Jews, foolishness to the Greeks, and an absurdity to the understanding. It cannot be expressed more strongly: Objectivity and faith are at complete odds with each other. What does objective faith mean? Doesn't it amount to nothing more than a sum of tenets?

Christianity is nothing of the kind. On the contrary, it is inwardness, an inwardness of existence that places a person decisively, more decisively than any judge can place the accused, between time and eternity, between heaven and hell in the time of salvation. But objective faith? It is as if Christianity was a little system of sorts, although presumably not as good as the Hegelian system. It is as if Christ – it is not my fault that I say it – had been a professor and as if the apostles had formed a little professional society of thinkers. The passion of inwardness and objective deliberation are at complete odds with each other. There is no way of getting around it. To become objective, to become preoccupied with the "what" of Christianity, instead of with the "how" of being Christian, is nothing but a retrogression.

Christianity is subjective; the inwardness of faith in the believer is the truth's eternal decision. Objectively there is no truth "out there" for existing beings, but only approximations, whereas subjectively truth lies in inwardness, because the decision of truth is in subjectivity. For how can decision be an approximation or only to a certain degree? What could it possibly mean to assert or to assume that decision is like approximation, is only to a certain degree? I will tell you what it means. It means to deny decision. The decision of faith, unlike speculation, is designed specifically to put an end to that perpetual prattle of "to a certain degree."

For an *existing* individual, therefore, there is no objective truth "out there." An objective knowledge about the truth or the truths of Christianity is precisely untruth. To know a creed by rote is, quite simply, paganism. This is because Christianity is inwardness. Christianity is paradox, and paradox requires but one thing: the passion of faith.

20 | The Folly of Proving God's Existence

Let us call the unknown *God.* It is only a name we give to it. Now it hardly occurs to the understanding to want to demonstrate that this unknown exists. If, namely, God does not exist, then of course it is impossible to demonstrate it. But if he does exist, then it is also foolishness to want to demonstrate it, for in the very moment the demonstration commences, you would presuppose his existence. Otherwise you would not begin, easily perceiving that the whole thing would be impossible if he did not exist.

One never reasons in conclusion *to* existence, but reasons in conclusion *from* existence. For example, I do not demonstrate that a stone exists but that something, which exists, is a stone. The court of law does not demonstrate that a criminal exists but that the accused, who does indeed exist, is a criminal. Whether you want to call existence an addition or the eternal presupposition, it can never be demonstrated.

If, for example, I wanted to demonstrate Napoleon's existence from his works, would this not be most curious? Isn't it Napoleon's existence which explains his works, not his works his existence? To prove Napoleon's existence from his works I would have in advance interpreted the word "his" in such a way as to have assumed that he exists. Moreover, because Napoleon is only a human being, it is possible that someone else could have done the same works. This is why I cannot reason from the works to *his* existence. If I call the works Napoleon's works, then the demonstration is superfluous, for I have already mentioned his name. If I ignore this, I can never demonstrate from the works that they are Napoleon's. At least I cannot guarantee that they are his. I can only demonstrate that such works are the works of, say, a great general. However, with God there is an absolute relation between him and his works. If God is not a name but a reality, his essence must involve his existence.

God's works, therefore, only God can do. Quite correct. But, then, what are God's works? The works from which I want to demonstrate his existence do not immediately and directly exist. Are the wisdom in nature and the goodness or wisdom in governance right in front of our noses? Don't we also encounter terrible tribulations here? How can I demonstrate God's existence from such an arrangement of things? Even if I began, I would never finish. Not only that, I would be obliged to continually live in suspense lest something so terrible happen that my fragment of demonstration would be ruined.

The fool says in his heart that there is no God, but he who says in his heart or to others: Just wait a little and I will prove it to you – ah, what a rare wise man he is! If, at the moment he is supposed to begin the demonstration, it is not totally undecided whether God exists or not, then, of course, he cannot demonstrate it. And if that is the situation in the beginning, then he will never make a beginning – partly for fear that he will not succeed, because God may not exist, and partly because he has nothing with which to begin.

In short, to demonstrate the existence of someone who already exists is the most shameless assault. It is an attempt to make him ludicrous. The trouble is that one does not even suspect this, that in dead seriousness one even regards it as a godly undertaking. How could it occur to anyone to demonstrate that God exists unless one has already allowed himself to ignore him?

A king's existence is demonstrated by way of subjection and submissiveness. Do you want to try and demonstrate that the king exists? Will you do so by offering a string of proofs, a series of arguments? No. If you are serious, you will demonstrate the king's existence by your submission, by the way you live. And so it is with demonstrating God's existence. It is accomplished not by proofs but by worship. Any other way is but a thinker's pious bungling.

21 | Answering Doubt

Have you ever doubted? I wonder whether you have ever born the marks of imitation? I wonder whether you have forsaken all to follow Christ? I wonder, whether your life has been marked by persecution?

Indeed, many have doubted. And there have been those who felt obliged to refute their doubt with reasons. But these reasons backfire and foster a doubt that gets stronger and stronger. Why? Because demonstrating the truth of Christianity does not lie in reasons but in *imitation:* what resembles the truth. Yet we Christians prefer to take this proof away. The need for "reasons" is already a kind of doubt – doubt lives off reasons. We fail to notice that the more reasons one advances, the more one nourishes doubt and the stronger doubt becomes. Offering doubt reasons in order to kill it is just like offering a hungry monster food it likes best of all in order to eliminate it.

No, we must not offer reasons to doubt – at least not if our intention is to kill it. We must do as Luther did, order doubt to shut its mouth, and to that end we must keep quiet.

Those whose lives imitate Christ's do not doubt such things as Christ's resurrection. And why not? Because their lives are so strenuous, so much expended in daily sufferings that they are unable to sit in idleness keeping company with reasons and doubt, playing at evens or odds. Secondly, need itself quenches the doubt. When it is for a good cause that you are despised, persecuted, ridiculed, in poverty, then you will find that you do not doubt Christ's resurrection, because you need it.

Without a life of imitation, of following Christ, it is impossible to gain mastery over doubts. We cannot stop doubt with reasons. Those who try have not learned that it is wasted effort. They do not understand that imitation is the only force that, like a police force, can break up the mob of doubts and clear the area and compel them to go home and hold their tongues.

Recall that the Savior of the world did not come to bring a doctrine; he never lectured. He did not try by way of reasons to prevail upon anyone to accept his teaching, nor did he try to authenticate it by demonstrable proofs. His teaching was his life, his existence. If someone wanted to be his follower, he said to that person something like this, "Venture a decisive act; then you can begin, then you will know."

What does this mean? It means that no one becomes a believer by hearing about Christianity, by reading about it, by thinking about it. It means that while Christ was living, no one became a believer by seeing him once in a while or by going and staring at him all day long. No, a certain setting is required – venture a decisive act. The proof does not precede but follows; it exists in and with the life that follows Christ. Once you have ventured the decisive act, you are at odds with the life of this world. You come into collision with it, and because of this you will gradually be brought into such tension that you will then be able to become certain of what Christ taught. You will begin to understand that you cannot endure this world without having recourse to Christ. What else can one expect from following the truth?

This is also what Christ says, and this is the only proof possible for the truth of what he represents: "If anyone will act according to what I say, he will experience whether I am speaking on my own." Venture to give all your possessions to the poor and you will certainly experience the truth of Christ's teaching. Venture once to make yourself completely vulnerable for the sake of the truth, and you will certainly experience the truth of Christ's word. You will experience how it alone can save you from despairing or from succumbing, for you will need Christ both to protect yourself against others and to maintain yourself upright when the thought of your own imperfection would weigh you down.

Yes, doubt will still come, even to the one who follows Christ. But the only person who has a right to leap forward even with a doubt is someone whose life bears the marks of imitation, someone who by a decisive action at least tries to go so far out that becoming a Christian can still be a possibility. Everyone else must hold his tongue; he has no right to put in a word about Christianity, least of all *contra*.

22 | Alone With God's Word

My listener, how highly do you value God's Word? Imagine a lover who has received a letter from his beloved. I assume that God's Word is just as precious to you as this letter is to the lover. I assume that you read and think you ought to read God's Word in the same way the lover reads this letter.

Yet you perhaps say, "Yes, but Scripture is written in a foreign language." Let us assume, then, that this letter from the beloved is written in a language that the lover does not understand. But let us also assume that there is no one around who can translate it for him. Perhaps he would not even want any such help lest a stranger be initiated into his secrets. What does he do? He takes a dictionary, begins to spell his way through the letter, looks up every word in order to obtain a translation.

Now let us imagine that, as he sits there busy with his task, an acquaintance comes in. He knows that the letter has come, because he sees it lying there, and says, "So, you are reading a letter from your beloved." What do you think the other will say? He answers, "Have you gone mad? Do you think this is reading a letter from my beloved! No, my friend, I am sitting here toiling and moiling with a dictionary to get it translated. At times I am ready to explode with impatience; the blood rushes to my head, and I would just as soon hurl the dictionary on the floor – and you call that reading! You must be joking! No, thank God, as soon as I am finished with the translation I shall read my beloved's letter; that is something altogether different."

So, then, with regard to the letter from his beloved, the lover distinguishes between reading with a dictionary and reading the letter from his beloved. The blood rushes to his head in his impatience when he sits and grinds away at reading with the dictionary. He becomes furious when his friend dares to call this the reading of a letter from his beloved. But when he is finished with the translation, he reads the letter. All the scholarly preliminaries were regarded as nothing but a necessary evil so that he could come to the point – of reading the letter from his beloved.

We must not discard this metaphor too soon. Let us assume that this letter contained not only an expression of affection, but also a wish, something the beloved wanted her lover to do. It was, let us assume, much that was required of him – so much so that any third party would have good reason to think twice about it. But the lover, ah, he is off at once to fulfill his beloved's wish. Now imagine that after some time the lovers meet and the beloved says, "But, my dear, that was not what I asked you to do. You must have misunderstood the word or translated it incorrectly." Do you think that the lover would now regret rushing off to obey the wish, do you believe that he regrets the mistake? And do you believe that he pleases his beloved less?

Think of a child, a bright and diligent student. When the teacher assigns the lesson for the next day, he says, "I want you to know your lesson very well tomorrow." This makes a deep impression on the pupil. He goes home from school and sets to work at once. But he has not heard precisely how far they were to study – so what does he do? It is the teacher's admonition that has impressed him. He probably reads twice as far as he actually had to. Do you think the teacher will think less of him for studying twice as hard? Think of another student. He, too, heard the teacher's admonition. He, too, did not hear exactly how far they had to study. When he came home, however, he says, "I must first find out how far we have to study." So he goes to one of his schoolmates, then to another. He doesn't get home until it is too late, and as a result he reads nothing at all!

Now think of God's Word. When you read it in a scholarly way, with a dictionary or a commentary, then you are not reading God's Word. Remember what the lover said, "This is not reading the letter from the beloved." If you happen to be a scholar, then please see to it that even with all your learned reading you do not forget to read God's Word. If you are not a scholar, rejoice! Be glad that you can listen to God's address right away! And if in the listening you hear a wish, a command, an order, then – remember the lover! – off with you at once to do what it asks.

"But," you say, "there are so many obscure passages in the Bible, whole books that are practically riddles. Won't the scholar help me?" To that I would answer (before I have anything to do with this objection): "Any objection must be made by someone whose life manifests that he has scrupulously complied with those passages that are already easy to understand. Is this the case with you?" Yet this is exactly how the lover would respond to the letter. If there are obscure passages but also clearly expressed wishes, he would say, "I must immediately comply with the wish – then I will see about the obscure parts. How can I ever sit down and ponder the obscure passages and not comply with the wish, the wish that I clearly understand?"

In other words, it is not the obscure passages in Scripture that bind you but the ones you understand. With these you are to comply at once. If you understood only one passage in all of Scripture, well, then you must do that first of all. It will be this passage God asks you about. Do not first sit down and ponder the obscure passages. God's Word is given in order that you shall act according to it, not that you gain expertise in interpreting it.

Again, let us not be too quick to discard the metaphor of the letter from the beloved. Would he not make sure to lock the door so as to not be interrupted? Would he not want to be alone, uninterruptedly alone with the letter? "Otherwise," he says, "I would not be reading the letter from my beloved." And so it is with God's Word. The person who is not alone with God's Word is not reading God's Word. Teachers and preachers beware!

Yes, alone with God's Word! My listener, allow me to make a confession about myself here. I still do not dare to be utterly alone with God's Word. I don't have the honesty and courage for it. I dare not! If I open it – any passage – it traps me at once. It asks me – indeed, it is as if it were God himself who does the asking – "Have you done what you read there?" And then I am trapped. Then either right into action or immediately a humbling confession. Oh, to be alone with Scripture; yet if you are not, then you are not truly reading.

Being alone with God's Word is a dangerous matter. Of course, you can always find ways to defend yourself against it: Take the Bible, lock your door – but then get out ten dictionaries and twenty-five commentaries. Then you can read it just as calmly and coolly as you read newspaper advertising. With this arsenal you can really begin to wonder, "Are there not several valid interpretations? And what about the prospect of new interpretations? Perhaps there are five interpreters with one opinion and seven with another and two with a strange opinion and three who are wavering or who have no opinion at all. So you calmly conclude, "I myself am not absolutely sure about the meaning of this passage. I need more time to form an opinion." Good Lord! What a tragic misuse of scholarship that it makes it so easy for people to deceive themselves!

Can't we be honest for once! We have become such experts at cunningly shoving one layer after another, one interpretation after another, between the Word and our lives, (much in the way a boy puts a napkin or more under his pants when he is going to get a licking), and we then allow this preoccupation to swell to such profundity that we never come to look at ourselves in the mirror. Yes, it seems as if all this research and pondering and scrutinizing would draw God's Word very close to us. Yet this interpreting and re-interpreting and scholarly research and new scholarly research is but a defense against it.

It is only all too easy to understand the requirements contained in God's Word ("Give all your goods to the poor." "If anyone strikes you on the right cheek, turn the left." "If anyone takes your coat, let him have your cloak also." "Rejoice always." "Count it sheer joy when you meet various temptations" etc.). The most ignorant, poor creature cannot honestly deny being able to understand God's requirements. But it is tough on the flesh to *will* to understand it and to then act accordingly. Herein lies the problem. It is not a question of interpretation, but action.

23 | Followers not Admirers

It is well known that Christ consistently used the expression "follower." He never asks for admirers, worshippers, or adherents. No, he calls disciples. It is not adherents of a teaching but followers of a life Christ is looking for.

Christ understood that being a "disciple" was in innermost and deepest harmony with what he said about himself. Christ claimed to be the way and the truth and the life (Jn. 14:6). For this reason, he could never be satisfied with adherents who accepted his teaching – especially with those who in their lives ignored it or let things take their usual course. His whole life on earth, from beginning to end, was destined solely to have followers and to make admirers impossible.

Christ came into the world with the purpose of saving, not instructing it. At the same time – as is implied in his saving work – he came to be *the pattern,* to leave footprints for the person who would join him, who would become a follower. This is why Christ was born and lived and died in lowliness. It is absolutely impossible for anyone to sneak away from the Pattern with excuse and evasion on the basis that It, after all, possessed earthly and worldly advantages that he did not have. In that sense, to admire Christ is the false invention of a later age, aided by the presumption of "loftiness." No, there is absolutely nothing to admire in Jesus, unless you want to admire poverty, misery, and contempt.

What then, is the difference between an admirer and a follower? A follower *is* or strives *to be* what he admires. An admirer, however, keeps himself personally detached. He fails to see that what is admired involves a claim upon him, and thus he fails to be or strive to be what he admires.

To want to admire instead of to follow Christ is not necessarily an invention by bad people. No, it is more an invention by those who spinelessly keep themselves detached, who keep themselves at a safe distance. Admirers are related to the admired only through the excitement of the imagination. To them he is like an actor on the stage except that, this being real life, the effect he produces is somewhat stronger. But for their part, admirers make the same demands that are made in the theater: to sit safe and calm. Admirers are only all too willing to serve Christ as long as proper caution is exercised, lest one personally come in contact with danger. As such, they refuse to accept that Christ's life is a demand. In actual fact, they are offended at him. His radical, bizarre character so offends them that when they honestly see Christ for who he is, they are no longer able to experience the tranquillity they so much seek after. They know full well that to associate with him too closely amounts to being up for examination. Even though he "says nothing" against them personally, they know that his life tacitly judges theirs.

And Christ's life indeed makes it manifest, terrifyingly manifest, what dreadful untruth it is to admire the truth instead of following it. When there is no danger, when there is a dead calm, when everything is favorable to our Christianity, it is all too easy to confuse an admirer with a follower. And this can happen very quietly. The admirer can be in the delusion that the position he takes is the true one, when all he is doing is playing it safe. Give heed, therefore, to the call of discipleship!

If you have any knowledge at all of human nature, who can doubt that Judas was an admirer of Christ! And we know that Christ at the beginning of his work had many admirers. Judas was precisely an admirer and thus later became a traitor. It is just as easy to reckon as the stars that those who only admire the truth will, when danger appears, become traitors. The admirer is infatuated with the false security of greatness; but if there is any inconvenience or trouble, he pulls back. Admiring the truth, instead of following it, is just as dubious a fire as the fire of erotic love, which at the turn of the hand can be changed into exactly the opposite, to hate, jealousy, and revenge.

There is a story of yet another admirer – it was Nicodemus (Jn. 3:1ff). Despite the risk to his reputation, despite the effort on his part, Nicodemus was only an admirer; he never became a follower. It is as if he might have said to Christ, "If we are able to reach a compromise, you and I, then I will accept your teaching in eternity. But here in this world, no, that I cannot bring myself to do. Could you not make an exception for me? Could it not be enough if once in a while, at great risk to myself, I come to you during the night, but during the day (yes, I confess it, I myself feel how humiliating this is for me and how disgraceful, indeed also how very insulting it is toward you) to say "I do not know you?" See in what a web of untruth an admirer can entangle himself.

Nicodemus, I am quite sure, was certainly well meaning. I'm also sure he was ready to assure and reassure in the strongest expressions, words, and phrases that he accepted the truth of Christ's teaching. Yet, is it not true that the more strongly someone makes assurances, while his life still remains unchanged, the more he is only making a fool of himself? If Christ had permitted a cheaper edition of being a follower – an admirer who swears by all that is high and holy that he is convinced – then Nicodemus might very well have been accepted. But he was not!

Now suppose that there is no longer any special danger, as it no doubt is in so many of our Christian countries, bound up with publicly confessing Christ. Suppose there is no longer need to journey in the night. The difference between following and admiring – between being, or at least striving to be – still remains. Forget about this danger connected with confessing Christ and think rather of the real danger which is inescapably bound up with being a Christian. Does not the Way – Christ's requirement to die to the world, to forgo the worldly, and his requirement of self-denial – does this not contain enough danger? If Christ's commandment were to be obeyed, would they not constitute a danger? Would they not be sufficient to manifest the difference between an admirer and a follower?

The difference between an admirer and a follower still remains, no matter where you are. The admirer never makes any true sacrifices. He always plays it safe. Though in words, phrases, songs, he is inexhaustible about how highly he prizes Christ, he renounces nothing, gives up nothing, will not reconstruct his life, will not be what he admires, and will not let his life express what it is he supposedly admires. Not so for the follower. No, no. The follower aspires with all his strength, with all his will to be what he admires. And then, remarkably enough, even though he is living amongst a "Christian people," the same danger results for him as was once the case when it was dangerous to openly confess Christ. And because of the follower's life, it will become evident who the admirers are, for the admirers will become agitated with him. Even that these words are presented as they are here will disturb many – but then they must likewise belong to the admirers.

24 | **Fear and Trembling**

When **Abraham and Isaac** reached the place that God had told him about, Abraham built an altar there and arranged the wood on it. He bound Isaac, lit the fire, drew his knife, and thrust it into Isaac!

At that moment God stood by Abraham's side in bodily form and exclaimed: "What have you done? Oh wretched old man! That was not what was asked of you at all. You are my friend, I only wanted to try your faith! I called to you at the last moment. Didn't you hear me? I cried, "Abraham, Abraham, refrain!" Didn't you hear my voice?

Then Abraham answered God with a voice that betrayed a half mystic adoration and a half disheveled weakness that belongs to mental derangement: "Oh Lord, I did not hear you. Yet now that you mention it, I seem to remember that I did hear some kind of voice. Oh when it is you, my God, who commands a father to murder his own child, then a man at such a time is under terrible strain. Therefore, I did not hear your voice. And if I had, dared I have believed it was yours? If you commanded me to sacrifice my child, which you did command me to do, and then at the decisive moment a voice is heard saying, 'Refrain,' am I not obliged to believe it is the voice of the Tempter that wants to keep me from fulfilling your will? I had journeyed long, and now, when the moment at last had come, I was intent on doing only one thing. My options were: Either I should have assumed from the start that the voice that spoke to me, 'Sacrifice Isaac,' was the Tempter's voice, and then not gone forth as I did, or when I had assured myself that it was indeed your voice from the start, I should have concluded that this other voice, this voice at the decisive moment, was the Tempter's. It was the latter I chose."

So Abraham went home, and the Lord gave him a new Isaac. But Abraham did not look upon him with any joy. When he looked on him he shook his head and said, "This is not my Isaac."

But to Sarah he spoke differently. To her he said: "This is all so very strange. That it was God's demand that I should offer Isaac is certain, absolutely certain. God himself cannot disavow that. Yet when I took it seriously, it was a mistake on my part. It was, in the end, not God's will."

Yet, as we know from the story (Gn. 22), it did not go like this with Abraham. His obedience lies just in the fact that at the very last moment he immediately and unreservedly obeyed as he did. This is amazing. When a person has for a long time been saying "A", then humanly speaking he is rather bothered at having to say "B." It is even harder, when one has actually drawn the knife, to be able and willing, with implicit obedience, to recognize that after all no demand is made, that it is not necessary after all to set forth to Mount Moriah with the purpose of sacrificing Isaac. The decision whether to sacrifice one's only child or to spare him, oh, this is indeed great! Greater still, however, is it to retain, even at the last moment, the obedience, and if I may venture to say so, the agile willingness of an obedient soldier. Such a one, even when he has almost reached his goal, does not mind having to run back again, even if it renders all his running in vain. Oh, this is great! No one was so great in faith as Abraham – who can comprehend him?

III | THE WORKS OF LOVE

25 | God's Triumphant Love

Suppose there was a king who loved a humble maiden and whose heart was unaffected by the wisdom that is so often loudly preached. Let then the harp be tuned. Let the songs of the poets begin. Let everyone be festive, while love celebrates its triumph. For love is over-joyed when it unites equals, but it is triumphant when it makes equal that which was unequal. Let the king's love reign!

But then there arose a sadness in the king's soul. Who would have dreamed of such a thing except a king with royal thoughts! He spoke to no one about his sadness. Had he done so, each courtier would doubtless have said, "Your Majesty, you are doing the girl a generous favor for which she could never thank you enough." This, however, would no doubt have aroused the king's wrath and, in turn, caused the king even more sorrow. Therefore he wrestled with the sorrow in his heart. Would the maiden really be happy? Would she be able to forget what the king wished to forget, namely, that he was the king and she a former lowly maiden? For if this happened, if the memory of her former state awoke within her, and like a favored rival, stole her thoughts away from the king, alluring her into the seclusion of a secret grief; or if this memory at times crossed her soul like death crossing over a grave – where then would the glory of their love be? She would have been happier had she remained in obscurity, loved by one of her own kind.

And even if the maiden were content to be as nothing, the king would never be satisfied, simply because he loved her so. He would much rather lose her than be her benefactor. What deep sorrow there is slumbering in this unhappy love! Who dares to rouse it?

When a believer sins he is still loved by God, God longs for him to know this, and is thus concerned to make him equal with himself. If equality cannot be established, love becomes unhappy and incomplete. The revelation of God's love becomes meaningless, the two cannot understand each other.

How then might this relationship be established? One way could be by the elevation of the disciple. God could lift the disciple up to his own exultant state and this could well divert the disciple with an everlasting joy. But God, the unselfish king, would find no satisfaction in this. He knows that the disciple, like the maiden, would be gravely deceived. For no deceit is so terrible as when it is unsuspected, when a person is, as it were, bewitched by a change of costume.

Perhaps unity could be brought about by God directly appearing to the disciple and receiving his unhindered worship. This would surely make the disciple forget about himself, much in the way the king could have appeared in all his glory to the humble maiden, making her forget herself in worshipping adoration. Alas! this might have satisfied the maiden but not the king, who desires not his own exultation but hers. Nor would she understand him, and this would make the king's sorrow even worse.

Not in this way, then, could love be made happy. Take an analogy. God has joy in arraying the lily in a garment more glorious than Solomon. But if a flower and a king could understand each other, what a sorry dilemma for a lily to be in! She would wonder whether it was because of her raiment that God loved her. What delusion! And whereas now she stands confident in the meadow, playing with the wind as carefree as the breeze, she would then languish and cease to have the courage to lift her head.

Who grasps the contradiction of this sorrow: not to disclose itself is the death of love; to disclose itself is the death of the beloved. It was God's longing to prevent this. The unity of love will have to be brought about in some other way. If not by way of elevation, of ascent, then by a descent of the lowest kind. God must become the equal of the lowliest. But the lowliest is one who serves others. God therefore must appear in the form of a servant. But this servant's form is not merely something he puts on, like the beggar's cloak, which, because it is only a cloak, flutters loosely and betrays the king. No, it is his true form. For this is the unfathomable nature of boundless love, that it desires to be equal with the beloved; not in jest, but in truth. And this is the omnipotence of resolving love, deciding to be equal with the beloved.

Look, then, there he stands – God! Where? There! Don't you see him? He is *the* God, and yet he has no place to lay his head, and he does not dare to turn to any person lest that person be offended at him. It is sheer love and sheer sorrow to want to express the unity of love and then to not be understood.

God suffers all things, endures all things, is tried in all things, hungers in the desert, thirsts in his agonies, is forsaken in death, and became absolutely the equal of the lowliest of human beings – look, behold the man! He yields his spirit in death, on a cross, and then leaves the earth. Oh bitter cup! More bitter than wormwood is the ignominy of death for a mortal. How must it be, then, for the immortal one! Oh bitter refreshment, more sour than vinegar – to be refreshed by the beloved's misunderstanding! Oh consolation in affliction to suffer as one who is guilty – what must it be, then, to suffer as one who is innocent!

God is not zealous for himself but out of love wants to be equal with the most lowly of the lowly. What power! When an oak seed is planted in a clay pot, the pot breaks; when new wine is poured into old wineskins, they burst. What happens, then, when God the king plants himself in the frailty of a human being? Does he not become a new person and a new vessel! Oh, this becoming – how difficult it really is, and how like birth itself! How terrifying! It is indeed less terrifying to fall upon one's face, while the mountains tremble at God's voice, than to sit with him in love as his equal. And yet God's longing is precisely to sit in this way.

26 | Neighbor Love

If anyone asks, "Who is my neighbor?" then Christ's reply to the Pharisee, who asked this same question, contains the only answer, for in answer to this question Christ turned everything around. Christ says: "Which of these three, do you think, proved neighbor to the man who fell among the robbers?" The Pharisee answers correctly, "The one who showed mercy to him" (Lk. 10:36). This means that by doing your duty you easily discover who your neighbor is. The Pharisee's answer is contained in Christ's question. He towards whom I have a duty is my neighbor, and when I fulfill my duty, I prove that I am a neighbor. Christ does not speak about recognizing our neighbor but about being a neighbor yourself, about proving yourself to be a neighbor, something the Samaritan showed by his compassion. Choosing a lover, finding a friend, yes that is a long, hard job, but your neighbor is easy to recognize, easy to find – if you yourself will only recognize your duty and be a neighbor.

In this way, Christ has thrust romantic love and friendship from the throne, the love rooted in mood and inclination, preferential love. He does so in order to establish a spiritual love in its place, love to our neighbor, a love which in all earnestness and truth is inwardly more tender in the union of two persons than romantic love is and more faithful in the sincerity of close relationship than the most famous friendship. Let us not confuse the matter. Christ does not ask for a higher love in addition to praising friendship and romantic love. No, Christian love teaches love for all people, unconditionally all.

The poet and Christ explain things in opposite ways. The poet idolizes feelings and since he has only romantic love in mind, believes that to command love is the greatest foolishness and the most preposterous kind of talk: Love and friendship contain no ethical task. Love and friendship are good fortune, the highest good fortune. To find the one and only beloved is good fortune, almost as great as to find the one and only friend. For the poet, the highest task in life is to be properly grateful for one's good fortune. But one's task can never be an obligation to find the beloved or to find this friend. This is out of the question.

Christianity, however, dethrones feeling and good fortune and replaces them with the *shall*. The point at issue between the poet and Christ may be stated precisely in this way: romantic love and friendship are preferential, the passion of preference; Christian love, however, is self-renunciation's love and therefore trusts in the *you shall*. According to Christ, our neighbor is our equal. Our neighbor is not the beloved, for whom you have passionate preference, nor your friend, whom you prefer. Nor is your neighbor, if you are well educated, the learned person with whom you have cultural affinity – for with your neighbor you have before God the equality of humanity. Nor is your neighbor one who is of higher social status than you, and you love him because he has higher social status. This is mere preference and to that extent self-love. Nor is your neighbor one who is inferior to you, and you love him because he is inferior to you, because such love can easily be partiality's condescension and to that extent self-love.

No, Christian love, this *you shall,* means equality. In your relationship to people of distinction you shall love your neighbor.

In relation to those who are inferior you are not to love in pity but shall love your neighbor. Your neighbor is every person, for on the basis of distinctions he is not your neighbor, nor on the basis of likeness to you as in contrast to others. He is your neighbor on the basis of equality with you before God.

We must take care not to be led into self-love. The more decisively and exclusively preference centers upon any one single person, including husband and wife, the farther it is from loving the neighbor. Husband, do not lead your wife into the temptation of forgetting your neighbor because of love for you. Wife, do not lead your husband into this temptation either! Lovers may think that in their love they have the highest good, but it is not so. No, love your beloved faithfully and tenderly, but let love to your neighbor be the sanctifier in your covenant of union with God. Love your friend honestly and devotedly, but let love to your neighbor be what you learn from each other in the intimacy of friendship with God!

Moreover, the person who does not see that his wife is first his neighbor, and only then his wife, never comes to truly love his neighbor, no matter how many people he loves, for he has made an exception of his wife. To be sure, one's wife or husband is to be loved differently than the friend and the friend differently than the neighbor, but this is not an essential difference. The fundamental equality in love lies in the category neighbor. Whatever your fate in romance and friendship, whatever your privation, whatever your loss, the highest still stands: love your neighbor! You can easily find him; him you can never lose. No change can take your neighbor from you, for it is not your neighbor who holds you fast – it is your love, this *you shall,* which holds fast your neighbor.

In this sense love is blind. Perfection in the object has nothing to do with perfection in love. Precisely because one's neighbor has none of the excellencies which the beloved, a friend, or an admired one may have – for that very reason love to one's neighbor has all the perfections which none of these others have. Let people debate as much as they want about which object of love is the most perfect – there can never be any doubt that love to one's neighbor is the most perfect love. Love to one's neighbor is determined by love. Since your neighbor is unconditionally every person, all distinctions are indeed removed from the object. True love is recognizable only by love.

Therefore he who in truth loves, loves his neighbor. And he who in truth loves his neighbor loves also his enemy. This is obvious; for the distinction of friend or enemy is a distinction in the object of love, but the object of love to your neighbor is always without distinction. Your neighbor is the absolutely unrecognizable distinction between one person and another; it is eternal equality before God – enemies, too, have this equality.

Distinction, this or that quality – be it a virtue or a vice – is selfishness' confusing element that marks every person as different. But neighbor is eternity's mark, a mark found on every human being. Take many sheets of paper and write something different on each one. They do not, at first glance, resemble each other. Then take every single sheet, do not let yourself be confused by the differentiating inscriptions, and hold each one up to the light and you shall see the same water-mark on them all. Thus is neighbor the common mark, but you can see it only by the help of the light of the eternal when it shines through every such distinction.

To love one's neighbor, therefore, means essentially to will to exist equally for every human being without exception. If then you really do meet the king, gladly and respectfully give him his due. You should see in him his inner glory, the equality of glory, the neighbor that his human magnificence only conceals. If you meet a beggar – perhaps suffering in sorrow over him more than he himself – you should nevertheless also see in him his inner glory, the equality of glory, the neighbor which his wretched outer garments conceal. Yes, then you shall see, wherever you turn your eye, your neighbor. In being king, beggar, scholar, rich man, poor man, friend, enemy, we do not resemble each other – in these ways we are all different. But in being a neighbor we are all unconditionally alike.

27 | The Greater Love

Worldly wisdom would have us believe that love is a relationship between one person and another. Christ's life teaches that love is a relationship between three: person-God-person. However beautiful a love-relationship is between two or more people – however complete all their enjoyment and all their bliss in mutual devotion and affection are for them, and even if all people praise this relationship – if God and the relationship to God is left out, then this is not love but a mutual and enchanting illusion. For only in love for God can one love in truth. To help another human being to love God is to love another person. And to be helped by another human being to love God is to be loved.

Love is by no means merely a human bond, no matter how faithful and tender it is. As soon as you leave God out, the power of human judgment becomes highest. Such judgment loses sight of love altogether. As soon as a love-relationship does not lead me to God, and as soon as I do not lead another person to God, this love – even if it were the most blissful and joyous attachment, even if it were the highest good in the lover's earthly life – nevertheless is not true love.

Not only should the celibate belong solely to God, so should the person who in love is bound to a woman or a man. He shall not first seek to please his wife, but shall strive first that his love may please God. Consequently, it is not the wife who shall teach the husband how he should love her, or the husband his wife, or a friend his friend, or associates their associates, but it is God who shall teach each individual how he or she should love. Only when the God-relationship determines what constitutes love is love prevented from being some illusion or self-deception.

Love that does not lead to God, love that does not have the single goal of leading us to love God, such love eventually comes to a standstill. Moreover, it escapes the ultimate and most terrible collision: in the love-relationship there is an infinite difference between God's conception of love and ours. A purely human conception of love can never comprehend that anyone, through being loved as completely as possible by another person, would be able to stand in the other person's way. And yet, Christianly understood, this very thing is possible, for to be loved thus can be a hindrance to one's God-relationship.

So what is to be done? Christ knows how to remove the collision without removing love. It demands only this sacrifice (in many cases it is the greatest sacrifice possible): being willing to accept that the reward for your love is to be hated. Wherever someone is loved in such a way as to endanger another's God-relationship, there is a collision. And wherever this collision occurs, there is the requirement of a sacrifice that cannot be humanly grasped. For the Christian view means this: to truly love oneself is to love God; to truly love another person is, though it mean being hated, to help the other person love God.

The world cannot seem to get it through its head that apart from God love is a chimera. For God alone *is* love. Where love is, God not only becomes the third party but essentially becomes the only loved object, so that it is not the husband who is the wife's beloved, but it is God, and it is the wife who is helped by the husband to love God, and conversely. The love-relationship is a triangular relationship of the lover, the beloved, and love –

not love by itself but love *in* God. For ultimately it is God who has placed love in us humans, and it is God who shall finally decide what is love.

In matters of love it takes no time at all to become deceived. It is so easy to get a quick, fanciful picture of what love is and then be satisfied with the fancy. It is still easier to get a few people to associate together in self-love, to be sought after and admired by them till the end. But if your ultimate and highest purpose is to have an easy and sociable life, then don't have anything to do with Christ or his love. Flee from him, for he will do the very opposite. He will make your life difficult and do this precisely by making you stand alone before God.

Thus when a friend, a beloved, or other lovers and associates notice that you want to learn from Christ what it is to love instead of learning from them, don't be surprised when they say to you, "Spare yourself. Give up this eccentricity. Why take life so seriously? Cut out the straining, and let us all live a beautiful, rich, and meaningful life in friendship and joy." And if you give in to the suggestions of this false friendship, you will surely be loved and praised for it. But if you don't, if in loving you will be a traitor neither to God nor to yourself nor to the others, you must expect your love to be refused and to be called selfish. Even if you say nothing, the others will notice that your life contains, if it is truly related to God's demand, an admonition, a demand on them. It is this they want to do away with.

How many have been corrupted – divinely understood – by such friendship, or by a woman's love, simply because, defrauded out of his God-relationship, he became far too attached to her while she in turn was inexhaustible in her praise of his love? How many have relatives and friends corrupted by their love because they got him to forget his God-relationship and changed it to something people could shout about, admire, without being sensitive to any admonition about higher things?

Do not appeal, therefore, to the judgment of others in order to prove your love. Human judgment has validity only as far as it agrees with God's demand. No love between one person and another can, in and of itself, ever be perfectly happy, ever perfectly secure. Even the happiest love between two people has still one danger, the danger that earthly love can become too intense, too important, so that the God-relationship is hindered. You must always watch apprehensively, lest this danger overtake you, lest you too should forget God, or that the beloved might do so. Such apprehension may mean being hated by the beloved. But only God, who is the one true source of love, is the continuously happy, the continuously blessed object of love. You should thus not watch too apprehensively; watch only in adoration.

28 | Love the Person You See

To love another in spite of his weaknesses and errors and imperfections is not perfect love. No, to love is to find him lovable in spite of and together with his weakness and errors and imperfections. Let us understand each other.

Suppose there were two artists, and the one said, "I have traveled much and seen much in the world, but I have sought in vain to find someone worth painting. I have found no face with such perfection of beauty that I could make up my mind to paint it. In every face I have seen one or another little flaw. Therefore I seek in vain." Would this indicate that this artist was a great artist? In contrast, the second one said, "Well, I do not pretend to be a very good artist, if one at all; neither have I traveled very much. But remaining in the little circle closest to me, I have not found a face so insignificant or so full of faults that I still could not discern in it a more beautiful side and discover something glorious. Therefore I am happy in the art I practice, though I make no claim to being an artist." Would this not indicate that precisely this one was the artist, one who by bringing a certain something with him found then and there what the much-traveled artist did not find anywhere in the world, perhaps because he did not bring a certain something with him! Was not the second of the two the real artist?

It is a sad upside-downness, altogether too common, to talk on and on about how the object of love should be before it can be loved. The task is not to find the lovable object, but to find the object before you lovable – whether given or chosen – and to be able to continue finding this one lovable, no matter how that person changes. To love is to love the person one *sees*. As the apostle John reminds us: "He who does not love his brother whom he has seen, cannot love God whom he has not seen." (1 John 4:20)

Consider how Christ looked on Peter, once he had denied Jesus. Was it a repelling look, a look of rejection? No. It was a look such as a mother gives her child when the child is in danger due to its own indiscretion. Since she cannot approach and snatch the child from danger, she catches him off guard with a reproachful but saving look. Was Peter in danger, then? Alas, we do not understand how serious it is for one to betray his friend. But in the passion of anger or hurt the injured friend cannot see that it is the denier who is in danger. Yet the Savior saw clearly that it was Peter who was in danger, not him, and that it was Peter who needed saving. The Savior of the world did not make the mistake of regarding his cause as lost because Peter did not hurry to help him. Rather, he saw Peter as lost if he did not hurry to save him.

Christ's love for Peter was so boundless that in loving Peter he accomplished loving the person one sees. He did not say, "Peter you must first change and become another man before I can love you again." No, he said just the opposite: "Peter, you are Peter, and I love you; love, if anything, will help you to become a different person." Christ did not break off his friendship with Peter, and then renew it again when Peter had become a different man. No, he preserved the friendship and in this way helped Peter to become another man. Do you think that Peter would have ever been won again without such faithful love?

We foolish people often think that when a person has changed for the worse we are exempted from loving him. What a confusion in language: to be exempt from loving. As if it were a matter of compulsion, a burden one wished to cast away! If this is how you see the person, then you really do not see him; you merely see unworthiness, imperfection, and admit thereby that when you loved him you did not really see *him* but saw only his excellence and perfections. True love is a matter of loving the very person you see. The emphasis is not on loving the perfections, but on loving the *person* you see, no matter what perfections or imperfections that person might possess.

He who loves the perfections he sees in a person does not see the person, and thus does not truly love, for such a person ceases to love as soon as the perfections cease. But even when the most distressing changes occur, the person does not thereby cease to be. Love does not vault into heaven, for it comes from heaven and with heaven. It steps down and thereby accomplishes loving the same person throughout all his changes, good or bad, because it sees the same person in all his changes. Human love is always flying after the beloved's perfections. Christian love, however, loves despite imperfections and weaknesses. In every change love remains with him, loving the person it sees.

Alas, we talk about finding the perfect person in order to love him. Christianity teaches us that the perfect person is the one who limitlessly loves the person he sees. We humans always look upward for the perfect object, but in Christ love looks down to earth and loves the person it sees. If then, you wish to become perfect in love, strive to love the person you see, just as you see him, with all his imperfections and weaknesses. Love him as you see him when he is utterly changed, when he no longer loves you, when he perhaps turns indifferently away or turns to love someone else. Love him as you see him when he betrays and denies you. Love the person you see and see the person you love.

29 | Love's Hidden Need

Love is like a spring that lures by the murmuring persuasion of its rippling. The stream almost begs one to go along the path, and yet it does not wish to be discovered or its secret revealed. Love is like the rays of the sun that invite us to observe the glory of the world but reproachfully punish with blindness the presumptuous who try, inquisitively and impudently, to discover the origin of the light. The suffering is always most painful when the surgeon penetrates into the more vital, hidden parts of the body. In the same way, the suffering is most painful and most devastating when someone, instead of rejoicing in the works of love, wants the pleasure of penetrating it, by disturbing it.

The hidden life of love, in its most inward depths, is unfathomable, and still has a boundless relationship with the whole of existence. As the quiet lake is fed by the flow of hidden springs, which no eye sees, so a human being's love is grounded in God's love. If there were no spring at the bottom, if God were not love, there would be neither a lake nor human love. As the still waters begin obscurely in the deep spring, so our love mysteriously begins in God's love.

The life of love is hidden, and yet its hidden life is itself in motion and has the eternal in itself. As still waters, however quietly they lie, are really running, so love flows, however still it is in its hiddenness. But the still waters can dry up if the springs stop; the life of love, on the other hand, has an eternal spring. This life is fresh and everlasting. No cold can freeze it – it is too warm for that; and no heat can dry it up – it is too fresh in its own coolness for that. Let us therefore not disturb this hiddenness or give ourselves over to mere observation or introspection.

This hidden life of love is knowable by its fruits. Yes, in love there is a need to be recognizable by its fruits. How beautiful it is – that which marks the deepest poverty also signifies the greatest riches! Need to have need and to be needy – how reluctantly we wish this to be said of us! Yet we pay the highest compliment when we say of a poet, "It is a need for him to write." Alas, even the most needy person has a rich life in comparison to the only really poor person, who lived out his life and never felt the need of anything! It is the lover's greatest treasure to need the beloved. It is the believer's highest and true wealth to need God. Ask the lover, or ask the believer if they could dispense with their need! It is the same with the recognizability of love by its fruits. It would be the greatest torture if love was required to keep hidden, to go unrecognizable. Would it not be as if a plant, sensitive to the vigor and blessing of life in itself, did not dare let it become known and kept the blessing to itself?

A tree, as Jesus puts it, is known by its fruits. But it is said of certain plants that they must form hearts. The same must be said of a person's love; if it is really to bear fruit and be recognizable by its fruit, it must *form a heart*. Love, to be sure, proceeds from the heart, but let us not forget that love itself forms the heart. This is the essential condition for bearing love's fruit.

As love itself is not to be seen, neither is it known by any single expression. There is no word, not even the most sacred word, which can guarantee that there is love in us. Likewise, there is no deed, not even the best, of which we dare announce: the one who does this is surely demonstrating love. No, it depends upon how each deed is done. True, there are special acts that we call works of love. But just because we make charitable contributions, because we visit those in prison and feed the poor does not necessarily mean we have love. Yes, it is quite possible to perform works of love in an unloving, yes, even in a self-loving way. When this is so, the "works of love" are in vain. Consequently, how something is said, how it is meant, and how the deed is done is the decisive factor in determining and recognizing true love. Yet even here there is nothing, no "in such a way," that unconditionally guarantees whether love is or is not.

Yes, love is known by its fruits. This does not mean we should now get busy judging one another. By no means! Even if love is recognizable by its fruits, let us not impatiently, suspiciously, judgingly demand to always see these fruit in our relationships with one another. We must believe in love. This is the first and last thing to be said about love if you are to ever know what love is. For where is love if there is miserable mistrust that insists upon seeing the fruits. If mistrust sees something as less than it actually is, then love sees something as greater than it is. Do not forget that it is more blessed to believe in love. Therefore, the last, the most blessed, the absolutely convincing evidence of love remains: love itself, which is known and recognized by the love in another. Like is known only by like. Only he who abides in love can recognize love, and in the same way his love is to be known.

30 | Love Builds Up

To build up is to construct something from the ground up. Everyone knows what the foundation of a house is. But spiritually speaking, what is the foundation of the life of the spirit? It is love. Love is the origin of everything, and love is the deepest ground of the life of the spirit.

The foundation – love – is laid in every person in whom there is love. And the edifice to be constructed, is love. It is love that edifies. Love builds up, and when it builds, it builds up love. Love is the ground; love is the building; love builds up. To build up another is to build up love, and it is love that does the building up. Love is the ground, and to build up means precisely to construct from the ground up.

When we speak about the works of love, it must mean either that we implant love in the heart of another or that we presuppose that love is in the other's heart and with this presupposition build up love in him. One of the two must exist for building up love. But can a person implant love in the heart of another? No. It is God alone, the creator, who can implant love in a person, he who himself is love. All energetic and self-assertive zeal in this regard, all thought of creating love in another person neither builds up nor is itself up-building. It is unthinkable. No, true love presupposes that love is in the other person's heart, no matter how hidden, and by this very presupposition builds love up – from the ground up.

Love is not what you try to do to transform the other person or what you do to constrain love to come forth in him; it is rather how you constrain yourself. Only the person who lacks love imagines himself able to build up love by constraining the other. The true lover always believes that love is present; precisely in this way he builds up. In this way he only entices forth the good; he "loves up" love; he builds up what is already there. For love can and will be treated in only one way – by being loved forth.

To love forth love means to believe that love is present at the base. The builder can point to his work and say, "This is my work." But love has nothing it can point to, for its very work consists only in presupposing. If a lover did succeed (by presupposing) in building up love in another person, when the building stands, he must step aside and humbly say, "Indeed, I knew it was there all the time." Alas, love has no merit at all, for love's building does not stand as a monument to the skill of the builder or, like the pupil, as a reminder of the teacher's instruction. The one who loves accomplishes nothing; he only brings forth the love that is already there. The lover works quietly and earnestly, and yet it is the powers of the eternal, not the strength of his love, which are set in motion. The humility in love is the secret of its power.

Love makes itself inconspicuous, especially when it works hardest. In love's work, our labor is reduced to nothing. The building-up of love can thus be compared to the work of nature. While we sleep, creation's vital forces keep on. No one gives a thought to how they carry on, although everyone delights in the beauty of the meadow and the fruitfulness of the field. This is the way love conducts itself. It presupposes that love is present, like the germ in a kernel of grain, and if it succeeds in bringing it to fruition, love is modest, as inconspicuous as when it worked day and night.

Therefore, "Love is patient." Patience means perseverance in believing that love is fundamentally present. He who judges that another lacks love takes the groundwork away, and thus cannot build up. Love builds up with patience. Neither "is it irritable or resentful," for irritability and resentment ultimately deny love in another. In fact, love bears another's misunderstanding, his thanklessness, and his anger.

"Love does not insist on its own way," neither does it "rejoice at wrong." He who seeks his own way pushes everything else aside. He demolishes in order to make room for his own way, which he wants to build up. Yes, the one who seeks to tear down must be said to rejoice at wrong. But love rejoices in knowing that love is already present; therefore it builds up. "Love bears all things." When we say of a very healthy person that he can eat or drink anything, we mean that in his strength he draws nourishment out of even the poorest food. In the same way love bears all things, continually presupposing that love is fundamentally present, despite resistance – and thereby it builds up.

"Love believes all things." Yes, to believe all things means to believe that love is there – even though love is not apparent, even though the opposite is seen. Mistrust takes the very foundation away. Unlike love, mistrust cannot build up. "Love hopes all things." Despite all appearances to the contrary, love firmly trusts that love will eventually show itself, even in the deluded, in the misguided, and in the lost. The father's love won the prodigal son again just because he hoped all things, believing that love was fundamentally present. What more can we say? "Love endures all things. It is not jealous or boastful; it is not arrogant or rude; it is not irritable or resentful..."

Love builds up simply because it knows beyond any doubt that love is present. Have you not, my reader, experienced this yourself? If any person has ever spoken to you in such a way or acted toward you in such a way that you felt yourself built up, was it not because you quite vividly perceived that he or she presupposed love to be present in you? We know that no one can bestow the ground of love in another person's heart. Love is the ground, and we build only from the ground up, only by presupposing love. Take love away, cease from presupposing it – then there is no one who builds up nor is there anyone who is built up.

31 | Love's Like-for-Like

Jesus says, "Forgive, and you will also be forgiven" (Mt. 6:14). That is to say, forgiveness *is* forgiveness. Your forgiveness of another is your own forgiveness; the forgiveness you give is the forgiveness you receive. If you wholeheartedly forgive your enemy, you may dare hope for your own forgiveness, for it is one and the same. God forgives you neither more nor less than *as* you forgive your trespassers.

It is an illusion to imagine that you have forgiveness while you are slack in forgiving others. No, there is not a more exact agreement between the sky above and its reflection in the sea below, than there is between forgiveness and forgiving. Is it not pure conceit to believe in your own forgiveness when you will not forgive others? For how in truth can you believe in forgiveness if your own life is a refutation of the existence of forgiveness?! Yes, to accuse another person before God is to accuse yourself, like-for-like.

People so gladly deceive themselves, so gladly imagine that they can have, as it were, a private relationship with God. But if you complain of your enemies to God, he makes short work of it and opens a case against you, because before God you too are a guilty person. To complain against another is to complain against yourself. You think that God should take your side, that God and you together should turn against your enemy, against him who did you wrong. But this is a complete misunderstanding. God looks without discrimination upon all. Go ahead. If you intend to have God judge someone else, then you have made God your judge as well. God is, like-for-like, simultaneously your judge. If, however, you refuse to accuse someone before God he will be merciful towards you.

Let me illuminate this with an example. There was once a criminal who had stolen some money, including a hundred-dollar bill. He wanted to get this changed into smaller bills and so he turned to another criminal to help him. The second criminal took the money, went into the next room as if to make change, then came out again and acted as if nothing ever happened. In short, he swindled the first criminal out of the hundred-dollar bill. The first man became so embittered over this that he brought the case to the authorities and reported how shamefully he had been deceived. Naturally the second man was imprisoned on the charge of fraud. Alas, in the trial the first question the authorities raised was: how did the accuser get the money in the first place? And so there were two trials. Thus it is with respect to God. When you accuse another person, there are immediately two cases; just because *you* come and reported another person before God, God happens to think of how it also involves you.

Like-for-like. Yes, Christ is so rigorous that he even affirms a radical inequality. He says, "Why do you see the speck that is in your brother's eye, but do not notice the log that is in your own eye?" (Mt. 7:3). And even if you do not see the log, even if no one else sees it – God sees it. Is this not rigorousness, this which makes a gnat into an elephant? But if you truly understand how God is continually present in everything, then you will indeed be able to understand this rigorousness, you will understand that seeing the speck in your brother's eye is always high treason. God is always present, and if he is present, he also sees you!

How rigorous is this Christian like-for-like! The world's like-for-like is: see to it that in the long run you do to others what others have done to you. But the Christian like-for-like is: as you do to others, God does to you in the very same mode. Christianly understood, what others do to you should not concern you. You should concern yourself with what you do to others and with the way you receive what others do to you. The direction is inwards; essentially you have only to do with yourself before God. To love human beings is to love God and to love God is to love human beings. What you do to others you do to God, and therefore what you do to others God does to you.

If you are embittered towards those who do you wrong, you are really embittered towards God, for ultimately it is God who permits wrong to be done to you. If, however, you gratefully take wrongs as if from God's hand, "as a good and perfect gift," you will not become resentful. If you will not forgive, you essentially want something else, you want to make God hard-hearted. How, then, should this hard-hearted God forgive you? If you cannot bear the offenses of those against you, how should God bear your sins against him? No, like-for-like.

God is himself the pure rendition of how you yourself are. If there is wrath in you, then God is wrath in you; if there is mildness and mercifulness in you, then God is mercifulness in you. You know well enough that echo which dwells in solitude. It corresponds exactly, oh, so exactly, to every sound, to the slightest sound, and duplicates it, oh, so exactly. If there is a word you prefer not be said to you, then watch your saying of it. Watch lest it slip out of you in solitude, for the echo duplicates it immediately and says it to *you*. If you have never been solitary, you have also never discovered that God exists. But if you have been truly solitary, then you have learned that everything you say and do to other human beings God simply repeats. He repeats it with the intensification of infinity.

32 | Love Abides – Forever!

The one who truly loves never falls away from love. He can never reach the breaking-point. Yet, is it always possible to prevent a break in a relationship between two persons, especially when the other has given up? One would certainly not think so. Is not one of the two enough to break the relationship? In a certain sense it is so. But if the lover is determined to not fall away from love, he can prevent the break, he can perform this miracle; for if he perseveres, a total break can never really come to be.

By abiding, the one who loves transcends the power of the past. He transforms the break into a possible new relationship, a future possibility. The lover who abides belongs to the future, to the eternal. From the angle of the future, the break is not really a break, but rather a possibility. But the powers of the eternal are needed for this. The lover must abide in love, otherwise the heartache of the past still has the power to keep alive the break.

How shall I describe this work of love; this work that transforms the past into the future? Oh, that I might be inexhaustible in describing what is so indescribably joyous and so edifying to reflect upon!

Let us consider the following. The breaking point between two lovers is reached. It was a misunderstanding; one of them broke the relationship. But the lover says, "I will abide" – therefore there still is no final break. Imagine a compound word which lacks the last word. There is only the first word and the hyphen. Imagine, then, the first word and the hyphen of a compound word. What will you say? You will say that the word is incomplete, that it lacks something. It is the same with the one who loves. The lover understands that the relationship which the other considers broken is a relationship which has not yet been completed. Although it lacks something, it is still not a total break. The whole thing depends upon how the relationship is regarded, and the lover – he abides.

Again, a relationship comes to the breaking point. There is an argument which separates the two. One breaks it off and says: "It is all over between us." But the lover abides: "No, all is not over between us. We are still midway in the sentence; it is only the sentence which is not complete." Is it not so? What a difference there is between an unfinished sentence and something we call a fragment because we know that nothing more is to come. If one does not know this, he says that the sentence is not yet completed. True, from the perspective of the past, one might well say, "It is a broken fragment." From the vantage point of the future, however, we await the next part, and say, "The sentence is not complete; it still lacks something."

Perhaps it is disharmony, a cooling-off, or indifference that separates the two. One makes the break saying, "I no longer speak to that person. I never see him anymore." But the one who loves says: "I abide. We shall yet speak with one another, because silence also belongs to conversation at times." Is this not so? Even if it is three years since they last spoke together, it doesn't make any difference. If you saw two people sitting silently together and you knew nothing more, would you thereby conclude that it was three years since they spoke to each other? Can anyone determine how long a silence must be in order to say, now there is no more conversation? Does the dance cease because one dancer has gone away? In a certain sense, yes. But if the other still remains standing in the posture that expresses a turning towards the one who has left, and if you know nothing about the past, then you will say, "Now the dance will begin just as soon as the other comes." Put the past out of the way; drown it in the forgiveness of the eternal by abiding in love. Then the end is the beginning and there is no break!

And so a relationship comes to a breaking-point, and one severs the relationship. It was terrible; hate, eternal and irreconcilable hate fills the other's soul. "I will never see that person any more. Our paths are forever separated; the abysmal depth of hate lies between us." To him the world is too small to house them both; to him it is agony to breathe in the same world where the hated one breathes. He shudders at the thought that eternity will house them both. But the one who loves abides. "I will abide," he says. "Therefore we are still on the path of life together." And is this not so? When two balls collide in such a way that the one, simply by repulsion, carries the other along in its path, are they not on the path together? That it happens through repulsion cannot be seen; for that is something past which must be known. But the one who truly loves moves beyond the past. He abides, he even abides on the path with the one who hates him. There is thus no break.

What marvelous strength love has! The most powerful word that has ever been said, God's creative word, is: "Be." But the most powerful word any human being has ever said is, "I abide." Reconciled to himself and to his conscience, the one who loves goes without defense into the most dangerous battle. He only says: "I abide." But he will conquer, conquer by his abiding. There is no misunderstanding that cannot be conquered by his abiding, no hate that can ultimately hold up to his abiding – in eternity if not sooner. If time cannot, at least the eternal shall wrench away the other's hate. Yes, the eternal will open his eyes for love. In this way love never fails – it abides.

33 | When Love Is Secure

Only when it is a duty to love, only then is love eternally secured; secured against the ravages of change, eternally and happily secured against despair. However joyous, happy, indescribably confident, instinctive and inclinational, spontaneous and emotional love may be – it still needs to establish itself more securely, in the strength of duty. Only in the security of the eternal is all anxiety cast out. For in spontaneous love, however confident it be, there still resides an anxiety, a dread over the possibility of change. Yet in the *you shall,* it is forever decided; one's love is forever secure. Every other love can be changed into something else.

Spontaneous, emotional love can be changed, for instance, to its opposite, to hate or by a kind of spontaneous combustion it can become jealousy. From being the greatest happiness it can change into the greatest torment. The heat of spontaneous love is so dangerous – no matter how great its passion – that it can very quickly become a poisonous fever.

Worst of all is how spontaneous love can gradually be changed through the years – as when a fire gradually consumes itself. Human love can lose its ardor, its joy, its desire, its originative power, its living freshness. As with the river which springs out of a rock and disperses farther down in the sluggishness of the dead-waters, so is love exhausted in the lukewarmness and indifference of habit. Alas, of all love's enemies habit is perhaps the most cunning. It is cunning enough never to let itself be seen, for he who sees the habit for what it is, is saved from it. Habit is not like other enemies we can see and against which we strive and defend ourselves. The struggle is really within ourselves – to see it. Ah, and how difficult this struggle is!

There is a preying creature, known for its cunning that slyly falls upon the sleeping. While sucking blood from its sleeping prey, it fans and cools him, making his sleep still more pleasant. This is how it is with habit – or maybe it is even worse! For the vampire seeks its prey among the sleeping, but it has no means to lull to sleep those who are awake. Habit, however, is quite adept at doing this. It slinks, sleep-lulling, upon a person, and then drains his blood while it coolingly fans him and makes his sleep all the more pleasant.

In this way human-inspired love can be changed into something else and made unrecognizable. Such is the way of habit. And when we become aware of how habit has changed our love, we long to make up for it, but do not exactly know how. We do not know where we can go to buy new oil to rekindle our love. Then we are liable to despair and to become weary of not ever being able to fan it into flame again. What sadness it is to encounter a poverty-stricken man who had once lived prosperously, and still, how much more sorrowful than this to see human-inspired love changed almost to loathsomeness!

Genuine love, love transformed and sustained by the eternal, however, will never become characterized by habit; habit can never get power over it. To what is said of eternal life, that there is no sighing and no tears, one can add: there is no habit. If you are to save your soul or your love from habit's cunning – though people blindly believe there are all kinds of ways of keeping oneself awake and secure – then you must heed to the eternal's *you shall*. This alone will preserve you. This alone will

keep your love alive. Let the thunder of a hundred cannon remind you three times daily to resist the force of habit. Have a
friend remind you every time he sees you. Have a wife who, in
love, reminds you morning and night – but be careful that all
this also does not become habit! For you can become accus-
tomed to hearing the thunder of a hundred cannon so that you
can sit at the table and hear the most trivial, insignificant things
far more clearly than the thunderous noise outside. No, only the
eternal's *you shall* and the hearing ear can save you from habit.

Behold, passion inflames, worldly sagacity cools, but neither
this heat nor this cold nor their blending is the pure air of the
eternal. There is something fiery in this heat and something
sharp in this cold, and in the blending an unconscious deceit-
fulness. But this "You shall love," this command from God, takes
all the unsoundness away and preserves for eternity what is
sound. This *you shall* is the saving element, purifying, elevating.
There where the merely human wants to storm forth, the command still holds. Just when the merely human would lose courage, the command strengthens. Just when the merely human
would become tired and clever, the command flames up and
gives wisdom. The command consumes and burns out what is
unsound and impure in your love, but through it you shall be
able to kindle it again, even when, humanly considered, all has
been lost.

IV | ANXIETY

AND

THE

GOSPEL

OF

SUFFERING

34 | Nebuchadnezzar

These are recollections of my life when I was a beast and ate grass, which I, Nebuchadnezzar, make known to all people and to every tongue.

Was not Babel the great city, the greatest of all the cities of the world? I, Nebuchadnezzar, built it. No city was so renowned as Babel, and no king so renowned through Babel, the glory of my majesty. My royal house was visible unto the ends of the earth, and my wisdom was like a dark riddle which no one could explain. So no one could interpret my dreams.

And the word came to me that for seven years I should be transformed and become like a beast that eats the grass of the field. And I heard a voice that came suddenly, and I was transformed as quickly as a woman changes color. Grass was my food, and dew fell upon me, and no one knew who I was. But I knew Babel and cried out, "Is not this Babel?" But no one paid attention to my word, for when I spoke I sounded like a bellowing beast. My thoughts terrified me, for my mouth was bound, and no one could grasp a thing I said.

And I thought to myself: Who is this Mighty One whose wisdom is like the darkness of the night, and like the deep sea unfathomable? No one knows where the Almighty resides, no one can point and say, "Behold, here is his throne." For he does not dwell on the confines of my kingdom as does my neighbor. And neither does he dwell in his temple, for I, I, Nebuchadnezzar, have taken his vessels of gold and silver, and have leveled his temple to ruins.

No one knows anything of him. Who is his father, and how did he come to acquire his power, and who taught him the secret of his might? He has no advisers from whom one might buy his secret for gold; no one to whom he says, "What shall I do?" and no one who says to him, "What are you doing?" He does not have spies who wait for the opportunity when one might catch him; for he does not say, "Tomorrow," he says, "Today." He makes no preparations like a man, and his preparations give the enemy no rest, for he says, "Let it be done," and it comes to pass.

It is he who has done this to me. He does not aim like the bowman, so that one can flee from his arrow; no, he speaks and it is done. In his hand, the brain of kings is like wax in the smelting oven, and their power is like a feather when he weighs it. And yet he does not dwell on earth that he might take Babel from me and leave me a small residue, or that he might take away everything from me in order to be the Mighty One in Babel.

This is how I thought in the secrecy of my mind, when no one recognized me and when my thoughts terrified me. This is how I thought of the Lord. But the seven years passed by and I became once again Nebuchadnezzar, and I called together all the wise men to see if they could explain to me the secret of that power, and how it was I had become a beast of the field. And they all fell down upon their faces and said, "Great Nebuchadnezzar, this is but a vision, an evil dream! Who could be capable of doing this to you?" But my wrath was kindled against them, and I had them put away for their folly. For the Lord possesses all might, as no human being possesses it, and I will not envy his power, but will laud it.

Babel has ceased to be the renowned Babel, and I, Nebuchadnezzar, am no longer Nebuchadnezzar, and my armies no longer protect me, for no one can see the Lord and no one can recognize him. Even if he were to come, the watchmen would give warning in vain, because I have already become like a bird in the tree, or like a fish in the water, known only to the other fish.

I no longer desire to be renowned through Babel, but every seventh year there shall be a festival in the land, a great festival among the people, and it shall be called the Feast of the Transformation. And an astrologer shall be led through the streets and be dressed like a beast, and he shall carry with him his calculations, torn to shreds like a bunch of hay. And all the people shall cry, "The Lord, the Lord, the Lord is the Mighty One. His deed is swift like the leap of the great fish in the sea."

My days have been numbered, and my dominion has gone like a watch in the night. I do not know where to go – whether it is to the invisible land in the distance where the Mighty One lives, that I might find grace in his eyes, or whether he will take the breath of life from me, so that I become like a cast-off garment like my predecessors, that he might find delight in me.

I, I, Nebuchadnezzar, have made this known to all people and to every tongue, and great Babel shall carry out my will.

35 | The War Within

Imagine a group of people who have come together to socialize. The conversation is in full swing, lively, almost out of control. One person can hardly wait to have his say till the other is through with his, and everybody takes part more or less actively as in a debate.

Then enters a stranger, who arrives in the midst of it all. Judging by the behavior of the group and the loudness of the talk, the stranger infers that the topic of conversation is one of great concern and importance. As it so often happens, however, the conversation is about a mere trifle. With perfect calmness, since he has not been in the heart of the conversation, he inquires about the subject of their conversation. The stranger, of course, cannot in the least be blamed for the effect his inquiry produces. He only assumed that what was being discussed was something of significance. But what a surprising effect, to become suddenly aware that what had so passionately absorbed the attention of the group was so unimportant that it can hardly be put into words. It turns out to be a mere nothing, and everyone gets annoyed.

Stranger still is the effect produced by God's word when it is heard in the midst of the world's talk. Think about it. In the world there is lots of talk about this or that strife. There is talk about this person who is in conflict with that person, about that man and that woman, although united in marriage, living in strife with one another, about the disagreement that has begun between this one and that, about this one challenging another to a fight, about there being unrest in the city, about a war that is impending, about the conflict of nature's elements that rage fearfully. Behold, it is this that is talked about everywhere, day in and day out. If there is a conflict to report, then there is always a listening audience. But if one should bring up or mention the strife and unrest that resides within every person with God – what an astonishing effect! To most people such talk is but nonsense, a mere trifle. There are too many other important things to talk about.

Travel the world over, get to know the most various cultures, go about and enter into conversation with all the different peoples, visit them in their houses, follow them to their meetings, and listen attentively to what they talk about. Now tell me if you ever hear anything said about the eternal strife, the war between God and man, the war within a person's soul. And yet this strife is the affair of every single person. In fact, there is no other strife that it is absolutely the affair of every person.

The strife between human beings – well, after all, there are many that live their lives rather peaceably without being in conflict with anybody. The strife between married people – well, after all, there are many happy marriages that go along without much tension. And after all it is a rare occurrence for a man to be challenged to a fight. And even during a war, yes, even if it was the most terrible war, there are still many who live in peace. But this strife, this fight with God is absolutely the affair of every single person, whether people recognize it or not. But beware lest you make the slightest mention of it!

Perhaps this strife is regarded as so sacred and so solemn that it is felt it should never be talked about. Perhaps it is like how God is manifested in creation. God is not directly visible so as to be noticed in the world. In fact, the beauty of creation attracts attention to itself, almost as if God did not exist at all. So maybe this strife is a kind of secret every person has, and because it is not directly visible, it never gets talked about. Everything else instead gets talked about, attracts attention to itself, as if this sacred strife did not exist. Perhaps so, perhaps.

But it is certain that every person, every sufferer has opportunity, in one way or another, to become aware of this strife. And it is this strife that underlies all others. Oh, whoever you are, pay heed to this sacred strife. This alone is the strife of eternity.

36 | Sickness Unto Death

Just as there isn't a single human being that enjoys perfect health, so there is not a single human being who does not despair at least a little. There is not a single human being whose innermost being is free of uneasiness, unquiet, discordance, or anxiety in the face of something unknown, something he doesn't even dare strike up acquaintance with. Everyone, in one way or another, is plagued with an anxiety about a possibility in life or about himself. We go about with a sickness – not unlike an illness of the body, which a physician has diagnosed – a sickness of the spirit that only now and then, in glimpses, reveals itself and with what is for him an inexplicable anxiety.

Despair differs from what we usually call sickness, because it is a sickness of the spirit. If for instance, a physician determines that so and so is in good health, and then later that person becomes ill, this doesn't mean that the physician was wrong. He may well have been right about his having been well at the time. Once despair makes itself known, however, it becomes apparent that the person was already in despair. Unlike a fever, which comes and goes, when someone falls into despair, it is immediately evident that he was already in despair. This is because despair is a characteristic of the spirit. It is related to the eternal, and therefore has something of the eternal in its dynamic.

We must not assume, therefore, that despair is something rare. On the contrary, it is quite general. And we cannot assume that just because someone doesn't think or feel he is in despair, he is not in despair. Nor should we think that only the person who says he is in despair is so. On the contrary, he who says without pretense that he despairs is, in actual fact, a little nearer, a step nearer to being cured than all those who do not regard themselves as being in despair. Yet we must concede that the normal situation is this: that most people live without being properly conscious of being spirit, and for this reason all the so-called security and contentment with life are actually forms of despair.

Ah! So much is spoken about human need and misery and how to overcome it. So much is spoken about wasting our lives. But the only wasted life is the life of him who has so lived it, deceived by life's pleasures or its sorrows, that he never became decisively, eternally, conscious of himself as spirit, as a self. Or, if I may put it another way, he has never become aware – and gained in the deepest sense the impression – that there is a God and that "he," himself, is answerable to and exists before this God, and that this God can only be met by way of despair. Alas! so many live their lives in denial, decapitated from eternity. So many are not aware of their true destiny, defrauding themselves of this most blessed of all realities.

Imagine a house consisting of a basement and a ground floor, designed in such a way that there is, or is meant to be, a difference of social class between the occupants of each floor. Imagine if we were to compare being a human being with such a house. The sorry and ludicrous fact with most people is that they prefer to live in the basement. Every human being is the synthesis of spirit and body, the infinite and finite, freedom and necessity, destined for spirit. This is the building, but we prefer living in the basement, that is, in the categories of the senses and in the abstractions of thought. We not only prefer living in the basement, we love it so much that we are indignant if anyone suggests we occupy the fine suite lying vacant above. After all we are living in our *own* house!

Yes, so many prefer to live in the basement, along life's surface. You can see amazing examples of this, which illustrate it on a stupendous scale. Take a thinker who erects a huge building, a system of thought, one that encompasses the whole of life and world history. Turn your attention to his personal life and you will discover to your astonishment, like among so many others, the appalling and ludicrous fact that he himself does not live in this huge, high-vaulted palace, but in a shack next door. If you took it upon yourself to draw attention to this deception, to this contradiction, he would be insulted. As long as he can complete the system – with the help of his error – being in error is not what he is afraid of. What sickness!

Or, take the industrious person who busily secures his life with this and that creature comfort but in a moment of illness or physical loss or adversity falls to pieces. If you took it upon yourself to ask, "What are you so busy for? What difference is all this activity if at a moment's notice you fall ill or fall dead?" you would surely be cursed. As long as this person can keep busy – without thinking too much about life's meaning – living in deception is the least of his fears.

All this is only to say that just because one is ignorant of his state as being one of despair, he *is* in despair all the same, and even more so. Beneath ignorance lies despair – spiritlessness – whether his state is one of total extinction, a merely vegetative life, or a life full of energy the secret of which is nevertheless despair. When the spell of illusion is broken, when life begins to quake, then it is immediately apparent that despair was lying beneath all the time. No wonder people prefer to live in the basement.

37 | The Dynamics of Despair

The human being is essentially spirit. But what is spirit? Spirit is to be a self. But what is the self? In short, the self is a synthesis of the infinite and the finite, of the temporal and the eternal, of freedom and necessity. The self is the conscious unity of these factors, which relates to itself, whose task is to become itself. This, of course, can only be done in relationship to God, who holds the synthesis together.

When is despair completely eradicated? It occurs when the self, in relating to itself and in wanting to be itself, is grounded nakedly in the power that established it. In other words, when it is related openly to and dependently on God. To transcend despair is neither to become finite nor to become infinite but to become an individual in their synthesis, which God alone holds together. In so far as the self does not become itself in this way, it is not itself. And not to be oneself, as God created you, is despair.

Finitude's Despair

Despair comes in different guises. To lack infinitude is a despairing confinement. It consists in ascribing infinite value to the trivial and temporal. Here the self is lost by being altogether reduced to the finite. Finitude's despair allows itself to be, so to speak, cheated of its self by "the others." By seeing the multitude of people and things around it, by being busied with all sorts of worldly affairs, by being wise in the ways of the world, a person forgets himself, forgets his own name, dares not believe in himself, finds being himself too risky, finds it much easier and safer to be like all the others, to become a repetition, a number along with the crowd.

Now this form of despair goes virtually unnoticed in the world. Precisely by losing oneself in this way, a person gains all that is required for a flawless performance in everyday life, yes, for making a great success out of life. One is ground as smooth as a pebble. Far from anyone thinking of such a person as being in despair, he is just what a human being ought to be. He is praised by others; honored, esteemed, and occupied with all the goals of temporal life. Yes, what we call worldliness simply consists of such people who, if one may so express it, pawn themselves to the world. They use their abilities, amass wealth, carry out enterprises, make prudent calculations, and the like, and perhaps are mentioned in history, but they are not authentic selves. They are copies. In a spiritual sense they have no self, no self for whose sake they could venture everything, no self for God, however self-consumed they are otherwise.

The Despair of Weakness

The despair of weakness is the despair of not wanting to be oneself. This kind of despair amounts to a passivity of the self. Its frame of reference is the pleasant and the unpleasant; its concepts are good fortune, misfortune, and fate. What is immediate is all that matters. The determining factor is what happens or does not happen to oneself.

To despair is to lose the eternal, but of this loss the one who despairs in weakness says nothing, it doesn't even occur to him. He is too preoccupied with securing his earthly existence against unnecessary deprivation. To lose the earthly, however, is not in itself to despair, yet that is precisely what this person speaks of and calls despair. What he says is in a sense true, only not in the way he understands it. He is turned around and what he says must be understood backwards. In other words, he stands there pointing to something that is not despair (e.g. a loss of some kind), explaining that he is in despair, and yes, sure enough, the despair is going on behind him but unawares. Therefore, if everything suddenly changes, once his external circumstances change and his wishes are fulfilled, then happiness returns to him, he begins life afresh. When help comes from outside, happiness is restored to him, and he begins where he left off. Yet he neither was nor becomes a self. He is a cipher and simply carries on living merely on the level of what is immediate and of what is happening around him.

This form of despair consists of not wanting to be a self, really. Actually, it consists of wanting desperately to be someone else. Such a self refuses to take responsibility. Life is but a game of chance. Hence, in the moment of despair, when no help comes, such a person wants desperately to become someone else. And yet a despairer of this kind, whose only wish is this craziest of all crazy transformations – to be someone else – is in love with the fancy that the change can be made as easily as one puts on another coat. Or to put it differently, he only knows himself by his coat. He simply doesn't know himself. He knows what it is to have a self only in externals. There could hardly be a more absurd confusion, for a self differs precisely, no, infinitely, from those externals.

And what if such a person was able to become somebody else, could put on a new self? There is the story of a peasant who had come barefoot to town but who made enough money to buy himself a pair of stockings and shoes and still have enough left over to get himself drunk. On his way home in his drunken state he lay down in the middle of the road and fell asleep. A carriage came along, and the coachman shouted to him to move aside or else he would drive over his legs. The drunken peasant woke up, looked down at his legs and, not recognizing them because of the stockings and shoes, said: "Go ahead, they aren't my legs." So it is with the immediate person who despairs in weakness of being a true self. It is impossible to draw a picture of him that is not comic.

The Despair of Defiance

Unlike the despair of weakness, the despair of defiance is the despair of wanting in desperation to be oneself. Here despair is conscious of itself as an activity. The self's identity comes not from "outside" but directly from the self. It is rooted in the consciousness of an infinitude, of being related to the infinite, and it is this self the despairer wants to *be*. In other words, such a self severs itself from any relationship to the power that has established it. It wants desperately to rule over itself, create itself, make this self what *it* wants it to be, and determine what it will have and what it will not have. The one who lives in defiance does not truly put on a self, nor does he see his task in his given self. No, by virtue of his own "infinitude" he constructs his own self by himself and for himself.

The defiant self recognizes no power other than its own. It is content with taking notice only of itself, which it does by means of bestowing infinite interest and significance on all its enterprises. In the process of its wish to be its own master, however, it works its way into the exact opposite; it really becomes no self, and thus despairs. As it acts, there is nothing eternally firm on which it stands. Yes, the defiant self is its own master, absolutely (as one says) its own master, and yet exactly this is despair. Upon closer examination it is easy to see that this absolute ruler is a king without a country. He really rules over nothing. His position, his kingdom, his sovereignty, is subject to the dictates of rebellion at any moment. This is because such a self is forever building castles in the air, and just when it seems on the point of having the building finished, at a whim it can – and often does – dissolve the whole thing into nothing.

When confronted with earthly need, a temporal cross, a thorn in the flesh that grows too deep to be removed, the defiant self is offended. It uses the suffering as an excuse to take offense at all existence. Such a person wants to be himself in spite of suffering, but not in "spite of it" in the sense of being without it. No, he now wants to spite or defy all existence and be himself *with* it, taking it along in steely resignation with him, almost flying in the face of his agony. Does he have hope in the possibility of help? No! Does he recognize that for God everything is possible? No! Will he ask help of any other? No! That for the entire world he will not do. If it came to that, he would rather be himself with all the torments of hell than ask for help.

Ah! Indeed, there is much, even prolonged and agonizing suffering that the defiant self fundamentally prefers so long as it retains the right to be itself. Ah, demonic madness! Such a self wants to be itself in hatred towards existence, to be itself according to its *own* misery. It does not even want so much as to sever itself defiantly from the power that established it but in sheer spite to push itself on that power, importune it, hold on to it out of malice.

In rebelling against existence, the defiant self will hear nothing about the comfort eternity offers. This comfort would be to his undoing, an objection to the whole of his existence. It is, to describe it figuratively, as if a writer were to make a slip of the pen and the error became conscious of itself as such and then wanted to rebel against the author. Out of hatred for him, the error forbids the author to correct it and in manic defiance says to him: "No, I will not be changed, I will stand as a witness against you, a witness to the fact that you are a second-rate author." Yes, this is the despair of defiance, and what despair it is!

38 | Consider the Lilies

Once upon a time there was a lily that stood in a secluded place' beside a little rippling brook. It lived in happy companionship with some nettles and a few other little flowers that grew nearby. The lily was more beautifully arrayed than Solomon in all his glory. Moreover, it was carefree and happy. One day a little bird came by to visit the lily. It came again the following day. Then it stayed away for several days before it came again. Now this seemed rather odd and baffling to the lily – strange that the bird did not remain in the same place like the little flowers nearby; how could the bird be so fickle? But as so often happens, the lily fell in love with the bird precisely because the bird was so fickle.

This little bird, however, was proud and naughty. Instead of delighting in the lily's beauty and sharing the joy of its innocent happiness, it would show off its freedom, making the lily feel its bondage. Not only that, the little bird talked fast and loose, of how in other places there were lots of lilies far more beautiful and in those places there was rapture and merriment, a fragrance, a splendor of colors, a singing of the birds that was beyond all description. This is how the bird spoke, and its stories usually ended with the remark – so humiliating for the lily – that in comparison with such glory the poor lily looked like nothing. Indeed, according to the bird, there was reason to wonder if it had any right to be called a lily.

So the lily began to fret. The more it listened to the bird the more worried it became. It no longer slept soundly at night. It no longer woke up happy in the morning. It felt imprisoned and bound. It found the purling of the water tiresome and the day long. In self-concern it began to be preoccupied with itself and the condition of its life. "To look so inferior as I do," said the lily to itself, "to be as insignificant as the little bird says I am – oh, why was I not placed somewhere else, under different conditions? Oh why did I not become a Crown Imperial?"

To make matters worse, the lily noticed that it was becoming exhausted from its worry. So it talked seriously to itself, yet not so seriously that it banished the worry out of its mind. Rather, it talked in such a way as to convince itself that its worry was justified. "After all," it said, "my wish is not an unreasonable one. I am not asking the impossible, to become what I am not – a bird, for example. My wish is only to become a beautiful lily, or even perhaps the most beautiful."

Amidst all this, the little bird flew back and forth, and with every visit and every departure the lily became more and more agitated. Finally it confided everything to the bird, and that evening they decided there had to be a change that would put an end to all the worry. So early the next morning the little bird came. He pecked away the soil from the lily's root so that it might become free. When this had been done, the bird took the lily under its wing and flew away. The decision was that the bird should fly with the lily to the place where the most beautiful lilies blossomed. Then the bird was to help the lily get planted down in the hope that with the change of place and the new surroundings it might succeed in becoming a magnificent lily in the company of all the others, or perhaps even a Crown Imperial envied by all the others. Alas, on the way the lily withered!

What does this have to say to us? The lily is we human beings. That proud, naughty little bird is the restless attitude of comparison, which roams far and wide, fitfully and capriciously, acquiring a diseased knowledge of distinction. And just as the bird did not put itself in the lily's place, comparison (or comparing) does the same thing by either putting us in someone else's place or putting someone else in ours.

In his preoccupation with comparisons, the worried person finally forgets altogether that he is a human being. He despairingly thinks of himself as being so different from others that he even believes he is different in his very humanity. That, of course, is what the little bird meant when he suggested that the lily was so insignificant that there was reason to doubt whether it really was a lily at all. And the typical defense for worrying (it seems so reasonable) is always that we are not asking anything unreasonable – such as to become a bird, for example. We only wish to fulfill an ambition we have not yet achieved, even if it seems so trivial to other worried people. If then, as with the movement of the bird to and fro, comparison incites worry to a passion and manages to tear us loose from the soil, for the soil is our willingness to be what we are created to be, then it seems as if comparison has now come to take us to our desired goal. And it certainly does come and fetch us, but only as death comes to fetch a person. It lets the worried one perish on the fluttering wings of despondency.

So what can the anxiety-ridden person learn from the lilies? He learns to be content with being a human being and not to worry about the differences between one person and another. He learns to speak just as concisely, just as solemnly, and just as inspiringly about being a human being as the Gospel speaks about the lilies. Let us consider Solomon. When dressed in royal splendor the one speaking says: Your Majesty. But when the most solemn speech of eternity is spoken, then we say: Man! And in the decisive moment of death when all differences are abolished, we say: Man! And in saying this we are not speaking disdainfully. On the contrary, we are uttering the highest of expressions. For to be a human being is not something lower than the differences we humans invent, but is high, high above them.

Worldly anxiety has its basis in a person's unwillingness to be content with being a human being and in his anxious craving for distinction by way of comparison. True, worry about making a living, or as it is more commonly put, worries about the necessities of life, is not exactly an invention of comparison. Nevertheless, should we not be able to learn a lot about this anxiety from the lilies and birds? If we cannot, without a smile, think of the lily's desire to become a Crown Imperial then think of its dying on the way. Oh, let us bear in mind that it is rather something to weep over that we too become just as foolishly worried, yes, just as foolishly.

39 | Behold the Birds of the Air

Once upon a time there was a wood dove. It had its nest in the fearsome forest, where wonder and apprehension dwelt together, among the erect, lonely trees. But nearby, where the smoke rises up from the farmer's house, lived some tame doves. The wood dove would often meet a pair of these. He would sit on a branch that stretched out over the farmyard, not far from the two tame doves on the ridge of the roof. One day they were talking together about how things were going and about making a living. The wood dove said, "Up until now I have made my living by letting each day have its own troubles, and in that way I get through life just fine." The tame dove, not without preening itself, answered: "No, we manage differently; with us, that is with the rich farmer with whom we live, our future is secure. At harvest time, my mate and I sit up on the roof and watch. The farmer brings in so many loads of corn that I know we are secure for a very long time. We two are well provided for and have our guaranteed security."

When the wood dove returned home he pondered the matter. It occurred to him that it must be a great comfort to *know* that one's living was secure for a long time, and what a wretched thing it was to always live in uncertainty. "It would be best," he told himself, "to gather a great stockpile and store it here or there in some safe place."

The next morning the wood dove woke earlier than usual. He got to work right away and was so busy gathering and storing that he scarcely had time to eat. But as fate seemed to hang over him, every time he had collected a little supply and hidden it away, when he came to look for it, it was gone! Meanwhile there was no actual change about making a living. He found his food every day as before. And yet a great change had taken place. He did not suffer actual want, but he had acquired the anticipation of need in the future. His peace of mind was lost. He had become anxious about the necessities of life.

From now on, the wood dove began to worry. His feathers lost their glint of color, his flight lost buoyancy. He was no longer joyful; indeed, he was almost envious of the rich, tame doves. He found his food each day, ate his fill, and yet he was not satisfied. In worrying about his needs he had trapped himself in a snare in which no birdcatcher could have trapped him, trapped as only a free creature can trap himself. "This securing of the future is constantly on my mind," he said. "Oh why am I a poor wood dove and not one of those rich ones?"

He saw plainly that anxiety was taking its toll on him, and so he spoke seriously to himself, yet not so seriously that he could drive away the worry from his mind and set his heart at rest. No, he only spoke in such a way that he convinced himself that his care was justified. "I am not asking anything unreasonable or impossible," he said. "I do not ask to become like the wealthy farmer, but only like one of the rich doves."

Finally, he contrived a scheme. One day he flew over and sat between the tame doves on the ridge of the farmer's roof. He noticed a place where they flew in, so he flew in too, because surely the storeroom had to be there. But when the farmer came home in the evening and shut the dovecote, he discovered the strange dove. He immediately put it into a little box by itself until the next day, when it was killed – and released from its worries about the necessities of life! Alas, the worried wood dove had not only trapped himself in worry but also in the dovecote – to its death!

The wood dove is like us silly human beings. When a person is content with the dignity of being human, then he understands that his heavenly Father feeds him. This he learns from the birds of the air. He does not live like the tame birds in the house of the wealthy farmer, but in the house of him who is richer than everyone, for heaven and earth are the house and possession of God, and humankind is his guest.

A person must be content to be as he is; a dependent being, as little capable of sustaining himself as of creating himself. If we choose to forget God and look after our own sustenance, then we are overcome with anxiety. It is certainly praiseworthy and pleasing to God when a person works for his food. But if he forgets God, and thinks that he himself is supporting himself, then he becomes burdened with the necessities of life. Let us not foolishly and small-mindedly say that the wealthy are spared this anxiety, while the poor are not. On the contrary, only he is spared who is content with being human and understands that his heavenly Father feeds him. And this is as possible for the wealthy as is it for the poor.

Worry about making a living, or not making a living, is a snare. In actuality, it is *the* snare. No external power, no actual circumstance, can trap a person. If a person chooses to be his own providence, then he will go quite ingenuously into his own trap, the wealthy as well as the poor. If he wants to entrench himself in his own plot of ground that is not under God's care, then he is living, though he does not acknowledge it, in a prison. When the farmer shut the door on the wood dove, the wood dove believed himself to be safe, when in fact he was caught. Or to put it another way, he was shut out from the care of Providence and trapped in a life of anxiety. In a spiritual sense he made himself a captive – trapped himself unto death.

40 | The Royal Coachman

It is the Spirit who gives life. The life-giving Spirit is not a direct heightening of our natural powers – what blasphemy! How horrible to understand the Spirit in this way! Christ brings *new* life! A new life, yes, and this is no platitude such as we use every time something new begins to stir in us. No, it is a new life, literally a new life – because, mark this well, death goes in between life and the new life on the other side of death. Yes, that is a new life.

Christianity teaches that you must die. Your power must be dismantled. And the life-giving Spirit is the very one who slays you. The first thing this Spirit says is that you must enter into death, you must die to yourself. The life-giving Spirit – that is the invitation. Who would not willingly take hold of it? But die first – there's the rub!

You must first die to every earthly hope, to every merely *human* confidence. You must die to your selfishness, and to the world, because it is only through your selfishness that the world has power over you. Naturally there is nothing a human being hangs on to so firmly – indeed, with his whole self – as to his selfishness! Ah, the separation of soul and body at the hour of death is not as painful as being forced to be separated from our flesh when we are alive! Yes, we human beings do not hang on to this physical life as firmly as we do to our selfishness!

What, exactly, does it mean to die to yourself? It is more than not seeing your wish fulfilled or to be deprived of the one that is dearest to you. True, this is painful enough, and selfishness is wounded. But it does not follow that you are dying. No, but personally to shatter your own fulfilled desire, personally to deprive yourself of the dearly desired one who is now your own: this is what it means to wound selfishness at the root, as it was with Abraham when God demanded that he sacrifice Isaac. Christianity is not what we are all too eager to make it. It is not a quack doctor who is promptly at your service and immediately applies the remedy but then bungles everything. Christianity waits before it applies its remedy. This is Christianity's severity. It demands a great sacrifice, one which we often despair of making and can only later see why it was necessary to hold out and wait.

Surely you have experienced, as I have, that when you begin to moan, and say, "I can't take any more," that on the next day you discover that you could. Consider a team of horses that groan and pant, feel exhausted, and feel that a handful of oats is just what is needed. However, they also don't realize that with only a momentary halt the heavily loaded wagon will roll back down the hill and plunge them and driver and everything into the abyss. Is it cruel of the driver that the lashes fall more dreadfully than ever before, especially on this team of horses who are as dear to him as the apple of his eye – is this cruel or is it kind? Is the driver cruel when the lashing is finally the only thing that can save the horses from ruin and help them pull through?

So it is with dying to yourself and to the world. But then, my listener, remember that then comes the life-giving Spirit. When? When you are dead to everything else. When does the Comforter come? Not until you have died to your selfishness and come to the end of your own strength. Not until you in love to

God have learned to hate yourself, even your ability, not until then can there be talk of the Spirit, of life, of *new* life.

Once upon a time there was a rich man. He purchased a team of entirely splendid horses, which he wanted for his own pleasure and the pleasure of driving them himself. A year or two passed by. If anyone who had known these horses earlier now saw him driving them, he would not be able to recognize them. Their eyes were now dull and drowsy, their gait lacked style and precision, they had no staying power, no endurance. Moreover, they had acquired all sorts of bad habits, and though they had plenty of feed, they grew thinner and thinner as each day passed by.

So he called in the royal coachman. The royal coachman drove them for a month. In the whole countryside there was not a team of horses that carried their heads so proudly, whose eyes were so fiery, whose gait was so beautiful. There wasn't a team that could hold out running as they did, even thirty miles in a stretch without stopping. How did this happen? It is easy to see: the owner, not being a coachman, drove the horses according to the horses' understanding of what it is to drive. The royal coachman, by contrast, drove the horses according to the coachman's understanding of what it is to drive.

So it is with us human beings. When I think of myself and the countless people I have come to know, I must confess that here are capacities and talents and qualifications enough, but the coachman is lacking. We humans have been, if I may put it this way (in order to carry on with the metaphor), driven according to the horses' (i.e., our) understanding of driving. We are governed, educated, and brought up according to the world's conception of what it means to be human. See, because of this we lack vitality and are unable to endure the sacrifice. We are impatient and impulsively use the means of the moment and, in turn, want instantly to see the reward for our work, which for that very reason is not very good.

Things were different once. There was a time when it pleased the Spirit himself to be the coachman. He drove the horses according to the coachman's understanding of what it is to drive. Oh, what a human being was capable of then! Ponder this! There sat twelve disciples, all of whom were of but a common social class. Their task, however, was to transform the world, and on the most appalling scale. And when the Spirit descended, the transformation indeed was set in motion.

They carried Christianity through. They were men just like us, but they were driven well! Yes, indeed, that they were! They were like that team of horses when the royal coachman drove them. Never has a human being lifted his head as high as did the first Christians in humility before God! And just as that team of horses could run if need be thirty miles without pausing to catch their wind, so also did they run; they ran seventy years at a stretch without getting out of the harness, without stopping anywhere. No, proud as they were in their humility before God, they exclaimed, "It is not for us to hold back and dawdle along the way. We will not stop – until eternity." They were driven well, yes, that they were!

Oh Holy Spirit, you who give new life, we pray for ourselves but also for all people. Here there is no want of capabilities, nor of education, nor of sagacity – indeed, there may rather be too much. But what is lacking is that you take away that which is corrupting us, that you take away our power and grant us new life. Certainly a person experiences a shudder like death's shudder when you, in order to become the power in him, take power away from him. So, help us also to die, to die to ourselves. If even the horses came to realize how good it was for them that the royal coachman took the reins, although it surely made them shudder at first and they at first rebelled, but in vain, should not we who are created in your image quickly come to understand what a blessing it is that you have the power and give life! Oh Holy Spirit, take the reigns of our lives and rule us. May it be you that has the power.

41 | The Invitation

Come here to me, all you who labor and are
burdened, and I will give you rest. (Mt. 11:28)

Come here! – Amazing! There is nothing especially amazing for a person in danger and in need of help to cry out, "Come here!" And ordinarily the person who can truly be of help must be searched for, and once he is found, it is often hard to gain access to him. But the one who sacrificed himself, he is the one who seeks out those who have need of help, he is himself the one who goes about and, calling, almost pleading, says, "Come here." He does not wait for anyone to come to him. He comes on his own initiative, for he is indeed the one who calls. He offers help – and such help!

"Come here to *me*." Amazing! Yes, human compassion does indeed do something for those who labor and are burdened. We feed the hungry, clothe the naked, give charity, build charitable organizations, and if the compassion is really heartfelt, we also visit those who are downtrodden. But to invite them to come to one, that is something that is not so easily done. It would mean that your household and way of life would be completely changed. To invite them in this way would mean to live together in entirely the same manner. You would have to become poor, sharing completely the same conditions as those who are distressed and burdened.

This invitation can only be made by changing your own conditions, so they are in keeping with theirs, provided that your life is not already like theirs, as was the case with him who says, "Come here to me, all you who labor and are burdened." This he said, and those who lived with him saw that there was not the slightest thing in his way of life that contradicts it. With the silent and faithful eloquence of action, his life expressed – even if he had never said these very words – his life expressed, "Come here to me, all you who labor and are burdened."

"I will give you rest." – Amazing! The words "Come here to *me*" should be understood to mean, "Remain with me, I *am* that rest." It is not as it usually is, when the helper who says "Come here" then says "Now leave" as he explains where the particular help a person might need is to be found, where, for example, the healing herb grows, or where there is a quiet place where he can relax from his labor. No, the helper is the help. Oh, how wonderful!

He who invites all and wants to help all treats the patient just as if he intended it for each one individually, as if each patient he had was his only patient. Ordinarily a physician must divide his help among his many patients. A physician, of course, cannot sit all day with one patient, even less have all his patients at home with him. How could he be all day with one patient without neglecting the others? The patient has the medicine the physician prescribes and uses it whenever he needs to. The physician checks on him occasionally, or the patient may visit the physician. But when the helper is the help, he remains with the patient all day long. How amazing, then, that this helper is the very one who invites all to remain with him!

The invitation goes out, along highways and down alleys. Yes, it goes out even to the path that is so lonely that only one solitary person walks it, so that there is only one track, that of the unhappy one who fled down it with his wretchedness (otherwise no track, and no track to show that anyone can come back along this way); there, too, the invitation finds its way and most easily when it brings back the fugitive to the Inviter. Come here, come here all of you – and you and you and you, too, you who are the loneliest.

This invitation stands at the crossroad, where temporal and earthly suffering has planted its cross, and there it beckons, "Come here, all you poor and miserable, you who must slave in poverty to eke out an existence with nothing more than a toilsome future. Come here, all you despised and discarded ones, whose existence no one cares about, not even as much as for a domestic animal, that has more value! All you sick, lame, deaf, blind, crippled, insane come here!" The invitation blasts away all distinctions in order to gather everybody together.

You sick at heart; you who through your anguish learn that a person's heart and an animal's heart are not the same; all you who have been treated unfairly, wronged, insulted, and mistreated; all you noble ones, you who were loving and unselfish and faithful, yet who deservedly reaped the reward of ingratitude – come here! All you victims of cunning and deceit and backbiting and envy, whom evil singled out and cowardice deserted, where no one asks what rights you have, where no one asks what wrong you have suffered, and where no one asks where it pains or how it pains, while the crowd tramples you into the dust – come here!

The invitation stands at the crossroad, where death separates. Come here, all you sorrowing ones, you who burdened labor in vain! Come here also you, you who have been consigned to live among the graves, you who are regarded as dead but are not missed, are not lamented, you to whom human society cruelly locks its doors and for whom no grave has yet mercifully opened; you, too, come here, here is rest and here is life!

The invitation stands at the crossroad, there where the road of sin veers away from the hedgerow of innocence. Come here, you who are so close and yet so far away. Come here, all you who are lost and gone astray, whatever your error and sin, whether hidden or revealed. Even if you have found forgiveness from others but do not have peace within, turn around and come here; here is rest! The invitation stands at the crossroad, there where the way of sin turns off for the last time and disappears from view in perdition. Oh, turn around, turn around, and come here. Do not shrink back, no matter how hard it is. Do not fear the narrow way of conversion that leads to salvation. Do not despair over every relapse. God in his mercy has the patience to forgive and a sinner should have the patience to humble himself. Do not despair. He who says, "Come here," is with you each step of the way. But come!

Come here, all of you; with him is rest. He adds no burden, he only opens his arms. He will not first ask you, as do the "righteous people" who try to help, "Are you not perhaps to blame for your misfortune?" It is so easy to judge by externals, to think that if someone does not get on well in the world that he is bad, or that he is an evil person that has done something wrong.

If you feel your need, he will not question you about it. He will not break the bruised reed even more but will lift you up when you accept him. He will not point his finger at you and thereby separate you from himself, so that your sin becomes even more terrible. He will provide you a hiding place with himself, and hidden in him he will hide your sins. For he is the friend of sinners. He does not merely stand still with open arms and say, "Come here." No, like the prodigal son's father he seeks the sinner, and like the good shepherd he seeks the lost sheep. He walks – no, he runs, but infinitely farther than any shepherd or any father. Indeed, he goes the infinitely long distance from being God to becoming man. And this he did to seek the lost!

The Inviter does not wait for those who labor and are burdened to come to him. He himself lovingly calls. He himself comes. He follows the urging ache of his heart, and his heart follows his words, "Come here!" If you follow these words, they in turn will follow you back again into his heart. Oh, that you would only accept the invitation, "Come here!"

42 | When the Burden Is Light

Christ does not lead people out of the world to paradise where there is no need or wretchedness. He does not, by magic, make this life into worldly delight and joy. No, he teaches what he demonstrates by example: that the burden is light even if the suffering is heavy.

Often, when we speak of carrying burdens, we distinguish between a light burden and a heavy one. We say that it is easy to carry the light burden and hard to carry the heavy one. But what about when a burden is both heavy and light? It is about this marvel I want to address.

When someone is on the verge of collapsing under a heavy burden, but the burden is the most precious thing he owns, he declares that in a certain sense it is light. When in distress at sea the lover is just about to sink under the weight of his beloved, the burden is most certainly heavy, and yet – yes, ask him about it – it is so indescribably light. He wants only to save his beloved's life. Therefore he speaks as if the burden did not exist at all; he calls her his life. How does this change take place? How is the heavy burden made light? Is it not because a great thought intervenes, a thought that marks his love? Is it not with the aid of the thought of being in love that the change takes place?

Similarly, Christ says, "My yoke is beneficial" (Mt. 11:33). There is only one thought, one single idea that contains faith's transformation of a heavy burden into a light one. This thought is that the burden is beneficial, that the heavy suffering laid on one can have a purpose.

But we must believe this. Later, perhaps, it can be seen that it has been beneficial, but at the time it cannot be seen, and neither can it be heard, even though countless people lovingly keep on repeating it. No, it must be believed. Faith's inward trusting must be there. Only faith's releasing power can loosen the yoke of thralldom so that the believer walks freely under the yoke. Only faith can loosen the tongue so that silence ends and the voice returns with adoration. It must be believed.

It is said of faith that it can move mountains. Even the heaviest suffering cannot be heavier than a mountain. And thus, if the sufferer believes that his suffering is beneficial to him – yes, then he moves mountains. In order to move a mountain you must get under it. Alas, that is the way – the sufferer gets under the heavy burden; this is the heaviness. But faith's perseverance lifts the mountain and moves it, precisely because it gets under it. However, this will happen only if the sufferer believes, only if *he* believes that it is beneficial, can he move the mountain.

When we, in faith, cling to the promise of moving mountains, our joy is so great that the yoke actually becomes light. When someone lifts up a feather, he says, "It is light." But when someone despairs of his lack of strength, but nevertheless tests the heavy weight and succeeds in lifting it, he becomes so joyful that he exclaims, "It is light!" Has he become rash; has he forgotten that he despaired; has he taken the divine help in vain? No, indeed, it is precisely in faith's blessed wonder that he speaks this way.

Christ says, "My burden is light." Christ summons his followers: "Learn from me, for I am meek and lowly of heart." Yes, Christ was meek. He did not assert his rights; he did not plead his innocence; he did not talk about how they were sinning against him. In fact, he did not point out their scandalous guilt with a single word (though surely such guilt was pointed out). Even in his last moment he said, "Father, forgive them, for they know not what they do." Does not his meekness conceal their guilt and make it far less than it is?

It is to this meekness, to this gentle courage that Christ calls us. And what else is meekness except, as it was for Christ on the cross, to carry the heavy burden lightly, just as impatience and sullenness carry the light burden so heavily. To deal harshly with iron strength with what is the hardest of all is not nearly as wonderful as it is to have iron strength and be able to deal gently with what is weakest of all, or to deal lightly with what is heaviest of all. Such is the way of Christ.

Meekness is perhaps the Christian's most distinguishing mark. "If anyone strikes you on the right cheek, turn to him the other also" (Mt. 5:39). Not to strike back is not, in itself, meekness. Nor is it meekness to merely put up with being wronged and accept it for what it is. But it is meekness to turn the left cheek. Pride also bears the wrong, but as it lifts itself above the wrong – usually in self-righteous judgment – it actually makes the wrong seem greater than it is. Patience also bears the wrong, but it does not make the wrong less than it is. Only meekness makes the wrong less, only meekness lightens the load. It takes the wrong into itself, be it injury, insult, or whatever, and in this way lessens it.

Meekness carries the heavy burden so lightly that it is as if the guilty party's fault became less. This meekness has but one glorious quality: it demands no reward on earth, and yet, it also has an even more glorious quality: that its reward is great in heaven. But is this not to make the heavy burden light? If you know of any other way to explain it then please explain it to me. I know of no other way than the simplicity of faith.

43 | A Dangerous Schooling

Scripture says that, "Jesus *learned* obedience from what he suffered" (Heb. 5:8). Now, if obedience directly followed suffering, it would be easy to learn. But learning obedience is not that easy. Humanly viewed, suffering is dangerous. But even more terrible is failing to learn obedience! Yes, suffering is a dangerous schooling, but only if you do not learn obedience – ah, then it is terrible, just as when the most powerful medicine has the wrong reaction. In this danger a person needs God's help; otherwise he does not learn obedience. And if he does not learn this, then he may learn what is most corrupting: to learn craven despondency, learn to quench the spirit, learn to deaden any noble fervor in it, learn defiance and despair.

Because the schooling of suffering is so dangerous, it is right to say that this school educates for eternity. This danger does not exist in any other school, but then there is not the gain either: the eternal. Of course, a person can learn a great deal without ever coming to know the eternal. He may learn how to cope outwardly, he may achieve amazing things in his suffering, encompass a mass of knowledge, understanding himself or his destiny. If in suffering you do not learn obedience, you will continue to be a riddle to yourself.

Suffering seeks to turn a person inward. If this happens, the school of suffering begins. You will not in despair mount a resistance, or seek to drown yourself and forget the suffering in the world's distractions, in amazing enterprises or in indifferent knowledge. Admittedly, suffering often comes from the outside, but it is not until you take the suffering into your inner being that the schooling begins. Many sufferings can assault a person, and worldly sagacity knows many remedies in defense. But all these remedies have the dismal quality that they save the body but kill the soul. They invigorate the body but deaden the spirit. Only inwardness, only in surrender can the eternal be gained.

Only when a person suffers and wills to learn from what he suffers does he come to know something about himself and about his relationship to God. This is the sign that he is being educated for eternity. Through suffering a person can come to know a great deal about the world – how deceitful and treacherous it is – but all this knowledge is not the schooling of suffering. No, just as we speak of a child being weaned from his mother's breast, so also, in the most profound sense, a person must be weaned by suffering, weaned from the things of this world, from loving it and from being embittered by it, in order to learn for eternity. For this reason, the school of suffering consists in a *dying to* – a dying to the world and to yourself. And in this school the lessons are always quiet. Here the attention is not dispersed by many subjects. No, here only one thing, the essential thing, is needful. Only one thing is learned: obedience.

Without suffering you cannot really learn obedience. Suffering is the very guarantee that obedience is not self-willfulness. Ordinarily we say that we must learn to obey in order to learn to be master, and this is indeed true. But we learn something even more glorious by learning obedience in the school of suffering. When this happens we learn to let God be master, to let God rule. And where else is this to be learned except in the school of suffering, where the child is weaned and self-willfulness dies and we learn the difficult lesson that it is indeed God who still rules, despite the suffering.

This is the key to finding rest in your suffering. There is only one way in which rest is to be found: to let God rule in everything. Whatever else you might come to learn only pertains to how God has willed to rule. But as soon as unrest begins, the cause for it is due to your unwillingness to obey, your unwillingness to surrender yourself to God.

When there is suffering, but also obedience in suffering, then you are being educated for eternity. Then there will be no impatient hankering in your soul, no restlessness, neither of sin nor of sorrow. If you will but let it, suffering is the guardian angel who keeps you from slipping out into the fragmentariness of the world; the fragmentariness that seeks to rip apart the soul. And for this reason, suffering keeps you in school – this dangerous schooling – so that you may be properly educated for eternity.

44 | To Suffer *Christianly*

What is decisive in Christian suffering? It lies in the fact that it is voluntary – "on account of the Word" and "for righteousness' sake." The disciples left everything to follow Christ. Their sacrifice was voluntary. Someone may be unfortunate to lose everything he owns and has; but he has not given up the least thing. Not like the Apostles! Herein lies the confusion.

In today's Christianity we take ordinary human suffering and turn it into a Christian example. "Everyone has a cross to bear." We preach unavoidable human trials into being Christian suffering. How this happens is beyond me! To lose everything and give up everything are not synonymous. To the contrary, the difference between them is infinite. If I happen to lose everything, this is one thing. But if I voluntarily give up everything, choose danger and difficulties, this is something entirely different. When this happens it is impossible to avoid the trial that comes with carrying Jesus' cross. This is what Christian suffering means, and it is a whole scale deeper than ordinary human adversity.

In ordinary human suffering there exists, unlike in Christian suffering, no *self*-contradiction. There is no self-denial in my wife's dying a natural death – after all, she is mortal. There is no self-denial in my losing my possessions – after all, they are perishable. In Christian suffering, however, self-contradiction is necessary. It is this that constitutes the possibility of offense.

This is why the remedy seems infinitely worse than the sickness. "But if your hand or your foot offends you, cut it off and throw it from you..." (Mt. 18: 8–9). Christ says: If you want to avoid the real offense, cut off your hand, tear out your eye, even let yourself be castrated for the sake of God's kingdom (Mt. 19:12). His word offends our sinful nature. Such a remedy, according to established wisdom, is nothing but madness, much worse than the sickness. Why should I do that? Christ answers: In order to avoid the real offense, that is, in order to become new and enter into life.

Nowadays we can become or live as Christians in the most pleasant way and without ever risking the slightest possibility of offense. All we have to do is start with the status quo and observe good virtues (good-better-best). We can continue to make ourselves comfortable by scraping together the world's goods, as long as we stir into the pot what is Christian as a seasoning, an ingredient that almost serves to refine our enjoyment of life. This kind of Christianity is but a religious variation of the world's unbelief, a movement without budging from the spot. That is to say, it is a simulated motion.

Jesus speaks of how tribulation and persecution come on account of the Word, and as a result, how one is immediately offended. The emphasis lies upon "on account of the Word." Let me clarify this. When in sickness I go to a physician, he may find it necessary to prescribe a very painful treatment. Here there is no self-contradiction in my submitting to his remedy, for it is only a matter of time before I am healed. On the other hand, if I suddenly find myself in trouble, an object of persecution, because I have gone to *that* physician, well, then there is a true *self*-contradiction. The fact that I get involved with this physician, the Great Physician, and attach myself to him, that is what makes me an object of persecution. Herein lies the possibility of offense; herein lies the terror.

Christ unabashedly speaks of what would await his disciples when they witnessed to him in the world. "This I have told you so that you will not be offended. They will exclude you from the synagogues; yes, the time will come when whoever kills you will think he is offering God a service" (Jn. 16:1; Mt. 16:23). The possibility of offense consists in being persecuted, ridiculed, cast out from society, misunderstood, and finally put to death – and in such a way that those who do it think they are doing God, or the cause of righteousness, a service. It is to this suffering Christ speaks and promises heaven's reward.

Whether you experience adversities in life, whether things perhaps go downhill for you, though you as a Christian will most assuredly bear these sufferings patiently, unlike many others in the world, however patiently you bear them, this suffering is not yet akin to Christ's suffering. To suffer Christianly is not to endure the inescapable but to suffer evil at the hands of people because you voluntarily will and endeavor to do only the good: to willingly suffer on account of the Word and for the sake of righteousness. This is how Christ suffered. This alone is Christian suffering.

V | CHRISTIAN COLLISIONS

45 | The Offense

When Christianity came into the world, it did not need to call attention (even though it did so) to the fact that it was contrary to human nature and human understanding, for the world discovered that easily enough. But now that we are on intimate terms with Christianity, we must awaken the collision. The possibility of offense must again be preached to life. Only the possibility of offense (the antidote to the apologists' sleeping potion) is able to waken those who have fallen asleep, is able to break the spell so that Christianity is itself again.

Woe to him, therefore, who preaches Christianity without the possibility of offense. Woe to the person who smoothly, flirtatiously, commendingly, convincingly preaches some soft, sweet something which is supposed to be Christianity! Woe to the person who makes miracles reasonable. Woe to the person who betrays and breaks the mystery of faith, distorts it into public wisdom, because he takes away the possibility of offense! Woe to the person who speaks of the mystery of the Atonement without detecting in it anything of the possibility of offense. Woe again to him who thinks God and Christianity are something for study and discussion. Woe to every unfaithful steward who sits down and writes false proofs, winning friends for themselves and for Christianity by writing off the possibility of offense. Oh, the learning and acumen tragically wasted. Oh, the time wasted in this enormous work of making Christianity so reasonable, and in trying to make it so relevant!

Only when Christianity rises up again, powerful in the possibility of offense, only then will it need no artful defenders. The more skillful, the more articulate, the more excellent the defense, however, the more Christianity is disfigured, abolished, exhausted like an emasculated man. Christianity ought not to be defended, at least not on the world's terms. It is we who should see whether we can justify ourselves. It is we who must choose: either to be offended or to accept Christianity.

Therefore, take away from Christianity the possibility of offense or take away from the forgiveness of sin the battle of an anguished conscience. Then lock the churches, the sooner the better, or turn them into places of amusement which stand open all day long!

46 | What Says the Fire Chief?

When a person suddenly falls ill, well-meaning people are quick to lend aid. The first proposes one thing, the next another. If all of them, however, had opportunity to advise all at once, the patient's death would be certain. Such well-meant advice may in itself be dangerous, for such bustling, flurried presence impedes the physician.

So also in the case of a fire. Hardly is the cry of "Fire!" heard before a crowd of people rush to the spot. One has a pitcher, another a basin, the third a squirter. All of them are nice, cordial, sympathetic, helpful people, so eager to help put out the fire.

But what says the Fire Chief? The Fire Chief, although normally a very pleasant and polite person, says, or rather he shouts, "Oh, to hell with all your pitchers and squirters!" Yes, the Fire Chief is generally a very pleasant and polite person who knows how to show everyone the respect due him, but at a fire he is rather different. He says, "Where the hell is the police force?" And when some policemen arrive he says to them, "Get rid of these damn people with their pitchers and squirters. And if they won't yield to words, then give them a whack or two, so that we may be free of them and get down to work."

At a fire the whole way of looking at things is not the same as in everyday life. This is quite natural, for a fire is a serious thing, and whenever things are really serious, honest good intentions never suffice. No, seriousness applies an entirely different law: either/or. Either you are the one who in this instance can actually do something, or if such be not your case, then the important thing for you to do is to get out. As it is in the case of a fire, so also in matters of the mind. Wherever there is a cause to be promoted, an undertaking to be carried out, an idea to be introduced, we can always be sure that when someone comes to the spot, he will find there before him a genial company of twaddlers who in the name of seriousness stand around and bungle things by wanting to serve the cause, promote the undertaking, introduce their own ideas. I say, when the right person comes along he will find things thus. And the fact that he is the right person can be determined precisely by how he understands his relationship to this company of twaddlers. If he has a notion that it is they who are to help, and that he must strengthen himself by union with them, he is not the right person. The right person sees at once, like the Fire Chief, that this company of twaddlers must get out, that their presence is the most dangerous assistance the fire could have.

As with matters of the mind, so also in the religious sphere. History is often compared with what the chemists call a process. The metaphor may be quite suggestive, if only it is understood correctly. Scientists speak of a filtering process: water is filtered, and in the process it deposits impure ingredients. It is precisely in an opposite sense that history is a process. The truth is introduced – and with that it enters into the process of history. But unfortunately this does not (as so many ludicrously assume) result in the purification of the idea, which never is purer than in its primitive form. No, it results, with steadily increasing momentum, in garbling the truth, in making it dull, trite, in wearing it out, in introducing impure ingredients that originally were not present. What happens is the very opposite of filtering, until at last, by the enthusiastic cooperation and mutual consent of a number of successive generations, the point is reached where the truth is entirely extinguished and its opposite embraced.

When at last the right one comes along, to set fire to this wilderness that is the asylum of all twaddle, all illusions, all clever tricks, he will, no doubt, already find there before him a company of twaddlers – a crowd. Such a mass have a notion that things are wrong, and often chatter about how dreadfully wrong everything is. But if we think, even for a single moment that this company will be a help, we are not the right man; divine governance will instantly let go of us as unfit. The right one always sees with half an eye, as does the Fire Chief. He understands that this company which well-meaningly offers help to put out a fire with pitchers and squirters, would lend help with a sulfur match. He knows full well that he must not have the least thing to do with this company, that he must be as harsh with them as possible. Everything depends upon getting rid of the crowd, for all the crowd does with its hearty sympathy is to eradicate the real seriousness from the cause.

Wherever true seriousness is called for, the law is this: either/or. Nothing is more detestable and disgusting, both betraying and bringing about a deeper demoralization than this: to somehow want a little part in that which must be either/or, all or nothing, and then with good-hearted moderation together rush about it, and by this prattle to pretend mendaciously that one is better than those who have nothing to do with the whole concern – pretend to be better, and thereby make the thing more difficult for those who properly have the task to do.

47 | Christianity Does Not Exist

Imagine someone who aspired to be a millionaire but as yet had managed to earn only three dollars. Were he to call himself a millionaire because he was trying, would we be foolish enough to go along with his use of language? Would it not be better for him – simply to keep him awake and alert for the exertion – to say to himself, "I am not a millionaire." By saying it to himself in this way, would he not guard against becoming a fool?

The point is this: if there is to be any meaning to it, if it is at all permissible to take the name of something simply because you are striving toward it, then you must at least resemble what you are striving toward. In order to hide the fact that Christianity simply does not exist we say, "I confess that in the strictest sense, in the New Testament sense, I am not a Christian, but I am trying." Having said that, or taking care to say it every Sunday year after year, or hearing it said, one concludes that one needs to do nothing. We are, after all, Christian.

Let me use an illustration. There is much talk these days about an expedition to the North Pole, an undertaking involving extreme exertion and danger. Now suppose that we had gotten the idea into our heads that taking part in such an expedition had significance for our eternal salvation. And let us assume that the clergy have also gotten into the affair and now are going to help us (out of love!). It is perfectly clear that in order to take part in such a North Pole expedition a person must first of all (if he lives in Europe) leave Europe, his home. Then he must travel a long way north before there can be any question of a North Pole expedition, which can be assumed to begin only with dangers and the initial exertion.

The clergy would make use of this. They know, of course, that those who would actually make the strenuous and dangerous journey will be few, an insufficient number to supply a living for the many pastors with their families. Consequently they change the terms. It now becomes a matter of changing "North Pole expedition" to "an effort in the direction of such a North Pole expedition" and then to babble on about it to those who pay money to listen. Managing to delude everyone into thinking that they, too, are striving in the direction of the North Pole, they manage to make everyone very happy and, in the process, to secure a living for themselves.

How this delusion is accomplished is clear enough. There is, for example, a man in Copenhagen. He travels by ship to London and back in the greatest comfort and ease, "and," says the pastor, "this was his North Pole expedition. No, he did not reach the North Pole, but he tried." "It is perfectly clear," expounds the preacher, "that if you are going to make an expedition to the North Pole and live in Copenhagen, you must first of all leave Copenhagen. This man did that. On the other hand, no one has yet reached the North Pole anyway. Even those who have gone the farthest have only made an effort. But so has this man. To travel to London is also an effort." Wonderful, tremendously popular! And to take a ride to the city park on Sunday afternoon, leaving one's home, is also an effort aimed at discovering the North Pole: ergo, we are all striving! This is the way all of us have become Christians, and paying Christians to boot!

48 | What Madness

We now have, unlike original Christianity, a complete cast of bishops, deans, and pastors; educated clergy, degree and all, talented, gifted, humanly well-meaning. They all preach with tremendous confidence – doing it well, very well, stupendously well, tolerably well, or badly – but not one of them lives in character with the Christianity of the New Testament. This grand cast of characters accomplishes one thing: it gives rise to a false impression that because we have such a complete cast we must of course have Christianity, too.

We also have what one might call a complete inventory of church buildings, bells, organs, pews, altars, pulpits, offering plates, and so on. But when Christianity does not exist, this inventory, so far from being an advantage, is a peril, because it is so very likely to give rise to the false impression that we must have Christianity, too.

The illusion of a Christian nation, a Christian "people," masses of Christians, is no doubt due to the power that numbers exercise over the imagination. And yet how many are able to say of their Christian acquaintances that they are truly Christians in the New Testament sense, or that their lives are even close to resembling those of the first disciples. But when there are thousands upon thousands who confess to being Christian, one becomes easily confused. Perhaps we are all Christians after all. Why be so harsh?

This brings to mind a ridiculous story about an innkeeper. It is said that this innkeeper sold his beer by the bottle for a cent less than it cost him. When a certain man said to him, "How does that balance the account? You're losing money," he replied, "No, my friend, it's the big number that counts."

When you have finished laughing at this story, you would do well to take its lesson to heart, which warns against the power that numbers exercise over the imagination. No doubt this innkeeper knew very well that one bottle of beer at 3 cents meant a loss of 1 cent since it cost him 4 cents. And, no doubt, he realized that selling 10 bottles also meant a loss. But 100,000 bottles! Here the big number stirs the imagination. The innkeeper becomes dazed. It's a profit, he says, for the big number does it. So also with every calculation that arrives at a Christian nation, and dare I also say at a church, by adding up units which are not Christian, getting impressed with the results by means of the notion that it is the big number that counts!

Numbers are the most dangerous of all illusions. Inasmuch as Christianity is spirit, the honesty of eternity, there is nothing its detective eye is so suspicious of as of Christian states, Christian lands, Christian endeavors, Christian movements, a Christian people, and (how marvelous!) a Christian world. Even if there were something true in this talk about Christian peoples and cultures, everything this world has up to this point seen in the way of criminal affairs is a mere nursery rhyme in comparison with this crime.

Christ requires *followers* and defines precisely what he means by this. They are to be salt, willing to be sacrificed. But to be salt and to be sacrificed is not something that the thousands naturally go for, still less millions, or (still less!) countries, kingdoms, states, and (absolutely not!) the whole world. On the other hand, if it is a question of size, mediocrity, and of lots of talk, then the possibility of the thing begins; then bring on the thousands, increase them to the millions – no, go forth and make the world Christian.

The New Testament alone, not numbers, settles what Christianity is, leaving it to eternity to pass judgment upon us. It is simply impossible to define faith on the basis of what people in general like best and prefer to call Christianity. As soon as we do this, Christianity is automatically done away with. There are, in the end, only two ways open to us: to honestly and honorably make an admission of how far we are from the Christianity of the New Testament, or to perform skillful tricks to conceal the true situation, tricks to conjure up a forgery whereby Christianity is the prevailing religion in the land.

Honestly, New Testament Christianity simply does not exist. If the human race would rise in rebellion against God and cast Christianity away from it, it would not be nearly so dangerous as this clever way of making Christians of everybody and giving this activity the appearance of zeal for the truth. This is nothing but a scoffing at God by offering him thanks for bestowing his blessing upon the progress that Christianity was making.

49 | The Echo Answers

Endless volumes have been written to show how one is to recognize what true Christianity is. This can be done in a far simpler way. Nature is acoustic. Pay attention to what the echo answers, and you will know at once what is what.

When one preaches Christianity in such a way that the echo answers: "Glorious, profound, brilliant, articulate Christian, you should be exalted with high praise," know that this signifies that this preaching is a base lie. Though it is not absolutely certain that he who walks with chains around his ankles is in fact a criminal (for there are many cases when the powers that be have condemned an innocent man), it is eternally certain that he who by preaching Christianity wins honor and prestige is a liar, a deceiver, who at one point or another has falsified the truth. It is simple: It is impossible to preach Christianity in truth without having to suffer for it in this world.

When one preaches Christianity in such a way that the echo answers, "He is mad," or "What nonsense," know then there are considerable elements of truth in his preaching. However, this is still not the Christianity of the New Testament. He may have hit the mark, but he does not press hard enough, especially not by the preaching of his life.

But when one preaches Christianity in such a way that the echo answers, "Away with that man, he does not deserve to live," know that this is the Christianity of the New Testament. Capital punishment is the penalty for preaching Christianity as it truly is. Does Christ's life indicate anything different? Hating oneself to love God; hating everything in which one's life consists, everything to which human beings cling. Capital punishment is the penalty for preaching Christianity in character. Preaching less, appealing to forms of the interesting, the relevant, or the controversial, is nothing but a religious falsification.

The merit of "Christendom" is that the world has now become so tolerant, has made such progress, that persecution can no longer take place. There is nothing to persecute. Oh, yes, Christianity is perfectible! And oh how the echo answers!

50 | The Tax Collector

In Luke's Gospel we read: "But the tax collector stood far off and would not even lift up his eyes to heaven, but beat upon his breast, saying, God be merciful to me a sinner" (Lk. 18:13). The tax collector stood far off. What does this mean? It means to stand by himself, alone with himself and God. Only when you are literally alone with God do you discover how far off you are. Oh, even though you are not as sinful as the tax collector, when you are alone with yourself before God, you also stand far off. And this is as it should be. For as soon as there is somebody between you and God, you are easily deceived, as though you were not so far off. You too easily use a deceitful standard of measurement, the standard of human comparison. It is as though you think you could measure how far away you are, which, of course, is never that far.

But the Pharisee also "stood by himself." Was he not also standing far off? Yes, if he had stood by himself. But the Gospel says that he stood by himself and thanked God "that he was not like other men." He did not stand by himself, for when we have others in view, we do not stand by ourselves. The Pharisee's pride consisted just in this – that he proudly used others to measure his distance. He held this thought fast, in order to stand proudly by himself in contrast to the rest. But this indeed is not to stand by yourself, least of all to stand by yourself before God.

The Pharisee stands by himself, the tax collector stands afar off – and yet, and yet, the Pharisee saw the tax collector but the tax collector did not see the Pharisee. When the Pharisee came home he knew very well that this tax collector had been in church, but this tax collector knew nothing of this Pharisee's having been in church. Proudly the Pharisee found satisfaction in seeing the tax collector; humbly the tax collector saw no one. With eyes cast down and turned inward he was in truth before God.

And so, "the tax collector went down to his house justified." With regards to this tax collector, the Scripture says of all tax collectors and sinners, that they draw near to Christ – just by standing afar off they draw near to him (whereas the Pharisee with presumptuous insolence stood far, yes far off). Thus the picture is inverted. It begins with the Pharisee standing near, the tax collector afar off; it ends with the Pharisee standing far off, the tax collector near. The tax collector went to his house justified. For he cast down his eyes; but such eyes *see* God, and in seeing God the heart is lifted up.

51 | Gospel for the Poor

Christ was not making a historical observation when he declared: The gospel is preached to the poor. The accent is on the gospel, that the gospel is for the poor. Here the word "poor" does not simply mean poverty but all who suffer, are unfortunate, wretched, wronged, oppressed, crippled, lame, leprous, demonic. The gospel is preached to them, that is, the gospel is for them. The gospel is good news for them. What good news? Not: money, health, status, and so on – no, this is not Christianity.

No, for the poor the gospel is the good news because to be unfortunate in this world (in such a way that one is abandoned by human sympathy, and the worldly zest for life even cruelly tries to make one's misfortune into guilt) is a sign of God's nearness. So it was originally; this is the gospel in the New Testament. It is preached *for* "the poor," and it is preached *by* the poor who, if they in other respects were not suffering, would eventually suffer by proclaiming the gospel; since suffering is inseparable from following Christ, from telling the truth.

But soon there came a change. When preaching the gospel became a livelihood, even a lush livelihood, then the gospel became good news for the rich and for the mighty. For how else was the preacher to acquire and secure rank and dignity unless Christianity secured the best for all? Christianity thus ceased to be glad tidings for those who suffer, a message of hope that

transfigures suffering into joy, but a guarantee for the enjoyment of life intensified and secured by the hope of eternity.

The gospel no longer benefits the poor essentially. In fact,
Christianity has now even become a downright injustice to
those who suffer (although we are not always conscious of this,
and certainly unwilling to admit to it). Today the gospel is
preached to the rich, the powerful, who have discovered it to be
advantageous. We are right back again to the very state original
Christianity wanted to oppose! The rich and powerful not only
get to keep everything, but their success becomes the mark of
their piety, the sign of their relationship to God. And this
prompts the old atrocity again – namely, the idea that the unfortunate, the poor are to blame for their condition; that it is
because they are not pious enough, are not true Christians, that
they are poor, whereas the rich have not only pleasure but piety
as well. This is supposed to be Christianity. Compare it with the
New Testament, and you will see that this is as far from that as
possible.

52 | How God Relates Inversely

The law for God's nearness and remoteness is as follows: The more the outward externals, the appearances, indicate that God cannot possibly be present here, the closer he is. The opposite is also true: the more the outward externals, the appearances, indicate that God is very near, the farther away he is. Consider the first case, and think especially of Christ. Whenever it appeared that this man could not possibly be the God-man, then people even refused to recognize him as a man. But it was then that God's actuality was most present. Now consider the law for God's remoteness (and the history of this is the history of Christendom). It is as follows: Everything that strengthens the appearance of God being present (in the worldly sense) distances God.

At the time when there were no churches and the Christians gathered together in catacombs as refugees and lawbreakers, God was close. Then came the churches, so many churches, such great, splendid churches and to the same degree God was distanced. For God's nearness is inversely related to externals, and this ascending scale (churches, many churches, splendid churches) is an increase in the sphere of appearance. Before Christianity became a doctrine, when it was only one or two affirmations expressed in one's life, God was closer. And with every increase and embellishment of doctrine, with every increase of "success," God was distanced. When there were no clergy and the Christians were all brothers, God was closer than when clergymen, many clergymen, a powerful ecclesiastical order, came into being. For clergymen are an increase in appearance, and God always relates inversely to outward show.

This is how Christendom has step by step become so distant from God. Christianity's history is one of alienation from God through the gradual strengthening of appearance. Or it might be said Christianity's history is one of the progressive removal of God – tactfully and politely by building churches and monumental buildings, by a monstrous doctrinal system, with an incalculable host of preachers and professors. Established Christianity is about as far away from God as one can possibly get.

Now if I say this to anyone, I will be surely be told, "True, something must be done, but the problem is that there are too few pastors in proportion to the population. Let's get a thousand more (Excellent – in order to get farther away from God!), a good many more churches (Excellent, in order to get farther away from God!), and a permanent alliance of pastors and professors to make the doctrine more strictly accurate (Excellent, in order to get farther away from God!)."

No, no, no! If you are really serious about getting God closer, then consign the whole system of established Christianity with its lying gang of preachers and professors, these Christian experts who *en masse* provide an excellent commentary on every Bible passage, to death and the devil. Seek first God's kingdom. The Christian rule for action is simple: Venture to act in accordance with the truth and at the same moment through this action you will collide with the environing world. Your action will be such that you will discover the collisions of the essentially Christian. In no other way can one enter into the situation where faith can come into existence. Venture right into the middle of actuality. Risk – and then God will truly come. But now God sits and watches to see if there is one single person who will venture.

Every single human being is able to venture, and God is willing to become involved with absolutely every human being who ventures. He is infinite love, but he is also majesty. And he is a connoisseur; with his dreadful sharp-sightedness he is able to see whether a person wants to exploit him or is venturing. But where is there one who will actually venture? Oh yes, there are ministers and professors and church workers by the thousands who make a profit, and who are willing to venture a tiny little bit as long as they can count on a proportionate increase in their income. But where is there one person who will actually venture, who trusting in God and in the power of God, will dare relate inversely to appearance – something Christians do not seem to accept, in fact can't stand.

No, Christendom would rather build great, spacious churches for God, presumably so that he (and we) can really have enough room. But in actuality even the smallest space is too large for God. One single, poor, abandoned, simple person, who trusting in God, will venture, will risk – there God is present and makes him, humanly, or paradoxically speaking, less unhappy. This is what God must do before he is able to be there – to such an extent does God relate negatively to externals. But we prefer to build huge edifices for him, and hundreds, yes, thousands of church professionals are summoned together in an enormous institution, convinced that when such a colossal body is assembled and sits together at an unbelievable cost that God is present, that he is closest there, that his cause is advanced there. No. God relates inversely to the outward show of externals.

53 | Undercover Clergy

S: Tell me, Preacher. What in the world are you doing in our neighborhood?

P: No, first things first. A glass of schnapps to open the meal and the heart. (Drinks a schnapps.) Well, to be brief, I am out here on behalf of the Temperance Society.

S: Ah, now I see why you had to have a glass of schnapps, for if you had not asked for one, I certainly would not have been able to have offered you a schnapps.

P: Please don't misunderstand me. I have by no means joined the Temperance Society. Anything but! I will drink a second glass in honor of the Temperance Society. I always drink a second glass in honor of the Temperance Society. (They clink their glasses, both drink and say: Long live the Temperance Society!) Now to the business at hand. You see, it is well known that I have an extraordinary speaking ability. The Temperance Society became aware of my talents and in the interest of the Society it decided not to let them go to waste. To put it briefly, I have been called and installed as "Pastor" to the Temperance Society. That I do not fully subscribe to the Temperance Society's explicit aims is understood. Yet, the Temperance Society Board is of the opinion, "What does it matter if the pastor drinks a schnapps or two? What does it matter as long as by using his gifts he is able to win scores of members for the Society?"

S: The Society is right about that. Even the strictest teetotaler knows that every such glass of schnapps for the pastor is well utilized, presupposing that you do get members for the Society.

P: So you agree. I, of course, am completely convinced it is right, and if I had not already done it I would drink another schnapps in honor of the Temperance Society. To go on with my story, I have made an agreement with the Society, whose activity involves diet, that I have my diet: four schnapps every day, two glasses of punch, and an extra glass for every one who signs up as a member. It all goes on the expense account. Just as I believe they are satisfied with me, so I am also satisfied with it. I really don't want to make any alteration or to leave. I even grieve to think of leaving a congregation which I love and esteem and which loves and esteems me in return.

S: You have become a "pastor" and somebody of influence in this world. Maybe you can tell me one more thing. I have often imaged myself as a pastor. It must be easy to stand and preach the very opposite of what you are doing – after all, you certainly cannot feel what you are saying.

P: Why do you say that? I can assure you – and every one of my many listeners is able to testify – that I sometimes am so moved that I can scarcely talk. In the first place, I think of the four schnapps, the two glasses of punch, an extra glass, and also the fact that I am successful in the world and have a good living – isn't that moving! Next I think of my useful and beneficial activity. While I stand there speaking I look at the people I am talking to and can read their eyes: there sits one who as sure as my name is Pastor H. will go right out of this meeting and sign up as a member. I can get so emotional over this that I sometimes start to cry, and this has such a powerful effect that I can see on his neighbor's face that he is going to do the same. Now, if that isn't moving then I don't know what is. If I were a saint do you think I would be able to produce such an effect? The people would quickly lose interest. Am I right?

S: Perhaps. But isn't it untrue to call yourself a pastor?

P: Not at all. If a person can proclaim the teaching that we should not aspire after earthly honor, esteem, wealth – if a person can proclaim this in such a way that he convinces people to live their lives accordingly, does it make any difference if he himself does just the opposite? Or isn't this the best proof of his extraordinary talent for speaking, of his being truly a great orator, the fact that although he doesn't exactly do what he preaches he still has such an enormous influence?

S: But doesn't it ever happen that people complain that you are not a member? Don't you get reproached for it?

P: Yes, of course, but I dismiss it. I explain it as a conflict of personalities, of style. Anyway, it is my job to preach, and one should stick to the subject of what I am teaching. That slays them.

54 | "*First* the Kingdom of God"

The theological candidate Ludvig From is seeking. And when one hears that a "theological" candidate is seeking, one need not have an especially vivid imagination to understand what it is he seeks. Of course it is the kingdom of God, which indeed one must seek first! No, it is not that after all. What he seeks is a living.

First he has to get properly educated. He must go to university. With that he is a theological candidate. And one would perhaps suppose that after he had *first* passed all his exams, he would finally be prepared to work for Christianity. But, no, *first* he must go on to seminary, and when that is finished eight years have gone by during which there was no question of being able to seek.

And now we have reached the beginning of the novel. The eight years are past, and Ludvig From seeks a position. He sends out his résumé. He fills out one application after another. He interviews with this congregation and that one. He recommends himself to the ministerial hierarchy. He is now entirely in the service of the Absolute. Thus the years pass by. And so our theological candidate really is in need of some rest. He needs to be nursed a little by his future wife, for meanwhile he *first* needs to become engaged.

Finally, the hour of his "redemption" strikes. With the power of conviction he is now able to "bear witness" before the congregation that in Christianity there is salvation and redemption – he lands a pastorate.

What happens? He discovers that his salary is 150 dollars less a month than he expected. The game is up. The unfortunate man is almost in despair. It's not quite what he expected. However, it remains at that, and he keeps the call. He is ordained, and the Sunday arrives when he is to be officially presented to the congregation. By a stroke of genius, the Dean chooses for his text the words of the Apostle Peter: "Lo, we have left all and have followed Thee." He then explains to the congregation that precisely in times such as ours there must be men like Ludwig who are knowledgeable in God's Word, and in this connection he recommends this young man – despite the fact that he is remiss about the 150 dollars.

Ludwig himself now mounts the pulpit, and strangely enough, the Gospel reading for the day is, "Seek first the kingdom of God." He delivers his sermon with all he's got. "A very good sermon," says the Bishop, who himself was present, "a very good sermon indeed, and it produced the proper effect – that whole part about *first* the kingdom of God, and the way you stressed the word *first*." You may be of the mind to question the Bishop, "But does it not seem to you that in this instance a correspondence between speech and life is called for? Upon me this word *first* made an almost satirical impression." "What an absurdity!" replies the Bishop, "Ludwig is called to preach the doctrine, the sound, unadulterated doctrine of seeking first the kingdom of God, and that he did very well." What a dreadful mockery!

Whoever you are, think only on this word of God, "First the kingdom of God." Then reflect on this little novel, which is so tragically true. You will soon realize that this whole official Christianity business is a morass of falsehood and illusion. It is something so unregenerate that the only thing that can truly be said about it is that by refusing to take part in the public worship of God as it now is, you have one sin the less, and that a great one: you do not take part in treating God as a fool.

God's Word reads, "Seek first the kingdom of God." We, however, prefer to read it as, first everything else, and *last* the kingdom of God. And we do this under the guise of religious piety. Only after the earthly life is first secured, then one should become a minister or a Christian. The clergy's whole profession (not to mention the rest of us good Christians) is a constant practice of this: first the earthly and then the kingdom of God, first regard for what the fear of man bids or forbids and then the kingdom of God, first a living and then a funeral oration, first a salary then a wedding sermon, first a pension then I will visit the sick, first money and then virtue. And the kingdom of God becomes something so last that it doesn't come at all. The whole thing stops with securing a living – the only case where one does not feel the need of "going further."

There is nothing so displeasing to God as taking part in all the "religious" Christianity with the claim that this is worshiping God. If you believe, as surely you must, that to steal, rob, commit adultery, and slander is displeasing to God, then official Christianity and its worship is infinitely more abhorrent to him. Again, it is my duty to exclaim, "Whoever you are, whatever in other respects your life may be, by refusing to take part in all this public worship of God as it now is, you have one sin the less, and that a great one." You have been warned.

55 | Childish Orthodoxy

The Christianity that is usually recited to a child is actually not Christianity but idyllic mythology. It is the idea of childlikeness raised to the second power. And, sadly, the child's lovable misunderstanding of what is essentially Christian often transmutes parental love into a piety that is nevertheless not actually Christianity.

A Christianity based on a child's piety is not the spirituality of a disciple. This gets everything mixed up – as if the mother should try to get nourished by the milk that nature provides the child. If this is the parents' entire religiousness, then they lack authentic faith. This "childlike" piety, which we so often laud, and this blessedness are lovely and lovable, but it is not really Christianity. It is Christianity in the medium of idyllic fantasy. It is a Christianity from which the cross has been removed. It is a sentimental view of faith which forgets that Christ's call provokes the consciousness of sin.

Let us look more carefully at what Christ actually says with regard to children: "Let the little children come and do not forbid them to come to me, for to such belongs the kingdom of heaven" (Mt. 19:14). The whole chapter speaks of the difficulty of entering the kingdom of heaven, and the expressions are as strong as possible: "There are eunuchs who have castrated themselves for the sake of the kingdom of heaven." "It is easier for a camel to go through the eye of a needle than for a rich man to enter the kingdom of God." It is no wonder that the disciples become so terrified that they exclaim: "Who then can be saved?"

After Christ answers the disciples, he goes on to speak of the reward awaiting those who have left houses and brothers or sisters or father or mother or wife or children or lands for the sake of his name. All of these teachings are salty expressions depicting the collisions in which a Christian can and will be tested. Consequently, Christ makes entering into God's kingdom as difficult as possible. But if entering this kingdom is supposed to be about the loveliness and innocence of being a little child, a proper little angel, then what could this possibly mean in the presence of the apostles who were called to pick up their cross and follow?

A childish view of Christianity is ludicrous. If the assertion about being a child must be understood literally, then it is nonsense to preach the cross of Christ to adults. Yet this is the way Christianity is defended by orthodox fencers. Childlike Christianity, which in a little child is lovable, in an adult is childish. Faith such as that confuses everything. If a little child (literally understood) is to provide the definition of what Christianity is, then there is no terror; it ceases to be an offense, as the apostle Paul says, to the Jews and foolishness to the Greeks.

When a child is told about Christ it naturally appropriates everything that is gentle, endearing, and heavenly. He lives together with the little Jesus-child, with the angels, and with the three kings. He sees the star in the dark night, journeys the long road, and now is in the stable, wonder upon wonder, and always sees the heavens open. With all the inwardness of the imagination he longs for these pictures. And now let us not forget the candy canes and all the other magnificent things that come along with such religiousness! Christ becomes the little divine child, or for the somewhat older child, the friendly figure with the kindly face. The child-conception of Christ is essentially a fantasy-perception.

With regard to being Christian, then, childhood is not the true age. On the contrary, adulthood – in the truest sense – is the time when it is to be decided whether a person will be a Christian or not. To become a Christian is a decision that belongs to a later age. The child's receptivity is so entirely without decision that it is no wonder people say: A child can be made to believe anything. This is because they do. This does not mean we should rigorously coerce a child into decisively Christian qualifications. By no means! If this happens, such a child will suffer a great deal. Such an upbringing will either plunge him immediately into despondency and anxiety or later into the anxiety of lust on a scale unknown even in paganism.

Even still, we must do everything we can to guard against changing Christianity into a beautiful, innocent recollection, instead of being what is most decisive in a person's becoming. Genuine Christianity is an offense to the religious and foolishness to the wise. It is not some complacent something that offends no one, where people smile at it instead, and where defense of it only incites them.

It is beautiful and lovable that Christian parents, just as they otherwise take care of the child, should also nourish the child with childlike ideas of the religious. But a stupid, sentimental, and clumsy misunderstanding of childhood is reprehensible. It is immense stupidity to say that childhood itself is the time for really deciding to become a Christian. And insofar as this urge and inclination to push becoming a Christian back into childhood becomes common, this in itself is proof that the decisiveness of Christian faith is on its way to dying out.

56 | Kill the Commentators!

Today's mass of Bible interpreters have damaged, more than they have helped, our understanding of the Bible. In reading the scholars it has become necessary to do as one does at a play where a profusion of spectators and spotlights prevent, as it were, our enjoyment of the play itself and instead we are treated to little incidents. To see the play, one has to overlook them, if possible, or enter by a way that has not yet been blocked. The commentator has indeed become a most hazardous meddler.

If you wish to understand the Bible, then be sure to read it without a commentary. Think of two lovers. The lover writes a letter to the beloved. Is the beloved concerned about what others think of it? Will he not read it all alone? In other words, would it ever occur to him to read this letter with a commentary! If the letter from the lover were in a language he did not understand – well, then he would learn the language – but he would certainly not read the letter with the aid of commentaries. They are of no use. The love for his beloved and his readiness to comply with her desires, makes him more than able to understand her letter. It is the same with the Scriptures. With God's help we can understand the Bible all right. Every commentary detracts, and he who sits with ten open commentaries and reads the Scriptures – well he is probably writing the eleventh. He is certainly not dealing with the Scriptures.

Suppose now that this letter from the lover has the unique attribute that every human being is the beloved – what then? Should we now sit and confer with one another? No, each of us should read this letter solely as an individual, as a single individual who has received this letter from God. In reading it, we will be concerned foremost with ourselves and with our relationship to him. We will not focus on the beloved's letter, that this passage, for example, may be interpreted in this way, and that passage in that way – oh, no, the important thing to us will be to act as soon as possible.

Isn't it something to be the beloved, and doesn't this give us something that no commentator has? Think about it. Aren't we each the best interpreter of our own words? And then next the lover, and in relation to God, the true believer? Lest we forget, the Scriptures are but highway signs: Christ, the beloved, is the way. Kill the commentators!

Of course, the commentators are not the only ones at fault. God wants to force each one of us out again into the essential, back to a childlike beginning. But being naked before God in this way, this we do not want at all. We all prefer the commentaries. So with each passing generation we grow more and more spiritless.

What we really need, then, is a reformation that sets even the Bible aside. Yes, this has just as much validity now as did Luther's breaking with the Pope. The current emphasis on getting back to the Bible has, sadly, created religiosity out of learning and literalistic chicanery – a sheer diversion. Tragically this kind of knowledge has gradually trickled down to the masses so that no one can read the Bible simply any more. All our Bible learning has become nothing but a fortress of excuses and escapes. When it comes to existence, to obedience there is always something else we have to first take care of. We live under the illusion that we must first have the interpretation right or the belief in perfect form before we can begin to live – that is, we never get around to doing what the Word says.

The Church has long needed a prophet who in fear and trembling had the courage to forbid people to read the Bible. I am tempted, therefore, to make the following proposal. Let us collect all the Bibles and bring them out to an open place or up on a mountain and then, while we all kneel, let someone talk to God in this manner: Take this book back again. We Christians, such as we are, are not fit to involve ourselves with such a thing; it only makes us proud and unhappy. We are not ready for it. In other words, I suggest that we, like those inhabitants whose herd of pigs plunged into the water and died, beg Christ "to leave the neighborhood" (Mt. 8:34). This would at least be honest talk – something very different from the nauseating, hypocritical, scholarship that is so prevalent today.

The matter is quite simple. The Bible is very easy to understand. But we Christians are a bunch of scheming swindlers. We pretend to be unable to understand it because we know very well that the minute we understand we are obliged to act accordingly. Take any words in the New Testament and forget everything except pledging yourself to act accordingly. My God, you will say, if I do that my whole life will be ruined. How would I ever get on in the world?

Herein lies the real place of Christian scholarship. Christian scholarship is the Church's prodigious invention to defend itself against the Bible, to ensure that we can continue to be good Christians without the Bible coming too close. Oh, priceless scholarship, what would we do without you? Dreadful it is to fall into the hands of the living God. Yes, it is even dreadful to be alone with the New Testament.

I open the New Testament and read: "If you want to be perfect, then sell all your goods and give to the poor and come follow me." Good God, if we were to actually do this, all the capitalists, the officeholders, and the entrepreneurs, the whole society in fact, would be almost beggars! We would be sunk if it were not for Christian scholarship! Praise be to everyone who works to consolidate the reputation of Christian scholarship, which helps to restrain the New Testament, this confounded book which would one, two, three, run us all down if it got loose (that is, if Christian scholarship did not restrain it).

In vain does the Bible command with authority. In vain does it admonish and implore. We do not hear it – that is, we hear its voice only through the interference of Christian scholarship, the experts who have been properly trained. Just as a foreigner protests his rights in a foreign language and passionately dares to say bold words when facing state authorities – but see, the interpreter who is to translate it to the authorities does not dare do so but substitutes something else – just so the Bible sounds forth through Christian scholarship.

We declare that Christian scholarship exists specifically to help us understand the New Testament, in order that we may better hear its voice. No insane man, no prisoner of the state, was ever so confined. As far as they are concerned, no one denies that they are locked up, but the precautions regarding the New Testament are even greater. We lock it up but argue that we are doing the opposite, that we are busily engaged in helping it gain clarity and control. But then, of course, no insane person, no prisoner of the state, would ever be as dangerous to us as the New Testament would be if it were set free.

It is true that we Protestants go to great efforts so that every person can have the Bible – even in their own tongue. Ah, but what efforts we take to impress upon everyone that it can be understood only through Christian scholarship! This is our current situation. What I have tried to show here is easily stated:

I have wanted to make people aware and to admit that I find the New Testament very easy to understand, but thus far I have found it tremendously difficult to act literally upon what it so plainly says. I perhaps could take another direction and invent a new kind of scholarship, bringing forth yet one more commentary, but I am much more satisfied with what I have done – made a confession about myself.

57 | Church Militant

A Church triumphant is nothing but a sham. In this world we can truthfully speak only of a militant Church. The Church militant is related to and feels itself drawn to Christ in humble obedience. The Church triumphant, however, has taken the Church of Christ in vain. How can we better grasp the difference?

Among other things, the Church militant never arrives. It is in the process of *becoming*. By contrast, an established Christianity *is*. It refuses to change. It is rooted in the conceit of human impatience that wants to take in advance that which ultimately comes later – the kingdom of God. It is blind to what Christ said about his kingdom not being of this world. Though his is truly enough a kingdom *in* this world, it is not *of* this world. His Church, therefore, is militant. As soon as Christ's church makes a deal with this world, Christianity is abolished.

The triumphant Church assumes that the time of struggle is over; that the Church, because it has expanded itself, has nothing more about or for which to struggle. With this, the Church and the achievements of the world become synonymous. This is not the way of Christ. He promised only one thing: hatred and opposition from the world. Christ's Church, therefore, can only endure by struggling – that is, by every moment battling the world and battling for the Truth.

The triumphant Church, or established Christianity, resembles the Church militant no more than a square resembles a circle. It would be utterly impossible for the first Christians to recognize Christianity in its current distortion. Yes, they would hear Christianity preached and hear that what was said was entirely true, but to their great horror they would see that the actual conditions for being a Christian are exactly opposite of what they were in their day. To be a Christian now is no more like being a Christian in their day than walking on one's legs is like walking on one's head.

To be a Christian in the Church militant means to exist or to place oneself within an environment that is the opposite of being Christian. To be a Christian in a triumphant Church, however, means to live within an environment that is more or less congruous with being Christian. In the first case, to be Christian is to be inversely recognizable by the opposition I experience. In the second case, being a Christian means to be directly recognizable by the favor, honor, and esteem I win in this world – all on account of good Christian virtue.

Imagine a youth that has been well taught in Christianity and has been told that the requirement for being Christian is to confess Christ before the world. Imagine too that he is well informed of what the result of this will be. Having well considered all this, the youth is determined to arrange his life according to these instructions. But what happens? He happens to live in established Christendom. As he makes a move to risk taking the step, a kindly man, a kind of spiritual mentor, comes to him and "delivers sort of a speech": "Young friend, you are striving under a delusion. You do not realize that you are among Christians, and there really is no need to confess Christ. Just between us, we are all Christians, we all affirm good Christian values, and the really serious Christian is the one who keeps all this most hidden."

Consider a youth brought up on fairy stories and thus familiar with the idea of monsters that lived in forests but who were slain. If that youth now started out into the real world armed for battle, with an enormous sword at his side and an equally enormous courage in his heart, nothing stranger could happen to him than happened to that youth who finds himself in established Christendom. In other words, if he were to encounter a monster even stranger than those about which he had heard or read, it would not amount to a thing in comparison with the strange thing that happens to him in Christendom – namely, that he could not catch a glimpse of anything that resembled a monster.

But then the kindly, elderly Christian mentor would come to him and say, "My young friend, you are striving under a delusion. You are not in the world of fairy tales but in the modern, scientific world, where there are no monsters like that, where you are living among well-educated Christian people, and where in addition, the police watch over your security and the clergy your morality, and where the lights make the night just as safe as the day. Therefore, put away your sword and learn that your task, now that the age of monsters is long since past, is to be polite and pleasant and civil just like the rest of us. Learn that you must now see yourself and God in every other person and that every other person must see himself in you. Don't you see how everything is now so nicely in order?"

Lest we forget, it was not some petty squabble between Christ and the world that put Christ on the cross. No, love of God is hatred of the world. And the day when Christianity and the world become friends – yes, then Christianity is abolished. Then Christ will have to be judged for being only a dreamer, a fanatic. If he had not been so intolerant, he would have gotten on quite well with the world and with its religious authorities;

he would then not have been put to death, something that would have been totally unnecessary. Instead, he would have become someone great, or at least much appreciated, just as his followers eventually became when the Church triumphed – an occurrence that indeed makes a lie of the saying that the pupil is not above the teacher.

But as long as this world lasts and Christ's Church is in it, it is to be a militant Church. Although it has the promise that the gates of hell shall not prevail against it, woe to the Christian Church when it is triumphant in this world, for then it is not the Church that has triumphed but the world. Then Christ is no longer the God-Man either but some kind of distinguished human being, a noble teacher whose life is but an example of what each of us and the human race can become. Then eternity is abolished, and the sphere for the completion of all things is transferred to the temporal order. Then the way to life is no longer narrow and the gate small, nor are there only a few who find it. No, the way is broad and the gate wide open. And the gates of hell prevail, and many, indeed all, are admitted. Is this what it means for Christ to be triumphant in this world? Did he not come into the world in order to suffer; is not *that* what he called being triumphant?

I do not assert nor have I ever asserted that every Christian must be a martyr, even though I think that every true Christian should – and here I include myself – make the humble admission that he has been let off far more easily than true Christians in the strictest sense. Without authority, Christianity now creeps around in worn-out, shabby clothes, and we do not know whether we should take our hats off to it in the name of progress, or whether it should bow to us, whether we need its compassion, or whether it needs ours.

VI | THOUGHTS THAT RADICALLY CURE: EXCERPTS AND APHORISMS

58 | Anxiety and Despair

Learn to be satisfied with little – will you deny that this is much?

It is not only the poor who hunger. There is a hunger that all the treasures of the world cannot satisfy, and yet this hunger is for them. There is a thirst that all the streams of overabundance cannot quench, and yet this thirst is for them. I know very well that there is an anxiety, a secret, private anxiety, about losing.

"Cast all your care upon God." You are to cast *all* care away; if you do not cast all care away, you retain it and do not become absolutely joyful. And if you do not cast it absolutely upon God, but in some other direction, you are not absolutely rid of it. In one way or another, it returns again, most likely in the form of a still greater and more bitter sorrow. For to cast care away, but not upon God – that is distraction. But distraction is a most doubtful and ambiguous remedy.

Anxiety for the next day is commonly associated with anxiety for subsistence. This is a very superficial view. The next day – it is the grappling-hook by which the prodigious hulk of anxiety gets a hold of the individual's light craft. If it succeeds, he is under the domination of that power. The next day is the first link of the chain that fetters a person to that superfluous anxiety that is of the evil one. The next day – it is strange indeed, for ordinarily when one is sentenced for life the sentence reads, "for life," but he who sentences himself to anxiety "for the next day," sentences himself for life.

One who rows a boat turns his back to the goal towards which he labors. So it is with the next day. When by the help of eternity one lives absorbed in today, he turns his back to the next day. The more he is absorbed in today, the more decisively he turns his back upon the next day, so that he does not see it at all. If he turns around, eternity is confused before his eyes, it becomes the next day. But if for the sake of laboring more effectually towards the goal (eternity) he turns his back, he does not see the next day at all. By the help of eternity he sees quite clearly today and its task.

If you are to labor fruitfully today, you must be in this position. It always involves delay and distraction to want to look impatiently every instant towards the goal, to see if you are coming a little nearer, and now a little nearer. No, be eternally and seriously resolved, turn completely to the labor and turn the back to the goal. Such is one's position in rowing a boat, but such is also the position when you believe.

You might think that the believer would be very far from the eternal when he turns his back to it and lives today, while the glimpser stands and looks towards it. And yet it is the believer who is nearest the eternal, while the apocalyptic visionary is farthest from the eternal. Faith turns its back to the eternal in order precisely to have this with him today.

Father in heaven! Draw our hearts to you so that our longing may be where our treasure is supposed to be. Turn our minds and our thoughts to where our citizenship is – in your kingdom, so that when you finally call us away from here our leave-taking may not be a painful separation but a joyful union with you. We do not know the time and the place, perhaps a long road still lies before us, and when strength is taken away from us, when exhaustion fogs our eyes so that we peer out as into a dark night, and restless desires stir within us, wild, impatient longings, and the heart groans in fearful anticipation of what is coming, oh Lord God, fix in our hearts the conviction that also while we are living, we belong to you.

59 | Becoming Christian

One best becomes a Christian – without "Christianity."

A Christian cannot be born. No, the individual *becomes* a Christian.

It is a dubious thing to bring up a child in Christianity. The child has no actual consciousness of sin. What then? Take an analogy. Describe the family physician to a child as a very rare and lovable man. What happens? The child thinks it is very possible that there is such a rare man. I would gladly believe it, but I would also rather stay clear of him. The fact that I might became the object of his special love means that I am sick, and to be sick is no fun. Therefore, I am far from being happy at the thought that he has been called.

When one is actually sick and the sickness is serious, then one is very happy that there is a physician, but when one is not sick, or has no idea at all of what it is to be sick, then "the physician" is really a disagreeable thought. In the Child's relation to Christianity, therefore, either what is really Christian must be left out, and then what does upbringing in Christianity mean? – or it must be taught the truth, and then the child is prompted more to be afraid of Christianity than to be happy for it.

If the whole matter of bringing up children in Christianity is not to be humbug, people need to be aware of this. Scholars want to make Christianity into mythology. We do not notice, however, that what generally passes as Christian education of children is also mythology.

Not until a person has become so wretched that his only wish, his only consolation, is to die – not until then does Christianity truly begin.

When Christianity entered into the world, people were not Christians, and the difficulty was to become a Christian. Nowadays the difficulty in becoming a Christian is that one must cease to become a Christian.

Everyone knows that to jump from the spot where you are standing and then to come down again on the same spot is one of the most difficult jumps to do. The jump becomes easier only if there is a space between the spot where your are standing and the spot where your jump is to be made. Similarly, the most difficult decision is the one in which the person deciding is not distanced from the decision (as is the unbeliever who has to decide whether he wants to be a Christian) and where the decision seems to have already been made.

If I am not a believer, and the decision is to become a Christian, then Christianity can help me make a decision. The distance between me and it helps just as the running start helps the jumper. But if the decision seems to have already been made, if I am already a "Christian" (that is, am baptized, go to church, etc., which is still only in the realm of possibility), then there is nothing to help me become properly aware of the decision. In short, it is easier to become a Christian if one is not a Christian than to become a Christian if one is already supposed to be one.

No one can make a direct transition into being a Christian. No, born in sin, every person lives in a sinful world. So-called natural human goodness is actually just as bad as defiance. As soon as authentic Christianity is brought into contact with this natural human goodness, this goodness becomes infuriated. Beware of human goodness!

Only a person of will can become a Christian; for only a person of will has a will that can be broken. But a person of will whose will is broken by God is a Christian. The stronger the natural will, the deeper the break can be and the better the Christian. This is what has been described by the expressive phrase: the new obedience. A Christian is a person of will who no longer wills his own will but with the passion of his crushed will – radically changed – wills another's will.

Christianity is not so much related to transforming the intellect – but to transforming the will. But this transformation is the most painful of all operations, comparable to a vivisection. And because it is so appalling, to become a Christian was changed long ago. Now it is only a matter of remodeling the intellect.

Biblical Christianity is concerned with our will, with changing the will. Everything touches this, all the instructions (renouncing the world, denying one's self, dying to the world, and so on, also to hate oneself, to love God) are connected with this fundamental idea: the transformation of the will.

To be a Christian is, in an upward sense, as different from being a human being as, in a downward sense, to be a human being is different from being a beast. A Christian is literally a stranger and a pilgrim. Everyone feels that this individual is a stranger to him.

Relationship to Christ is the decisive thing. You may be thoroughly informed about Christianity as a whole, may know how to explain it, to present it and to expound it – but if with all this you think that your own relationship to Christ is a matter of indifference, you are a pagan.

This is Christianity: Let a person begin seriously to realize his need for Christ. Let him literally give all his fortune to the poor, literally love his neighbor, and so forth, and he will soon learn to need Christ. Christianity is a suit that at first glance seems attractive enough, but as soon as you actually put it on – then you must have Christ's help in order to be able to live in it.

On the subject of pilgrimages, Gregory of Nyssa says most excellently: "You do not come closer to God by changing your place." Oh no, it is all too clear that this is done only by changing yourself.

Christianity did not come in order to develop the heroic virtues in the individual but rather to remove selfishness. It is not a matter of improving yourself up to a certain maximum. Why, this can so easily be nothing but selfishness and pride.

To stress that mankind needs Christianity and then prove it and demonstrate it is all wrong. The Christian stress is: *I* need Christ.

The will of Christ is this: an examination in which one cannot cheat.

Although the scribes could say where the Messiah should be born, they remained quite unperturbed in Jerusalem. They did not accompany the Wise Men to seek him. Similarly one may know the whole of Christianity, yet make no movement. What a difference! The three kings had only a rumor to go by. But it moved them to make that long journey. The scribes were much better informed. They sat and studied the Scriptures like so many scholars, but it did not make them move. Who had more truth? The three kings who followed a rumor, or the scribes who remained sitting with all their knowledge?

What a vexation it must have been for the kings, that the scribes who gave them the news remained quiet in Jerusalem! We are being mocked, the kings might have thought. For indeed it is serious self-contradiction that the scribes had the knowledge and yet remained still. It is just as serious as if a person knows about Christianity, and his own life expresses the opposite. We are tempted to suppose that he wishes to fool us, unless we admit that he is only fooling himself.

In following Christ, there is no chattering about what happens afterward.

60 | The Bible

What must you do to look honestly in the mirror of the Word? The first requirement is that you must not look *at* the mirror but look *in* the mirror and see yourself. God's Word is indeed the mirror. But oh how enormously complicated we make it. How much belongs to God's Word? Which books are authentic? Are they really written by the apostles, and are the apostles really trustworthy? As for ways of reading, there are thirty thousand different ways. And then there is this crowd or rush of scholars and opinions, and learned opinions and unlearned opinions about how the particular passage is to be understood. Is it not true that all this seems to be rather complicated? God's Word is the mirror – in reading it or hearing it, I am supposed to see myself in the mirror – but look, this business of the mirror is so confusing that I very likely never come to see myself.

If God's Word is merely a doctrine, then it is no mirror. An objective doctrine cannot be called a mirror. It is just as impossible to look at yourself in a doctrine as to look at yourself in a wall. And if you want to relate intellectually to God's Word, there can be no question of looking at yourself in the mirror. It takes a personality, an I, to look at oneself in a mirror. While reading God's Word you must incessantly say to yourself: It is *I* to whom it is speaking; it is *I* about whom it is speaking.

What makes such great confusion is how everyone feels compelled to formulate a theory and obligate everyone else to it. Someone gets an impression of Christianity. Presto! Now there has to be a theory, and everyone must subscribe to his theory. Then he gets busy developing his theory further. Then his theory is attacked, and he defends it – constantly moving away from true religiousness. He does not personally get around to acting according to the theory but manages to introduce a theory about the opposition to the theory.

No, what should be insisted upon is that I feel obligated to obey the New Testament, not to theorize about it. I cannot obligate others. I simply say: I feel obligated in this way and will express it in action. Truth does not try to get a random bunch of people obligated to me or to my conception. No, each person must be alone before God and become obligated by it.

What is the New Testament? A handbook for those who are to be sacrificed.

According to the mentality of our day one would think that God might have postponed being born until after the invention of the printing press, that he then would have gotten himself one, two, three high-speed presses. What a satire on the human race that God's word was put into the world as it was! What a satire on the human race that everything grows worse and worse as the means of communication grow greater and greater!

Father in heaven! You, oh God, you give your Word as a gift. And if you find only some willingness on our part, you are promptly at hand. With divine patience you spell out the Word for us so that we may understand it aright; and then you are the one who, again with more than human – indeed, with divine – patience takes us by the hand, as it were, and helps us when we strive to act according to it. You, our Father in heaven!

A young girl is at age sixteen and it is her confirmation day. Among various other gifts she also receives a beautifully bound New Testament. Look, this is what we call biblical Christianity! Actually we do not expect her to read it, not any more than the rest of us. She receives this book as a safeguard in her life: "Here you will find consolation if you should ever need it," we tell her. Of course we do not expect her to really read it, otherwise she might discover that here are true terrors. For in comparison to the persecutions witnessed here, the ordinary hardships of this world are but a jest.

To see yourself is to die, to die to all illusions and all hypocrisy. It takes great courage to dare look at yourself – something which can take place only in the mirror of the Word. You must want only the truth, neither vainly wish to be flattered nor self-tormentingly want to be made a pure devil.

61 | Christ

The birth of Christ is an event not only on earth but also in heaven. Our justification is likewise an event not only on earth but also in heaven.

Christ is God just as much as he is man – just as the sky seems to be deep in the sea as it is high above the sea.

Christ walks in history as he walked in life – between two thieves.

Christ does not always sit at the Father's right hand. No, when dangers threaten, he arises, he stands erect, just as Stephen saw him standing at the right hand of the Father.

Christ is not love, according to the human notion of love. He is the truth, absolute truth. Therefore he does not defend himself. He permits us to become guilty of his death which reveals the truth in the most radical way.

Why cannot Christ be called a martyr? Because he was not a witness to truth but *was* "the truth", and his death was not a martyrdom but the Atonement.

Christ is the paradox, the God-man. He is the very compounding of God and a socially insignificant man. But this is not the way we Christians like to think about it. We regard Jesus Christ as a great man who lived misunderstood, but after his death became somebody great. And this is how we want to be. Aha! This is why today's Christianity is nonsense. All the danger is taken away. No, Jesus Christ is the sign of offense and the object of faith. Only in eternity is he in his glory. Here upon earth he must never be presented in any other way than in his social insignificance – so that everyone can be offended or believe.

Christ willed to be the socially insignificant one. The fact that he descended from heaven to take upon himself the form of a servant is not an accidental something which now is to be thrust into the background and forgotten. No, every true follower of Christ must express existentially the very same thing – that insignificance and offense are inseparable from being a Christian. As soon as the least bit of worldly advantage is gained by preaching or following Christ, then the fox is in the chicken house.

Christ humbled himself – not: was humbled.

It must be firmly maintained that Christ did not come to the world only to set an example for us. If that were the case we would have law and works-righteousness again. He comes to save us and in this way be our example. His very example should humble us, teach us how infinitely far away we are from resembling him. When we humble ourselves, then Christ is pure compassion. And in our striving to approach him, he is again our very help. It alternates: when we are striving, then he is our example; and when we stumble, lose courage, then he is the love that helps us up. And then he is our example again.

Christ is anything but an assistant professor who teaches to parroters or dictates paragraphs for shorthand writers – he does exactly the very opposite, he discloses the thoughts of hearts.

Christ is himself the way. There were not many ways, of which Christ took one – no, Christ is the way.

Lord Jesus, there are so many things that attract us, and each one of us has his own particular attraction. But your attraction is eternally the strongest! Draw us, therefore, the more powerfully to you.

Whenever I think of the insipid, sweet, syrupy concept of the Savior, the kind of Savior Christendom adores and offers for sale, reading his own words about himself has a strange effect: "I have come to set afire," come to produce a split which can tear the most holy bonds, the bonds God himself has sanctified, the bonds between father and son, wife and husband, parents and children.

Christ did not teach about dying-to-the-world; he is himself what it means to die to the world.

When the doors were locked, Christ came to his disciples. So the doors must be locked, locked to the world – then Christ comes, through the locked doors; in fact, he also comes from the inside.

One might ask: How was it possible that Christ could be put to death, one who never sought his own advantage? How is it possible that any power or person could come into collision with him? Answer: It was precisely for this reason that he was put to death. This is why the lowly and the powerful were equally exasperated by him, for every one of them was seeking his own advantage and wanted him to show solidarity with them in self-ishness. He was crucified precisely because he was love, that is, because he refused to be selfish. He was as much of an offense to the powerful as to the lowly. He did not belong to any party, but wished to be what he was, namely, the Truth and to be that in love.

Christ was born in a stable, wrapped in rags, laid in a manger – so unimportant was this child apparently, so meagerly valued. And immediately afterward this child was so valuable that it costs the lives of the children in Bethlehem. Such is the squan-dering that can take place in connection with this child.

62 | Christendom and Counterfeit Christianity

Gold and silver I do not have, but I give you what I have; stand up and walk," said Peter. Later on the clergy were saying: Gold and silver we have – but we have nothing to give.

The existence of the Established Church is a money question, and the solemn silence of the clergy has a perfectly simple explanation, corresponding to what happens in business when a debtor is asked for money and perhaps first tries to get out of it by pretending he did not hear.

Christendom is a society of people who call themselves Christians because they occupy themselves with obtaining information about those who a long time ago submitted themselves to Christ's examination – spiritlessly forgetting that they themselves are up for examination.

One would think that the omnipotence of money would run aground on the rock of Christianity, which proclaimed that a rich man would have difficulty entering the kingdom of God. Yes, so it was originally, but then the ordained hired-servants, the money changers of Christianity, got hold of things, and

Christianity was improved practically and it triumphantly spread over kingdoms and countries.

The established Church is far more dangerous to Christianity than any heresy or schism. We play at Christianity. We use all the orthodox Christian terminology – but everything, everything without character. Yes, we are simply not fit to shape a heresy or a schism. There is something frightful in the fact that the most dangerous thing of all, playing at Christianity, is never included in the list of heresies and schisms.

Imagine a fortress, absolutely impregnable, supplied with provisions for an eternity. A new commandant comes. He gets the idea that the right thing to do is to build bridges over the ditches – in order to be able to attack the besiegers. Charming! He transformed the fortress into a village, and the enemy captured it, naturally. So it is with Christianity. We changed the method – and the world conquered, naturally.

Christianity has been abolished somewhat as follows: life is made easier.

Christendom plays the game of taking God by the nose: God is love, meaning that he loves me – Amen!

When we receive a package we unwrap it to get at the contents. Christianity is a gift from God, but instead of receiving the gift, we have undertaken to wrap it up, and each generation has furnished a new wrapping around the others.

Imagine a family of noble blood demoted to slavery as punishment for a crime. Imagine someone of the tenth generation with a background of eight or nine generations who have lived as slaves. The result will probably be that the tenth-generation man is well satisfied with the conditions of life, he feels at home in his station by birth, which was his father's before him, and grandfather's before him. Now if someone were to come to this tenth-generation man and explain to him that he is of noble lineage, he would be laughed to scorn and would discover that the persons involved care least of all. Yes, they even become embittered because someone seeks to disturb their routine, the routine in which they had contentedly lived for a long time.

So it is with Christianity. Christianity points to the fall (Gn. 3) as its presupposition. But in the meanwhile, through the consequences of repetition, the fall has burgeoned into such a frightful habit that it is like an enormous parenthesis, so colossal that no one has sufficient range of vision to see that it is a parenthesis. And within this parenthesis life goes on lustily. The degradation continues, and in constantly increasing proportion from generation to generation. The next generation becomes less significant than its predecessor, with whose insignificance it began, and also more numerous. And now the two greater powers, insignificance and numbers, join to reduce humanity to such a triviality that the Christianity of the New Testament, if brought into touch with it, is looked upon as nonsense.

We, however, have long ago forgotten that the fall is a parenthesis into which we have entered, and that Christianity was introduced precisely as the divine in-breaking. No, we live pleasantly within the parenthesis, propagate the race, and organize world history – and it is all a parenthesis. Question: is a parenthesis-man immortal?

Think of a very long railway train – but long ago the locomotive ran away from it. Christendom is like this. Generation after generation has imperturbably continued to link the enormous train of the new generation to the previous one, solemnly saying: We will hold fast to the faith of the fathers. Thus Christendom has become the very opposite of what Christianity is. Christianity is restlessness, the restlessness of the eternal. Any comparison here is flat and tedious – to such a degree that the restlessness of the eternal is restless. Christendom is tranquillity. How charming, the tranquillity of literally not moving.

In so-called Christianity we have made Christmas into a great festival. This is quite false, and it was not at all so in the Early Church. We mistake childishness for Christianity – what with all our sickly sentimentality, our candy canes, and our manger scenes. Instead of remaining conscious of being in conflict that marks a life of true faith, we Christians have made ourselves a home and settled down in a comfortable and cozy existence. No wonder Christmas has become little more than a beautiful holiday.

Think of a hospital. The patients are dying like flies. Every method is tried to make things better. It's no use. Where does the sickness come from? It comes from the building, the whole building is full of poison. So it is in the religious sphere. One person thinks that it would help if we got a new hymnal, another a new altar-book, another a musical service, and so on. It's no use. It comes from the building. This whole pile of lumber of an established Church, which from time immemorial has not been ventilated, spiritually speaking – the air confined in this lumber room has developed poison. And for this reason the religious life is sick or has died out.

In talking with a pupil, a teacher sometimes expresses himself in lower terms while meaning something higher, but he does so in such a way that the pupil understands it. He says, for example, "Tomorrow will be a fun day" and means by this that it will be a rigorous day with much to do, which in a certain higher sense can also be fun. But suppose that a pupil takes the liberty of pretending he did not understand and loafs all day long. When the teacher rebukes him he answers, "Didn't you say that tomorrow should be a fun day?" Would the teacher put up with this?

So it is with Christianity. In his majestic language God has proclaimed a great joy to us – a great joy. Yes, God cannot speak in any other way about the high goal he has for us. And what is Christendom? Christendom is a tricky boy who pretends he does not understand what God meant but thinks that since it is a great joy the task must be to enjoy life thoroughly. Does God put up with this?

Once upon a time learning to read was a rigorous matter; it took a lot of hard work. But eventually the theory was devised that everything ought to be enjoyable. So the practice of having a little party after each hour of reading was introduced, and the A B C's were decked out with pictures, etc. Ultimately that hour was also dropped, and the A B C's became simply a picture book. But still people went on talking about learning to read, even though the children did not learn to read at all. Learning to read was now understood to mean eating cookies and looking at pictures, which became an even more pleasant experience just because it was called "learning to read." So also with the transformation of Christianity in Christendom, except that here (which is not the case in the illustration) "the teacher" (i.e. preacher) is also interested in this transformation, it suits him best of all.

Christianity is proclaimed in Christendom in such a way that obedience is taken away and reasoning put in its place.

No one can be the truth; only the God-man *is* the truth. Then comes the next: the ones whose lives express what they proclaim. These are witnesses to the truth. Then come those who disclose what truth is and what it demands but admit that their lives do not express it, but to that extent still are striving. There it ends. Now comes the sophistry. First of all come those who teach the truth but do not live it. Then come those who even alter the truth, its requirement, cut it down, make omissions – in order that their lives can correspond to the requirement. These are the real deceivers.

The world does not want to eliminate Christianity, it is not that straightforward, nor does it have that much character. No, it wants it proclaimed falsely, using eternity to give a flavor to the enjoyment of life.

Just as the statement, "Everything is true," means that nothing is true, so to exclaim that all are Christians means that no one is a Christian.

Christianity has been made so much into a consolation that people have completely forgotten that it is first and foremost a demand.

We humans have ingeniously turned God into a humbug. We talk about the fact that God is love, that we love God (who does not love God, what "Christian" does not love God, etc.) and even rely on him, and yet we refuse to see that our relationship to him is purely and simply a natural egotism, the kind of love which consists of loving oneself. We try to get this loving God's assistance, but only to lead a right cozy, enjoyably religious life.

Think of a father. There is something he wishes his child to do (the child knows what it is); so the father has a plan: I will come up with something that will really please my child and give it to him. Then, I am sure, he will love me in return. The father believes that his child will now do what he asks. But the child takes his father's gift and does not do what he wills. Oh, the child thanks him again and again and exclaims: "He is such an affectionate father"; but he continues to get his own way.

And so it is with us Christians in relationship to God. Because God is love, we turn to him for help but then go our own way. Although we dance before him and clap our hands and blow the horn and with tears in our eyes exclaim, "God is love!" we go on our merry way doing what it is that we want.

The apostasy from Christianity will not come about by everybody openly renouncing Christianity; no, but slyly, cunningly, by everybody assuming the name of being Christian.

When there is something distasteful to us we look to see if the power that commands us is not too great for us to pit our power against it. If we are convinced that it is not too great, we revolt in defiance. But if the power is so superior that we despair of making a revolt, we resort to hypocrisy. This certainly applies to Christianity. The fact that the apostasy from Christianity occurred long ago has not been noticed because the apostasy came about, the revolt was made, in hypocrisy. Christendom is precisely this apostasy.

Think of a fisherman who owns a splendid net that he inherited from his father. Year after year he puts out his net – but gets no fish. What is the matter? What can it be? "Sure enough, I know," says the fisherman. "The fish have changed; in the course of time they have decreased in size. If I want to catch them, I must get hold of a net that is not made for large fish."

Now think about eternity in terms of salvation. From generation to generation, steadily, incessantly, the cost of being Christian has become cheaper and cheaper, the terms of salvation have become easier and easier. A generation of jubilant millions, served by huckster clergy, has replaced Christianity with a religion of easy terms. It has rendered Christianity worthless and taken Christianity in vain, all in the name of perfecting Christianity. Eternity quietly looks on and observes: I am catching no one. But eternity is not like the fisherman. It does not need us. It is we who need eternity, to be caught is to be saved. Moreover, eternity is at one and the same time the fisherman and the net – consequently it does not change.

The Moral: The fisherman needs the fish; ergo, he changes the net. If, on the contrary, it is the fish that need to be caught – and this is the Christian way – then to be caught is to be saved.

But then the fish must change, which is impossible as far as the metaphor is concerned but not in respect to what the metaphor signifies.

The definition of "Church" found in Protestant Confessions, that it is the communion of saints where the Word is rightly taught and the sacraments rightly administered, grasps only two of the points. It overlooks the foundation, the *communion* of saints.

It is simply comical to think that one can "introduce" Christianity into this or that situation, just as one introduces improved sheep breeding. Christianity is precisely the one thing that cannot be introduced.

Christianity received its first blow when the emperor became a Christian. The second, and far more dangerous blow, came when the "extraordinary Christian" emerged. The error lay not in entering the monastery but in the title of extraordinary Christian.

Everything has become reversed. There was a time when the world wanted to fight Christianity – then Christianity fought back. Now the world is in fraudulent possession of Christianity. Its tactics are, with all its power and at any price, to prevent a showdown. It is as when a swindler has misgivings – if the matter goes to court, he has lost – and therefore all his tactics are directed toward keeping it from going to court. In the realm of the spirit this happens far more easily than in the actuality of civil life, for the technique consists in the world continually counterfeiting Christ's position so that it is kind of saying the same thing – but good God, then the world and Christ are agreed!

63 | The Cross

Christ has not only spoken *to* us by his life but has also spoken *for* us by his death.

Christ certainly died for all people, and also for me; but that "for me" must be understood in the sense for "all people."

As far as power is concerned, to rule the whole world with a scepter is nothing compared to ruling it with a reed – that is, by impotence – that is, divinely.

The objective reality of Christ's atonement, independent of its personal appropriation, is most clearly shown in the history of the ten lepers. All of them were healed, though only of the tenth, who thankfully returned to give honor to God, is it said: your faith has made you whole. What was it that cured the others?

Just try to imagine that the Pattern is called a "Lamb." That alone is a scandal to the natural mind. Who has any desire to be a lamb?

Just because Christ was upon the cross proves that he is the Son of God. But humanity cannot grasp the divine mind. It would rather conclude that he was the Son of God, if only he had come down from the cross.

You have no doubt felt that however wearing the grief of repentance is, the grief that seizes us when we suffer innocently – when we bear the consequences of other's guilt – is far deeper. Such is Christ's sorrow.

The desire to make Christ king is itself a part of his being crucified.

"Our Lord Jesus Christ, in the night he was betrayed…" Must not the thought of that night knit the church together, make it watch carefully to see whether the night of betrayal threatens once more?

When God had created the world, he looked at it and, behold, it was very good. When Christ died upon the cross, he said – "It is finished."

When Christ had drunk the vinegar offered to him, he said: It is finished, that is, now the law's requirement is fulfilled. But these were not Christ's last words. He also prayed for his enemies, and this is of the gospel.

Lord Jesus! How often have I gone astray from the right way or, even if I remained on the right path, nevertheless stumbled along the right way or gone creeping forward so slowly on the right way. Infinite patience! Infinite suffering of patience! How many times have I been impatient, wishing to forsake you, wishing to give up, to take the terribly easy way out, the way of despair: but you did not lose patience. Alas, the words of your servant Paul that he "filled up that which was lacking in your sufferings" do not apply to me. No, I can only claim that I have increased your sufferings, added new ones to those you once suffered in order to save me.

64 | The Crowd

God is as infinitely concerned with one person of intensity, yes, as he is infinitely indifferent to the millions and trillions. We humans believe numbers mean something. For God, it is precisely numbers that mean nothing, nothing at all.

To compensate for the emptiness of nuts, we clever human beings get all the more of them. This is ridiculous compensation and also a curse. If the nuts are hollow, it would be better if there were just three or four of them. What agony to have to crack a million empty nuts in order to be convinced that they are hollow! So it is with us human beings: compensation for specimens or copies devoid of ideas – we get all the more of them. Everyone is in the service of the substitute, served by multiplying. The numerical is the most ridiculous parody of the truth. By addition we are supposed to achieve that for which addition is really subtraction. But, of course, in the brute sense, numbers have power.

The specimen-man tranquilizes himself with human numbers. If something is true, he needs no higher proof than that such and such a number have regarded it as true.

There are insects that protect themselves against attackers by raising a cloud of dust. Likewise man instinctively protects himself against truth and spirit by raising a cloud of numbers. If you want to be insured against having to deal with truth, with spirit, simply get together battalions, legions, millions who strive, perhaps with united powers – then spirit vanishes and you achieve what you really want: a life lived on the animal side of human nature.

Animal-man has the courage to do the most frightening things as long as he simply has human numbers with him. Christ points to the very opposite. To suffer courageously means precisely to fear God in contrast to fearing the crowd, in contrast to what we as animal-creatures fear most of all – human numbers.

No one dares to be himself; everyone is hiding in "togetherness."

There are people who have the fortunate gift of managing successfully with everyone – they have no sharp edge. Such people God never uses. God is no friend of the cozy human crowd – no, the one he wants to use is promptly blocked off.

We are no longer salt, we are a mass.

The numerical is the conspiracy. Just as in civil life, when crowds of people collect in the street, the police respond immediately, regardless of whether or not a crime has been committed – for the massing together of lots of people is suspect – so also, and with a completely different kind of right, the higher police immediately and directly attack wherever a hoard of Christians show up. The greater the number, the more certain the lie, the more certain that there is a falsification. Let this be regarded as a counter-proposition to what has delighted the clergy for a long time now – the spread of Christianity.

The single individual is decisive in forming community. He can at any moment become higher than community, specifically, as soon as "the others" fall away from the eternal. The cohesiveness of community comes from each one's being a single individual before the eternal. The connectedness of a public, however, or rather its disconnectedness, consists of the numerical character of everything. Only the single individual guarantees community; the public is a chimera. In community the single individual is a microcosm who qualitatively reproduces the cosmos. Community is certainly more than a sum, but yet it is truly a sum of ones. The public, on the other hand, is nonsense – a sum of negative ones, of ones who are not ones.

If someone in public happens to pass gas loudly, people are so startled, it is as if it were the voice of a spirit. So intoxicated are we when we are a public.

The majority of the people are not so afraid of holding a wrong opinion, as they are of holding an opinion alone.

To be like the others is humankind's degeneration, the degradation to copies.

If it is true that human beings alone have received speech in order to conceal their thoughts or, as I put it, in order to conceal the absence of thoughts, then something like this can truthfully be said about the crowd: The crowd is used in order to conceal how empty all existence is. The "many" transfer us into an exalted state just as opium does, and we are tranquilized by the tremendous trustworthiness of millions.

The crowd is like an envelope. One receives a large package, thinks it is something important, but look, it is a package of envelopes.

Everything that needs numbers in order to become significant is by that very fact insignificant. Everything that can be arranged, executed, completed only with the help of numbers, the sum of which startles people in amazement, as if this were something important – precisely this is unimportant. The truly important is inversely related, needs a progressively smaller and smaller number to implement its completion. And for the most important of all, that which sets heaven and earth in motion, only one person is needed. And what is most important of all? What interests angels and demons most is that a person is actually involved with God – for this one single human being is enough.

It occurs to me that we would be quite happy if we managed to find a way for everyone to be a virtuoso in ventriloquism – how satisfied we would be with anonymity!

When it has come to the point where the majority decides what constitutes truth, it will not be long before they take to deciding it with their fists.

Every future effort at reformation, if it is genuine, will be directed against the crowd, not against the government.

Instinctively "man" has a tactic he uses against "spirit": Let us form a crowd! This is our tactic, our mode of defense. It is done cunningly this way: Let us join together in order to strive toward the ideals. But to form a crowd is precisely the way to get rid of the ideals. Just as the ostrich sticks its head into the ground and thinks it is invisible, so we form a crowd and think no one can see us. We speak of not being able to see the woods for the trees, and by this tactic we hope that one cannot see the trees for the woods. Just like the person who says he is not at home to visitors, we are not at home whenever we lose ourselves in the crowd – instead of being an *I*.

If Christ lived today, attention would surely make the most desperate effort. Every day every paper would have an article on him. Every insignificant detail about him would be spread all over the country in thousands of copies. Everything possible would be dug up to make the situation demented, and harmless! Everything possible would be done to dismiss him.

Of all the tyrannies, fear is the most dangerous. The communists fight for human rights. Good, so do I. Precisely for that reason I fight with all my might against the tyranny of the fear of man.

Something to chatter about! The crowd demands only something to chatter about, and this is understood to mean finding something about each other to chatter about, something about our meaningless lives, particularly the trivialities in our lives. Anything else nauseates the public, which knows only one lust – the desire for self-pollution by talking, a lust in which it indulges with the help of the journalist.

Journalists are animal-keepers who provide something for the public to talk about. In ancient days people were cast to the wild animals. Now the public devours the people – those tastefully prepared by the journalists.

If you want to be loathsome to God, just run with the herd.

65 | Decisiveness

I will work on with energy and not waste time looking back, not like the man who was caught in quicksand and began calculating how far down he had already sunk, forgetting that all the while he was sinking still deeper. I will hurry along the path I have discovered, not looking back as did Lot's wife, but remembering that it is a hill up which we have to struggle.

A golden key, it is said, fits every lock. But decision and determination also unlock doors, and that is why they are called resolution. With resolution the door is opened to the noblest powers of the soul.

As a rule, to go to school means that I go wherever the teacher is. Spiritually it means that I act decisively. At once, there is the teacher. I desire to be educated spiritually – and yet I do not desire to act decisively? Nonsense!

Good intention makes a person think that everything is settled by a resolution. But if anyone allows himself to be nourished by good intentions, the resolution itself becomes a seducer and deceiver instead of a trustworthy guide.

It is a proud thing to dive into danger, and it is a proud thing to battle with untold horrors, but it is also wretched to have an abundance of intentions and a poverty of action, to be rich in truths and poor in virtues.

We creep before we learn to walk, and to want to fly is always precarious. To be sure, there are great decisions, but even in regard to them the main thing is to activate your resolution, lest one become so high-flying in the resolution that one forgets to walk.

Many have gone astray through not understanding how to continue a good beginning.

A conviction is not firmly fixed when everyone presses upon it equally and holds it firm. No, its true stability is revealed when everything is in question.

If it is hard to bear the world's persecution, it is harder still to bear the responsibility for not having acted, to stand ashamed in eternity because you did not win the bold confidence that transforms shame into honor.

Ah, how many ways there are to choose in the hour of decision! And yet there is only one true way; the others are deviations.

By God's help and by your own faithfulness something good will always come from the uncompromising beginning.

Decision is the eternal protest against fictions.

Do you think that just as the Israelites brought Jehovah a tenth of the fruits of the earth and of the flocks you are to bring him only one-tenth of your heart? Do you think that just as the Jews labored six days out of the week and rested on the seventh, you are to think about the world and its activities six days out of the week but about God on the seventh? No, the Christian's tenth and the Christian's sacrifice is his whole heart. The Christian's holy day is every day. And if you bring God a tenth, watch out lest God open his window, as the prophet says, and look down and see you.

Only when he becomes the way, the truth, and the life for you, only then does he become everything to you. Christ must be all or nothing for you. But only when his mighty voice speaks to you and says, "I will be everything to you," will he be everything for you.

Nothing, neither the most trifling nor the most important thing, must stand between you and Christ. No, the commitment must be unconditional. Only then can you pray that you won't be treated too unjustly. Committing yourself to Christ, which is a matter of the spirit and of dying to the world, means that you run the risk of Christ making things so tangled for you that you almost despair. This is what is so appalling to the flesh. So must it be, but at the same time remember that Christ is grace, that it is to grace that you can so commit yourself.

Take a combination of five people, each of whom puts 5/8 of his capability into working jointly for the same cause, and take one person who does not have more ability than each of these five but puts all his abilities to work. Who will achieve the most? All sensible people will unanimously bet on the combination. I bet on the one person. Putting all you have into something is vastly different from a high total of fractional efforts. The one is dedication, it is spirit – the other is human muddling.

Simplicity is to do what one says. To act is to make simple; what I carry out in action is simple, for it cannot be done otherwise.

Imagine a well trained hunting dog. He accompanies his master on a visit to a family where, as all too often in our time, there is a crowd of ill-behaved youths. Their eyes barely notice the hound before they begin to terribly mistreat it. The hound, which is well trained, as these youths are not, fixes his eye at once upon his master to ascertain from his expression what he expects him to do. And he understands his master's glance to mean that he is to put up with all the ill-treatment. Thereupon the youths become still rougher, and finally they agree that it must be a prodigiously stupid dog that puts up with everything.

The dog meanwhile is concerned with only one thing, what his master's glance commands him to do. And, lo, that glance suddenly alters; it signifies – and the hound understands it at once – use your strength! That instant he seizes the biggest lout and throws him to the ground – and now no one stops him, except the master's glance, and at the same instant he is as he was a moment before.

Suppose that there are two opposing armies drawn up in the field. A soldier arrives whom both parties invite to fight on their side. He makes his choice, is vanquished and taken prisoner. As prisoner he is brought before the victor, to whom he foolishly presumes to offer his services on the same terms as were extended to him before the battle. Would not the victor say to him, "My friend, you are now my prisoner. There was indeed a time when you could have chosen differently, but now everything is changed…" One who throws a stone has power over it until he has thrown it, but not afterwards.

When it is a question of making a resolution the calculation of probability is a contemptible fellow, a bungler, a peddler. It seeks to trick people out of something more than money is worth. Anyone who seeks the aid of probability is lost in imagination, whatever else he may try to do. When making a resolution, if you do not meet up with God, you might as well have never lived. Probability is a commercial paper not quoted in heaven. In making a resolution, therefore, let God overawe probability and render it speechless.

When the castle door of inwardness has long been shut and finally is opened, it does not move noiselessly like an apartment door that swings nicely on hinges. No, No! Either/or is the word before which the folding doors fly open. Oh blissful sight! Either/or is the token that insures bold entrance into the unconditional. God be praised! Yes, either/or is the key to heaven! On the other hand, what is, was, and continues to be our misfortune is this "to a certain degree," this paltriness or cowardly shrewdness, which being applied to Christianity transforms it into twaddle! No: Either/or!

However tenderly the actor and actress embrace one another and caress one another on stage, it remains only a theatrical union, a theater-marriage. So also in relation to the unconditional. All this thing of "to a certain degree" is theatrical, it grasps an illusion. Only either/or is the embrace that grasps the unconditional.

Father in heaven! Teach me to walk in your sight and let not my thoughts and deeds be as strangers from afar paying a brief visit to your mansions. Let me never forget that faith is a life course, so that even if I stand at the farthest border of your kingdom, far away by myself like the publican of old, I only stand with my face toward you with staff in hand ready to go – not like him who put his hand to the plow and then turned around.

In the world of the spirit, there is neither luck nor chance. The only one who is shut out is the one who shuts himself out. In the world of the spirit, all are invited; if spirit pertains to one single person it pertains to all.

In making a choice it is not so much a question of choosing the right as of the energy, the earnestness, the passion with which one chooses. This is how personality is consolidated. Even if a person chooses the wrong, he will nevertheless discover precisely by reason of the energy with which he chose, that he has chosen the wrong.

66 | Doctrine and Theology

Christ did not establish any doctrine; he acted. He did not teach that there was redemption, he redeemed. Christ's relationship to God, nature, and the human situation was conditioned by his activity. Everything else is to be regarded only as introduction.

Christianity should not be lectured about. Christ says, my teaching is food. Christ has not appointed assistant-professors – but followers.

Christianity is not the doctrine of denying oneself. Christianity is to deny oneself.

When Christianity becomes nothing but doctrine, the test is nothing but a scholarly examination.

No one can lecture himself into eternity.

What is needed is not professors but witnesses. No, if Christ did not need scholars but was satisfied with fishermen, what is needed now is more fishermen.

The Law of Existence: First life, then theory. Then, as a rule, there comes still a third: an attempt to create life with the aid of theory, or the delusion of having the same life by means of the theory. This is the conclusion, the parody, and then the process ends – and then there must be new life again.

Take Christianity, for example. It came in as life, sheer daring that risked everything for the faith. The change began when Christianity came to be regarded as doctrine. This is the theory; it was about that which was lived. But there still existed some vitality, and therefore at times life-and-death disputes were carried on over "doctrine" and doctrinal formulations. Nevertheless doctrine became more and more the distinctive mark of being a Christian. Everything then became objective. This is Christianity's theory. Then followed a period in which the intention was to produce life by means of the theory; this is the period of the system, the parody. Now this process has ended. Christianity must begin anew as life.

Fixed ideas are like a cramp in your foot: the best remedy is to stomp on them.

A dogmatic system ought not be erected in order to comprehend faith, but in order to comprehend that faith cannot be comprehended.

To treat Christianity as a science is to change it into something of the past and to admit that it is no longer something present.

When a lark wants to pass gas like an elephant, it has to blow up. In the same way, all scholarly theology must blow up, because it has wanted to be the supreme wisdom instead of remaining what it is, an unassuming triviality.

The theological world is like the road along the coast on a Sunday afternoon during the races. People storm past one another, shouting and yelling, laugh and make fools of each other, drive their horses to death, upset each other, are run over, and when at last they arrive, covered with dust and out of breath – they look at each other – and go home.

Someone has the following invitation advertised in the newspaper: "If there are five or six like-minded people who together with me and without any solemn ceremonies will pledge themselves simply to try to understand the New Testament and strive to express its demands in action, I propose to start religious meetings. If by any chance a theological professor should want to attend these meetings, the price for him will be twenty dollars each time. This does not seem unreasonable to me when one considers that to become a full professor is to make a living off the fact that Christ was crucified."

67 | Doubt and Skepticism

All the objections to Christianity – what are they, after all, to the person who in truth is conscious of being a sinner and who has experienced belief in the forgiveness of sins and in this faith is saved from his sin? One conceivable objection might be: Yes, but is it not still possible for you to be saved in some other way? But how can one reply to this? One cannot. It is just like a person in love. If someone were to say: Yes, but you could perhaps have fallen in love with another – then he must answer: To this I cannot reply, for I know only one thing, that this is my beloved. As soon as the person who is in love tries to reply to this objection, he is by that very fact not a believer.

It is claimed that arguments against Christianity arise from doubt. This is a complete misunderstanding. The arguments against Christianity arise out of rebellion, out of a reluctance to obey. The battle against objections is but shadow-boxing, because it is intellectual combat with doubt instead of ethical combat against mutiny.

Christ says: Do according to what I say – then you shall know. Consequently, decisive action first of all. By acting, your life will come into collision with existence, and then you will know the reality of grace. Nowadays we have turned the whole thing around. Christianity has become a world view. Thus, before I get involved I must first justify it. Good night to Christianity! Now doubt has surely conquered. And this doubt can never be halted by reasons, which only nourish doubt. No, doubt can only be halted by imitation.

The objections to Christianity may be dismissed with one single comment: Do these objections come from someone who has carried out the commands of Christ? If not, all his objections are nonsense. Christ continually declares that we must do what he says – and then we will know that it is truth.

Since Descartes, skeptics don't dare express anything definite with regards to knowledge. Yet they dare to act, and in this respect are satisfied with probability. What an enormous contradiction! As if it were not far more dreadful to do something about which one is doubtful (thereby incurring responsibility) than to assert an idea. Or is it because the ethical is in itself certain? But then there is something that doubt cannot reach!

The method of beginning with doubt in order to philosophize seems as appropriate as having a soldier slouch in order to get him to stand erect.

God cannot be an object of study, since God is subject. For this very reason, when you deny God, you do not harm God but destroy yourself. When you mock God, you mock yourself.

A conviction is called a conviction because it is over and above proof. Proof is given for a mathematical proposition in such a way that no disproof is conceivable. For that reason there can be no conviction with respect to mathematics. But as far as every existential proposition is concerned, for every proof there is some disproof, there is a pro and a contra. The person of conviction is not ignorant of this; he knows full well what doubt is able to assert: a contra. For that very reason he is a person of conviction, because he has made a resolution and voluntarily raises himself higher than the logical maneuvers of proofs and is convinced.

It is good that Christianity still has enemies, because for the longest time they have been the only ones from whom it has been possible to get any trustworthy information about what Christianity is. Yet I dare say Christianity will soon become so meaningless that it will not even be able to make enemies.

It is wrong of established Christendom to say that Feuerbach (an atheist) is attacking Christianity. It is not true; he is attacking the Christians by demonstrating that their lives do not correspond to the teachings of Christ. This is quite different. What Christianity needs are more such traitors. Christendom has insidiously betrayed Christianity by not wanting to be truly Christian but to have the appearance of being so. Now "traitors" are needed.

If you suffer because you do good, because you are in the right, because your are loving; if it is because you are for a good cause that you live despised, persecuted, ridiculed, in poverty, then you will find that you do not doubt Christ's resurrection. Why? Because you need it.

If Christianity is viewed as history, the important thing will be to obtain a completely reliable report. But if the inquiring subject is infinitely interested in his relation to Christianity's truth and tries to rely on history, he will despair at once. With regard to the historical the greatest certainty is only an approximation, and an approximation is too little to build one's happiness on. Even with the most stupendous learning and perseverance, and even if the heads of all the critics were mounted on a single neck, one would never arrive at anything more than an approximation. There is an essential misrelation between all that and a personal, infinite interestedness in one's own eternal happiness.

One who truly believes that Christ was and is God, who prays to him repeatedly every day, who finds all his joy in association with him and thinking of him – such a person comes to terms with the historical. How silly to be upset if one gospel writer said one thing and a second another. You can turn to Christ in prayer and say, "This disturbs me, yet you are still with me." It is nonsense that the significance of historical details should be decisive with respect to faith. How could this matter? Is Christ not with us when we turn to him daily?

Believe that Christ is God – then call upon him and pray to him. The rest comes by itself. When the fact that he is present is more intimately and inwardly certain than all historical information, then you will come out all right with the details of his historical existence – whether the wedding was at Cana or perhaps somewhere else, whether there were two disciples or only one. The historical details are not nearly so important simply because Christ is Christ, the eternally present one who is true God and true man.

Faith's conflict with the world is not a battle of thought with doubt, thought with thought. It is a battle of character. The person of faith is a person of character who does not insist upon comprehending everything. Now comes the conflict. The world insists that to believe what you cannot comprehend is not only blind obedience but obscurantism, stupidity, and so on. The world wants to alarm the believer against such foolishness. This is precisely why faith is a task for the person of character.

Teach me, Lord, that the fight of faith is not a fight with doubt, thought against thought, but a fight for character. Enable me to see that human vanity consists in having to understand. Save me from the vanity of not being willing to obey like a child, and of wanting to be like a grown man who has to understand. Help me to realize that he who will not obey when he cannot understand does not, in any essential sense, obey you at all. Make me a believer, a "character man," who, unreservedly obedient, sees it as necessary for his character's sake that he must not always understand. Make me willing to believe even when I cannot understand.

68 | The Eternal

When a ship is put to sea, the end of a cable is cast out and fastened to a tugboat – and in this way the ship is drawn. When a human life is to be commenced and continued without too much dependence upon the temporal, a cable must be cast out. Christ alone is the drawing power from eternity to all eternity.

Have you lived in such a way that truth was in you, that there was something higher for which you actually suffered? Or has your life revolved around profitable returns? The fact that you got along well only makes matters worse. This distinction the eternal cannot and will not take away, it will not contradict itself. Two such individuals can never in all eternity come to an understanding with each other.

Most people think, speak, and write the way they sleep, eat, and drink, without any question ever arising as to their relationship to the eternal.

Becoming nothing in this world is the condition for becoming something in the other world.

The eternal is acquired in one way, and it is different from everything else precisely because it can be acquired only in one single way. It is the difficult way that Christ indicated by the words: "Small is the gate and narrow the way, that leads to life, and few are they that find it." The comfortable – precisely the thing in which our age excels – absolutely cannot be applied with respect to an eternal blessedness. When, for example, the thing you are required to do is to walk, it is no use to make the most astonishing inventions in the way of the easiest carriages and to want to transport yourself in these when the task prescribed to you is walking. And if the eternal is the *way* in which it is acquired, it doesn't do any good to want to alter this way, however admirably, in the direction of comfort. The eternal is acquired only in the difficult way.

If there is no eternal consciousness in a human being, if at the bottom of everything there is only a wild ferment, a power that, twisting in dark passions, produces everything great or inconsequential; if an unfathomable, insatiable emptiness lies hidden beneath everything, what would life be then but despair? If this is the way life is, if there is no sacred bond uniting mankind, if one generation rises up after another like the leaves of the forest, if one generation succeeds the other as the songs of birds in the woods, if the human race passes through the world as a ship through the sea or the wind through the desert, a thoughtless and fruitless whim, if an eternal oblivion always lurks hungrily for its prey and there is no power strong enough to wrest it from its clutches – how empty and devoid of consolation life would be!

A person seated in a glass case is not put to as much embarrassment as is one in his transparency before God. This is the factor of conscience. By the aid of conscience things are so arranged that the judicial report follows at once upon every fault, and that the guilty one himself must write. Everyone arrives in eternity already bringing with him and delivering the most accurate account of every least insignificance that he has committed or has left undone. Therefore to hold judgement in eternity is a thing a child could manage; there is really nothing for a third person to do. Everything, even to the most insignificant word is counted and in order.

The guilty person's journey through life to eternity is like that of the murderer who got on a train to flee from the place where he perpetrated his crime. Alas, just under the railway coach where he sat ran the electric telegraph with its signal and the order for his apprehension at the next station. When he reached the station and stepped off the coach he was arrested. The denunciation was waiting there for him.

One has at most seventy years for enjoyment – but an eternity for remembering. And pleasure does not show up at all well in memory.

In the temporal world, the main thing is to be able to talk, to have a regular devil's gift of gab. This is the case all down the line, right from the merchant talking up his wares and someone buttering up the women and the agitator soft-soaping the public, right up to the poet, speaker, and scholar. It's a matter of talk, not character-transformation.

If eternity were allowed to rule, there would be no verbosity, which is just what temporality loves – it loves appearance, procrastination, and most of all, talk. But eternity has an eye for action, character-transformation. Every change along the line of talk is of no assistance whatsoever when it comes to eternity.

Let us never deceive youth by foolish talk about the matter of accomplishing. Let us never make them so busy in the service of the moment, that they forget the patience of willing something eternal.

Several families can join together for a box at the theater, and three single gentlemen can join together for a riding horse so that each one rides every third day. But this is not the way it is with immortality. The consciousness of my immortality belongs simply and solely to me.

Immortality is the Judgment. Immortality is not a life indefinitely prolonged, but the eternal separation between the just and the unjust. Immortality is not a continuation that follows as a matter of course, but a separation that follows as a consequence of the past.

In this world, Truth walks in meekness and humiliation. It does not have a place to lay its head, and it must be thankful if one will give it a cup of water. But if one does this, confessing it for what it is in public, then this lowly figure, this humble, despised, mocked, persecuted wretch, the Truth, has, if I may say so, in its hand an ink pen and writes upon a little tablet: "For eternity."

69 | Existence and the Existential

Philosophy is perfectly right in saying that life must be understood backwards. But then it forgets the other side – that it must be lived forwards.

Life can be explained only after it has been lived.

On the whole there can be no schoolmaster, strictly understood, in the art of existing. With respect to existing, there is only the learner; for anyone who fancies that he is in this respect finished – that he can teach others and on top of that himself forgets to exist and to learn – is a fool. In relation to existing there is for all persons one schoolmaster – existence itself.

The essential sermon is one's own existence. A person preaches with this every hour of the day and with power quite different from that of the most eloquent speaker in his most eloquent moment. To let your mouth run with eloquent babbling when such talk is the opposite of your life is in the deepest sense nonsense. You become liable to eternal judgment.

What really counts in life is that at some time you have seen something, felt something which is so great, so matchless, that

everything else is nothing by comparison, that even if you for-
got everything you would never forget this.

It is one thing to introduce a new doctrine into the world, it is
something else to live it.

All this talk about wanting to know the truth is gibberish, illusion, and hypocrisy. Every person understands the truth a good
deal more than he lives it. Why does he not do more, then? Ah,
there's the rub!

The lives of most people are like the grass – only the trees catch
the storm, and they experience a great deal, but the grass experiences practically nothing.

There are many people who arrive at conclusions in life much
the way schoolboys do; they cheat their teachers by copying the
answer book without having worked the problem themselves.

What I really lack is to be clear in my mind what I am to do, not
what I am to know, except in so far as a certain understanding
must precede every action. The thing is to understand myself,
to see what God really wants me to do. The thing is to find a
truth that is true for me, to find the idea for which I can live and
die. What would be the use of discovering so-called objective
truth, of working through all the systems of philosophy and of
being able, if required, to review them all and show up the in-
consistencies within each system; what good would it do me to
be able to develop a theory of the state and combine all the de-

tails into a single whole, and so construct a world in which I did not live, but only held up to the view of others; what good would it do me to be able to explain the meaning of Christianity if it had no deeper significance for me and for my life; what good would it do me if truth stood before me, cold and naked, not caring whether I recognized her or not, and producing in me a shudder of fear rather than trusting devotion?

I certainly do not deny that there is an imperative of understanding, but it must be taken up into my life, and that is what I now recognize as the most important thing. That is what I lack, and that is why I am left standing like a man who has a rented house and gathered all the furniture and household things together, but has not yet found the beloved with whom to share the joys and sorrows of his life.

Everyone, even the most industrious, is in imagination, feelings, thought and speech, a good bit in front of himself, beyond what he is in action and reality. The majority of us are like a train from which the locomotive has run away – we are so far ahead of ourselves, we are so far behind.

The easiest thing of all is to die; the difficult thing is to live.

It is one thing to let ideas strive with ideas, to battle and be victorious in a dispute; it is something else entirely to be victorious over your own mind in the battle of life. For however close one battling idea comes to another in life, however close one combatant comes to the other in an argument, all this strife is still at a distance and like shadow-boxing. The measure of a person's fundamental disposition is determined by how far is what he understands from what he does, how great is the distance between his understanding and his action.

It would indeed be a ludicrous contradiction if an existing person asked what Christianity is and then spent his whole life deliberating on that. In that case, when would he ever exist in it?

To say that Christianity is empty of content because it is not a doctrine is only chicanery. When a believer exists in faith, his existence has enormous content, but not in the sense of a yield in paragraphs.

If an *existing* person relates himself with passion to eternal happiness, then his life will express the relation. If the eternal does not absolutely transform his existence, then he is not relating himself to it.

A speculative thinker has finished on paper and mistakes this for existence.

To be finished with life before life is finished with you is not to finish the task at all.

The true is not superior to the good and the beautiful. The true and the good and the beautiful belong essentially to every human existence and are united not in thinking them but in living them.

The difficulty is not to understand what Christianity is but to become and to be a Christian.

If a person does not become what he understands, then he does not understand it either.

Between understanding and willing lie excuses and evasions.

Just as air in a sealed space becomes poisonous, so the imprisonment of reflection develops a culpable resentment if it is not ventilated by action.

In the world of spirit, to change place is to be changed yourself.

The passion of faith lies not in testifying to an eternal happiness but in transforming one's own existence into a testimony to it.

Seeking the truth means that the seeker himself is changed, so that he may become the place where the object of his search can be.

70 | Faith and Reason

It is in the interest of faith to make a final, absolute decision. It is in the interest of the understanding to keep "deliberation" alive. Just as the police would be embarrassed if there were no crimes, so the understanding is embarrassed if deliberation were completed. Faith wants the absolute; the understanding wants prolongation of thought.

What then is the absurd? Quite simply, it is that I, a rational being, must act in the situation where my understanding says to me both: you can just as well do the one thing as the other – and you cannot act but you must act. Thus the absurd is to act in this situation in an unwavering confidence in God. Quite simply, I must act, but my intellect has blocked the passage, so I take one of the possibilities and turn pleadingly to God and say: This is how I am doing it; please bless it. I cannot do otherwise, for I am brought to a halt by my understanding.

Enormous treatises have been written that try to demonstrate the truth of Christianity. Behind these we feel perfectly convinced and secure against all attack. With every demonstration we end with: Ergo, Christ was the one he claimed to be. It is just as certain as two plus two equals four and as easy as putting one's foot in a sock. With this irrefutable "ergo" the professor bids defiance, and the missionary confidently goes forth to convert the unbelieving. But not Christ! He never says: Ergo, I am the expected one. No, he says, "Blessed is he who is not offended at me." That is, we do not come to him by means of proofs, but by picking up his cross.

Demonstrations are ultimately ambiguous, the loquacious understanding's "for and against." Only in choosing is the heart disclosed and this, indeed, was why Christ came to the world – to disclose the thoughts of the heart. Proofs are able to lead someone – not to faith, far from it, but to the point where faith might come into existence. At best they are able to help someone become aware and come into the tension where faith breaks forth: Will you believe or will you be offended?

Can the absolute be praised, commended, served by reasons? No. Anyone who does this reveals that he is a blockhead who cannot think two thoughts together. "Reasons" transpose the absolute into relativity. The absolute must not be intellectually speculated about in the remotest way, researched, chattered about – no, it is the unconditional, so hold your tongue.

There is only one proof – that of faith. It is impossible for a person to hold back his conviction and push ahead with reasons. If I actually have a firm conviction, then it is higher than reasons; it is actually the conviction that sustains the reasons, not the reasons which sustain the conviction. "Reasons" can lay an egg no more than a rooster can, at most a wind egg, and no matter how much intercourse they have with each other they never beget or bear a conviction. A conviction arises elsewhere.

There is only one proof for the truth of Christianity – the inward proof, *argumentum spiritus sancti* (the argument of the

Holy Spirit). The Apostle John intimates this: "If we receive the testimony of men" (this is all the historical proofs and considerations) "the testimony of God is greater" – that is, the inward testimony is greater. And then: "He who believes in the son of God has the testimony in himself" (1 Jn. 5:9–10).

It is not reasons that justify faith in God's son, but just the opposite – faith in God's son *is* the testimony. Faith is the movement of infinity within itself, and it cannot be otherwise. Everything previous is preparatory, preliminary, something which disappears as soon as the conviction arrives. Otherwise, there would be no resting in a conviction, for then to have conviction would mean perpetually to repeat the reasons. Faith itself is the testimony, faith is the justification.

Have you seen a ship aground in a spongy bog? It is almost impossible to get it afloat again because it is impossible to drive piles. No pile reaches ground firm enough so that one can rely on it. In just the same way our whole generation is stuck fast in the spongy bog of reason; and there is no grief over it – no, there is self-satisfaction and conceit, which always accompanies reason and the sin of reason. Oh, the sins of the heart, the sins of passion – how much closer they are to salvation than the sin of intellect!

By faith Abraham went out from the land of his fathers and became a sojourner in the land of promise. He left one thing behind, and took one thing with him. He left his earthly understanding behind and took faith with him. Otherwise he would have never gone forth.

In the New Testament faith possesses an ethical character. The apostle speaks of the obedience of faith. Faith is set to a test, is tested, not by reasons, but by life.

Christ uses only one proof: "If you do my father's will, he shall know whether the teaching is from God or whether I am speaking on my own authority." This implies that an action-situation is necessary before the decision of faith can come into existence; it is a venture. It is not a matter of proof first and then the venture. No, first the venture, then the proof.

When a rich man goes driving at night with lights on his carriage, he sees a small area better than the poor man who drives in the dark – but he does not see the stars. The lights prevent that. It is the same with all intellectual understanding. It sees well close at hand but takes away the infinite outlook.

When Christianity entered the world it presupposed want, distress, the suffering of the anguished conscience, the hunger that cries out only for food – and then Christianity *was* the food. Nowadays we think that we have to offer appetizers before we can get people to enter into faith. What appetizers? The preaching of the law? No, no! Christianity must be served with such appetizer seasonings as proofs, grounds, probability, and the like. This means we betray Christianity, we actually deny that it is unconditionally the food, that the fault lies in men, that they should be properly starved out.

We have changed Christianity from a radical cure into a minor precaution, like something used to prevent colds, toothaches, and the like. And strangely enough, although every inventor of drops, pills, and so on, "which do neither good nor harm," trumpets his medicine as a miracle balm, Christianity is proclaimed in very muted tones. A host of grounds and reasons march right up in order to make it somewhat probable that there is something to Christianity. Truly, if worst comes to worst, I believe that Christianity would be better off served by a charlatan than by a legion of witnesses of this sort.

God can no more prove his existence by way of something else than he can swear; he has nothing higher than himself to swear by.

Take all the skeptics who have difficulties with Christianity and all the apologists who strive to defend it, and see how the whole thing is a false alarm. The difficulties are simply introduced by God in order to make sure that he can become the object of faith. This is why Christianity is a paradox; this explains the contradictions in Scripture. But the intellectual approach wants to abolish faith. It has no inkling of God's sovereignty nor what the requirement of faith means.

In teaching a child to walk you get in front of the child and turn towards it. You do not walk alongside the child but are the goal toward which the child is to walk. Even though you stand so far away that you cannot reach the child, you stretch out your arms and motion with them as if you already embraced the child, although there is still some distance between you and the child. That much solicitude you have, but more solicitous you cannot be, for then the child does not learn to walk. So it is with Christ. Christ gets in front of us, does not walk beside his disciples, but is himself the goal toward which we are to strive while we are learning to walk alone. There he stands at the goal, turning toward us and stretching out his arms – just as a mother does.

The widow who put three pennies in the temple treasury box performed a miracle just like the miracle of the five loaves and three fish; her three pennies were transformed into abundance.

You can either employ all your acumen to show the unreasonableness of a miracle and then on that basis (that it is unreasonable) conclude that it is no miracle – but would it be a miracle if it were reasonable? – or you can employ all your profundity and acumen to understand the miracle, to make it understandable, and then conclude that it is a miracle because it is understandable – but then it is indeed no miracle. No, let miracle be what it is: an object of faith.

We should either abandon miracles completely or act accordingly.

You must venture out into life, out on the sea, and lift up your voice, even though God does not hear it, and not stand on the shore and watch others fighting and struggling. Only then does the understanding acquire its official sanction. To stand on one leg and prove God's existence is a very different thing from going on your knees and thanking him.

Faith is a restless thing. It is health, but stronger and more violent than the most burning fever.

Faith simply means that what I am seeking is not here, and for that very reason I believe it. Faith expressly signifies the deep, strong, blessed restlessness that drives the believer so that he cannot settle down at rest in this world. He who has settled down has ceased to be a believer, because a believer cannot sit still – a believer travels forward in faith.

One person can do much for another, but he cannot give him faith.

What is the eternal power in a human being? It is faith. What is the expectancy of faith? Victory – or, as Scripture teaches, that all things work together for good for those who love God. Faith is an expectancy of the future that expects victory. Faith conquers the future. The believer, therefore, is finished with the future before he begins with the present, and this victory can only make him stronger for the present work.

What modern philosophy and theology understand by faith is really what is called having an opinion, or what in everyday language we call "to believe." Christianity is thus made into a teaching. Then the next stage is to "comprehend" this teaching, and this philosophy and theology are supposed to do. All this would be entirely proper if Christianity were a teaching. But it's not. Faith is related to the God-man, not a doctrine.

What faith it takes to believe that this life is noticed by God and that this is enough!

Imagine a violinist. If, without having learned the least bit of music, he were to take his seat in the orchestra and right away begin playing, he would not only be disturbed but would disturb others. No, for a long time he practices by himself, alone. As far as possible not a thing disturbs him there; he sits and beats time etc. But his aim is to play with the orchestra. He must be able to tolerate the profusion of the most varied instruments, this interweaving of sounds, and yet be able to attend to his violin and play along just as calmly and confidently as if he were home alone in his room. Oh, this again makes it necessary for him to be by himself to learn to be able to do this – but the aim is always that he play in the orchestra. It is the same with faith and the task of living it out.

He who loves God without faith reflects upon himself; he who loves God in faith reflects upon God.

Ethically speaking, what Abraham planned to do was to murder Isaac. Religiously, however, he was willing to sacrifice Isaac. In this contradiction lies the very anguish that can indeed make anyone sleepless. And yet without that anguish Abraham is not the one he is. Neither would faith be what it is.

Resignation by itself does not require faith. It has only to comply with the eternal. It renounces, but does not gain. Faith, however, does not renounce anything. On the contrary, in faith I receive everything. Herein lies the crucial difference. It takes a purely human courage to renounce the world of temporality in order to win eternity; but it takes a humble and paradoxical courage to take hold of what is temporal and to do so for the sake of the eternal. That courage is the courage of faith. Through faith Abraham did not renounce his claim on Isaac. No, through his faith he received Isaac.

In relation to Christ, there is only one time, the present. Eighteen hundred years makes absolutely no difference; they neither change Christ nor reveal who he was, for who he is is revealed only to faith.

71 | Following Jesus

Christ's entire life must supply the norm for the Christian and for the life of the whole Church. One has to take every particular aspect of Christ's life straight from his baptism to his resurrection and show correspondence. What else does it mean to be a Christian?

What is Christianity? Simple: to be like Christ.

It does not say that you should try to resemble Christ. No, you are to put on Christ, put him on yourself – as when someone goes around in borrowed clothing – put him on, as when someone who looks strikingly like another not only tries to resemble him but represents him. Christ gives you his clothing (the satisfaction of atonement) so that you might represent him.

Imitation of Jesus! I do not mean the kind of imitation consisting of fasting and flagellation, and so on. No, imitation means following the example, being willing to witness for the truth and against untruth, and to do so without seeking any support whatsoever from any external power, neither attaching oneself to any power nor forming a party. No wonder we humans are unable to get involved with this imitation.

There are this many children baptized every year, that many confirmed, and how many become theological professors and Bible teachers? There are a thousand pastors. Everything is in place – if only following Christ existed.

People seem to forget that there is a limit to the passion of making assurances and that this limit lies where the passion of action should begin. And when this is lacking, verbal assurances become the more vehement and shrill, all the more a declaration that what is said is a lie in the assurer's throat.

We congratulate ourselves on having explained away all asceticism from Christianity, showing how far Christianity is from the foolishness of such things as monastic flagellation. But wait a little! Something is always left out, and that is the Pattern: the Lord of Lords in the form of a poor servant without a place to lay his head, the self-denial exemplified by Christ's example that Christianity requires. The one who remains in the world to suffer for the truth is always in the right over against the hermit's flight from the world. But the sociable, happy-go-lucky person who remains in the world to enjoy himself in the completely ordinary human sense has absolutely no right to castigate the monastic. Let us not deceive ourselves.

Christianity is a believing and a very particular kind of existing corresponding to it – imitation. We can put faith first and imitation second, inasmuch as it is necessary for me to have faith in that which I am to imitate. But we must also put imitation first and faith second. I must, by some action, be marked in some measure by conformity to Christ, and thus collide with the world. Without some kind of situational tension, there is no real opportunity of becoming a believer.

We could at least be truthful before God and admit our weakness instead of reducing the requirement.

Imitation is not a requirement of the law, for then we would have the burden of law again. No, imitation begins with the joy over being loved – and then comes the striving to please.

Christ comes to the world as the example, constantly enjoining: Imitate me. We humans prefer to adore him instead.

Genuine faith is never satisfied with the religious way of doing things – Sabbath worship or an hour or a half-hour of each day. Christianity is nothing else but faith right in the middle of actual life and weekdays. But we have reduced it to quiet hours, thereby indirectly admitting that we are not really being Christians. That we should have quiet times to think about God – this seems so elevated and beautiful, so solemn. It is so hypocritical, because in this way we exempt daily life from the authentic worship of God.

Anyone who does not take up the task in everyday life and in the living room should just keep quiet, because Sunday vistas into eternity are nothing but air. Of course, he should not remain in the living room. However, it is in the living room that the battle must be fought, lest the skirmishes of piety become a changing-of-the-guard parade one day a week. It is in the living room that the battle must be fought, not imaginatively in church, with the pastor shadowboxing and the listeners looking on. It is in the living room that the battle must be fought, because the victory must be that the home becomes a shrine.

Christianity entered into the world not to be understood but to be existed in.

Some suggestions by way of a few questions: Can one be a Christian at all without being a disciple? Can Christianity, which came into the world to strengthen and inspire us morally, be changed in such a way that it demoralizes us with the help of easy "grace"? – Can one be a Christian in that manner? Is it all right to take from the world the promises for this life, which it has because it has no eternal salvation to point to, and to take from Christianity the promises of eternity, which it has because it demands renunciation of this life, and mix these together so it gets to be really bonbon (twice as sweet) – is it all right to call this Christianity and be a Christian in this way? And if by virtue of "grace" it can be done, must not one thing at least be demanded, that we realize clearly what we have done and how hypnotically we are drawing upon "grace"?

When we see someone holding an axe wrong and chopping in such a way that he hits everything but the block of firewood, we do not say, "What a wrong way for the woodcutter to go about it," but we say, "That man is not a woodcutter."

Now for the application. When we see thousands and thousands and millions of Christians whose lives do not resemble in the remotest way what – and this is decisive – the New Testament calls a Christian, is it not tampering with the meaning to talk as one does in no other situation and say: "what a mediocre way, what a thoroughly inexpressive way these Christians have." In any other situation would one not say, "These people are not Christians." Now be earnest about it and say: We are not Christians. Let this become ordinary language usage and you will have a world-transformation.

Just as the name of Christ is the one and only name in heaven and on earth, so also is Christ the one and only predecessor who has gone ahead to prepare a place. Between heaven and earth there is only one road: to follow Christ. In time and eternity there is only one choice: to choose this road. There is only one eternal hope on this earth: to follow Christ into heaven. There is one lasting joy in this life, to follow Christ; and in death there is one final blessed joy – to follow Christ to life!

In a verbal dispute there is no essential difference between an admirer and an imitator, except that perhaps the imitator does not have such a copious vocabulary and is not at all inclined to give assurances.

Lord Christ, you did not come to the world to be served nor to be admired either, or in that sense worshipped. You yourself were the way and the life – and you require only followers. If we have dozed off into this infatuation, wake us up, rescue us from this error of wanting to admire or adoringly admire you instead of wanting to follow you and be like you.

You who yourself once walked the earth and left footprints that we should follow; you who from heaven still look down on every pilgrim, strengthen the weary, hearten the disheartened, lead back the straying, give solace to the struggling. You who will come again at the end of time to judge each one individually, whether he followed you – our God and our Savior – let your example stand very clearly before the eyes of the soul in order to dispel the mists, strengthen in order to keep this alone unaltered before our eyes so that by resembling you and by following you we may be able to stand rightly before you in judgment – oh, but may we also be brought by you to the eternal happiness with you in the life to come.

Christ did not say to the rich young man, "If you want to be perfect, then sell all your property and give it to the poor." Christ speaks in another way and says, "Go, sell what you have and give it to the poor and come, take up the cross and follow me" (Mk. 10:21). To sell one's property and give it to the poor is at most a beginning. To give all to the poor, that is the first step; it is to take up the cross. The next step, the protracted continuation, is to carry your cross. It must take place daily, not once and for all, and there must not be anything, anything at all, that you would not be willing to give up in self denial.

As Nicodemus came at night, so a king comes to Christ at night and wants to be a disciple. I wonder what Christ might say to him. "If you want to continue being what you are – a king – then fear nothing from me; my kingdom is not of this world. I will be your subject like anyone else, will be your humble and loyal subject, and I will teach my disciples to be the same. But if you want to be a disciple – oh, man, then I am the king. Take off your crown, give everything away, follow me."

72 | Forgiveness

That Jesus Christ died for my sins certainly shows how great his grace is, but it also shows how great my sins are.

The forgiveness of sins is not a matter of particulars – as if on the whole one were good. (This is childish, for the child always begs forgiveness for some particular thing which it did yesterday and forgets today, etc.; it could never occur to a child, in fact, the child could not even get it into its head, that it is actually evil.) No, it is just the opposite. It pertains not so much to particulars as to the totality. It pertains to one's whole self, which is sinful and corrupts everything as soon as it comes in slightest contact with it.

Forgiveness of sins cannot be such that God by a single stroke, as it were, erases all guilt, abrogates all its consequences. Such a craving is only a worldly desire that has no idea of what guilt is. Forgiveness does not mean to be placed in more fortunate circumstances but to become a new person in the reassuring awareness that your guilt is forgiven even if the consequences of guilt remain. Only the person who grasps the fact that guilt is something completely different from and more terrible than the consequences of guilt (regarded as misfortune, suffering), only he repents, only he is forgiven.

Christ abandoned "an eye for an eye, a tooth for a tooth," and turned the relationship around. He introduced a different like-for-like: as you relate yourself to others, so God relates himself to you. Forgiveness is to forgive.

Where reconciliation takes place, there the altar is.

You rest in the forgiveness of sins when the thought of God does not remind you of the sin but that it is forgiven, when the past is not a memory of how much you trespassed but of how much you have been forgiven.

The need for forgiveness is a sign that one loves God. But both parts correspond to one another – when a person does not comprehend what a great sinner he is, he cannot love God; and when he does not love God, he cannot comprehend how great a sinner he is. The consciousness of sin is the very passion of love. Truly the law makes one a sinner, but love makes one a far greater sinner! It is true that the person who fears God and trembles feels himself to be a sinner, but the person who in truth loves feels himself to be an even greater sinner.

Consider Giordano Bruno or someone like him, who became a martyr for an idea. In a weak moment he yielded and hid himself in order to avoid danger. He then is betrayed, his hiding place discovered, and he is seized.

Now imagine him before the judge. He demands to know who has given away his hiding place and betrayed him. It proves to be his servant. He is confronted by the servant, who is extremely dejected since he himself now clearly feels his guilt.

Then he says to the servant, "Don't be distressed. I completely forgive you. Certainly not many servants would have acted differently than you did, for I know very well that you were bribed. Incidentally, how much did I cost?" The servant replies, "I got 250 dollars." "Well, now," says the master, "that is a pretty good payment. You understand, however, that you are rather lucky that I am not angry with you, for in my will I designated for you 500 dollars payable upon my death. If I had become angry, you would have been a fool: you would have only received 250 dollars for betraying me, a 250 dollar bribe – a crime. Otherwise you would have received 500 dollars without any misconduct, and if I were angry you would have lost more than half. Now, on the contrary, because of the will you get 500 after my death, 250 extra as something you have earned on the side. My friend, those who paid you 250 dollars probably did not admonish you to use the money well. Take my advice, then, and use the money well. Do not despair because you were weak enough to betray men, be strong enough to believe both that God will forgive you entirely and that I have entirely forgiven you."

To forgive sins is divine not only in the sense that no one is able to do it except God, but also because no one can do it without God.

It is God's joy to forgive sins. Just as God is almighty in creating out of nothing, so he is almighty in uncreating something; for to forget is indeed to uncreate something.

When I hate someone or deny that God is his Father, it is not he who loses, it is I. It is I who have no Father. With unforgiveness there is always the reversed echo.

You may think that the sin remains just as great whether it is forgiven or not, since forgiveness neither adds nor subtracts. But this is not so. Rather, when you refuse to forgive you increase the sin. Does not your hardness of heart become yet one more sin? Ought this not be brought into the reckoning as well?

The anguished conscience alone understands Christ.

If the forgiveness of sins was intended to make good works superfluous, then it should not be called the forgiveness of sins but the permission of sins.

If we fail to understand that forgiveness is also a burden that must be carried, even though a light burden, we take forgiveness in vain. Forgiveness is never earned – it is not that heavy. But neither is it to be taken in vain, for it is not that light either. Forgiveness is not to be paid for – for it is not that costly and it cannot be paid for. But neither is it to be treated as nothing; it is bought at too high a price for that.

The Law is no longer the only disciplinarian to lead us to Christ. Forgiveness through Christ is the gentle disciplinarian who does not have the heart to remind us of what has been forgotten but still reminds us of what has been forgiven. Every time you remember his forgiveness, your sins are forgotten. But when you forget his forgiveness, your sins are not forgotten, and then his forgiveness is wasted.

When the Pharisees surrounded that woman, they discovered an enormity of sin, but Christ wrote in the sand – and hid it. In Christ everything is revealed – and everything is hidden.

My reader, there was a woman who was a sinner, but by her great love she made herself, if I dare say so, indispensable to the Savior. You can call her blessed because her many sins were forgiven, or you can call her blessed because she loved much. Substantially you are saying the same thing – if only you note well that he whom she loved much was Christ, and if at the same time you don't forget that Christ is grace and the giver of grace.

Is this the test: to love Christ more dearly than mother and father, than gold and goods, than honor and reputation? No, the test is this: to love the Savior more than your sin.

God creates out of nothing – marvelous, you say. Yes, of course, but he does something more marvelous – he creates saints out of sinners.

You will get a deep insight into the state of Christianity in each age by seeing how it treats Judas.

God will be just as severe with us as we are with others. How devastating! For we know well enough how severe we can be. But the whole point is that God is playing with us when he does toward us what we do toward others. He could be far more severe.

Oh God, you are great, the Creator and Sustainer of the world. But when you, oh God, forgive the sin of the world and reconcile yourself with the fallen race, ah, then you are still greater. You are inconceivable compassion!

Father in heaven! Hold not our sins up against us but hold us up against our sins, so that the thought of you when it wakens in our soul, and each time it wakens, should not remind us of what we have committed but of what you forgave, not of how we went astray but of how you saved us!

73 | Freedom

Unconditional freedom, freedom which equally well chooses the good or the evil, is nothing but an abrogation of freedom and a despair of any explanation of it. Freedom means to be capable.

Christianity teaches that you should choose the one thing needful, but in such a way that there must be no question of any choice. That is, if you fool around a long time, then you are not really choosing the one thing needful. Consequently, the very fact that there is no choice expresses the tremendous passion or intensity with which one chooses. Can there be a more accurate expression for the fact that freedom of choice is only a formal condition of freedom and that emphasizing freedom of choice as such means the sure loss of freedom? The very truth of freedom of choice is that there must be no choice, even though there is a choice.

Freedom really is freedom only when, in the same moment, the same second, it rushes with infinite speed to bind itself. Freedom is the choice whose truth is that there can be no question of any choice.

In staring fixedly at freedom of choice instead of choosing, we lose both freedom and freedom of choice. The most tremendous thing given to a human being is – choice, freedom. If you want to rescue and keep it, there is only one way – in the very same second unconditionally in full attachment give it back to God and yourself along with it. If the sight of what is given to you tempts you, if you surrender to the temptation and look with selfish craving at freedom of choice, then you lose your freedom. And your punishment then is to go around in a kind of confusion and brag about having freedom of choice.

Woe to you, this is the judgment upon you. You have freedom of choice, you say, and yet you have not chosen God. Then you become ill; freedom of choice becomes your fixed idea. Finally you become like the rich man morbidly imagining that he has become impoverished and will die of want. You sigh that you have lost the freedom of choice, and the mistake is merely that you do not sorrow deeply enough so that you get it back again.

What Augustine says about true freedom (distinguished from freedom of choice) is very true and very much a part of experience. Namely, that a person has the most lively sense of freedom when with completely decisive determination he impresses upon his action the inner necessity which excludes the thought of another possibility. Then freedom of choice or the "agony" of choice comes to an end.

People want to eliminate injunctions and constraints in order to play the game of being independent. In the old days people believed that it was the conscience that gave freedom of conscience, that if one had conscience, freedom was sure to come along. But to eliminate every constraint, to loosen every bond, meant at best to make it as free and as convenient as possible for everyone to have no conscience while imagining that he had one. All this talk about eliminating constraint comes either from the coddled or from those who perhaps once felt the power to fight but are now exhausted and find it nicer to have all constraints taken away.

Certainly, Mary was the chosen one, and so decidedly so that she was chosen. But there is also another factor, freedom and the moment of choice, where we see that such a one is the right one. Had the angel not found her as he did find her, she would not have been the right one.

God's education consists in leading one to being able to do freely what at first one had to be compelled to do.

The opposite of freedom is not necessity, but guilt.

Who does not want to be free? Wishing to be free is an easy matter, but wishing is the most paltry and unfree of all performances.

In all our own "freedom," we actually seek one thing: to be able to live without responsibility.

That which distinguishes the Christian way from the common way is the voluntary. Christ was not someone who coveted earthly things but had to be satisfied with poverty – no, he *chose* poverty.

A person is a slave of what he is unfreely dependent upon. But our freedom-loving age thinks otherwise; it thinks that if one is not dependent, then one is not a slave either. If there is no ruler, then there is no slave either. One is scarcely aware that precisely here a bondage is being created. This bondage is not that one person wants to subjugate many, but that individuals, when they forget their relation to God, become mutually afraid of one another.

We read that Christ after his resurrection came through closed doors, where the disciples were assembled. This is sometimes mistakenly used as a picture of how eagerly Christ seeks the soul, how he can even get through the closed doors of hearts that are indifferent or hardened. But this is untrue. Rather, he stands before the door and knocks.

That God could create beings free over against himself is the cross that philosophy could not bear but upon which it has remained hanging.

The whole question of God's omnipotence and the relation of goodness to evil may perhaps be resolved quite simply in this way. The highest that conceivably can be done for a being is to make it free. But it requires omnipotence for this. It may seem strange, since omnipotence would seem to require dependence. But if one will think carefully about omnipotence, he will perceive that the distinctive characteristic of omnipotence is the ability to withdraw itself again. It is precisely for this cause that what comes into existence by omnipotence can be independent.

Only omnipotence is able to withdraw (take itself back) in giving out, and it is this relationship precisely which constitutes the independence of the recipient. Hence God's omnipotence is his goodness. For goodness means to give out completely, but in such a way that withdrawing it makes the recipient free. Omnipotence is not merely able to produce the most imposing phenomenon, the totality of the visible universe, but also the most fragile thing of all: a being that in the very face of omnipotence is independent. It is but a worthless and worldly conception of the dynamic of power that it is greater and greater in proportion as it can compel and make dependent. No, the art of true power is precisely to make free.

74 | God

The law of relationship between us humans and God is as follows: Major Premise: There is an infinite, radical, qualitative difference between God and humans. This means that we can achieve absolutely nothing; it is God who gives everything. It is he who brings forth a person's faith, and so forth. This is grace, and this is Christianity's major premise. Minor Premise: Although we can merit nothing, unconditionally nothing, we can, in faith, dare in all childlikeness to be involved with God.

If the major premise is everything, then God becomes so infinitely great that there can be no relationship between God and the individual human being. The life of the single individual never gets off the ground. It can be fraud to elevate God so high. The difficulty is to have an infinite conception of God's majesty and of Christ's glory and then the childlike openness to become involved with them in your own personal life in a wholly childlike way.

Yes, who in all the world can or dares risk involvement with God when you consider that your serial number in the race is, for example, No. 27,000,000,000 and so on? But you ought not think this way. You should simply shut your eyes, think only of God, become a poor single human being to whom God's infinite love gives childlike openness, and above all rejoice in the fact that every human being has permission to do this – yes, he shall do this.

Oh, that you would learn to think humanly of God! I do not mean that you should become buddy-buddy with God. No, first of all, first the infinite conception of God's infinite majesty, and then, then the next, the childlike openness to become involved with him earnestly and in truth. Unfortunately Christianity has made God so sublime that in the long run we really have spirited him away and smuggled him out of life.

If a desert Arab looking for water suddenly discovered a spring in his tent, so that he would always have spring water in abundance – how fortunate he would consider himself! It is the same with a person who is always turned outward, thinking that his happiness lies outside himself. If only he would turn inward and discover that the springs lie within, to say nothing of discovering the spring that God offers in a relationship.

"He must increase, but I must decrease" is the law for all drawing near to God. But then in a way do I lose God? How? For indeed, he increases! No, if I lose anything, I lose only myself.

The longer one lives with God the more infinite God becomes – and the less one becomes. Alas, as a child one thinks that God and man can play happily together. As a youth one dreams that if he really and truly makes an effort, like someone passionately in love, then that relationship to God might still be achieved. Alas, when one matures he discovers how infinite God is, discovers the infinite distance.

God is personal. That matter is certain enough. But unless something else happens, you have not advanced. No, God is indeed personal, but it still does not follow that he is straightway personal for you. Take a human relationship. A superior person is certainly personal, but does he not have it in his power to be personal in relation to the inferior one or to relate himself objectively to him?

So it is with God. Yes, he is personal, but whether he will be that toward you depends on whether it so pleases God. It is the grace of God if he will be personal in his relation to you. And if you throw away his grace, he punishes you by relating to you objectively. And in this sense it can be said that the world (despite all proofs!) does not have a personal God. The truth is that long ago there ceased to be people capable of bearing the pressure and the weight of having a personal God.

God is the only power who does not hold sales or reduce the prices; his prices remain eternally unchanged.

The goal is not to merge into God through some fading away or in some divine ocean. No, in an intensified consciousness "a person must render account for every careless word he has uttered." Even though grace blots out sin, the union with God still takes place in the personality clarified and intensified to the utmost.

God is unchanging. But this changelessness is not a chilling indifference, a devastating loftiness, an ambiguous distance, which the callous understanding lauds. No, on the contrary, this changelessness is intimate and warm and everywhere present. God is unchanging love.

Imagine a solitary traveler, a desert wanderer. Almost burned by the heat of the sun, languishing with thirst, he finds a spring. Oh refreshing coolness! Now God be praised, he says – and yet it was merely a spring he found. What then is he who finds God! He too must say, "God be praised, I have found God – now I am well provided for. Your faithful coolness, oh beloved well-spring, is not subject to any change. In the cold of winter, if winter visited this place, you would not become colder, but would preserve the same coolness unchanged, for the waters of the spring do not freeze! In the midday heat of the summer sun you preserve precisely the same coolness, for the waters of the spring do not become lukewarm!" There is nothing untrue in what he says, no false exaggeration in his eulogy.

You, oh God, you who are unchangeable, you are always and invariably to be found, and always to be found unchanged. Whether in life or in death, no one journeys so far afield that you are not to be found by him, that you are not there, you who are everywhere. It is not so with the well-springs of earth, for they are to be found only in special places. And besides – overwhelming security! – you don't remain, like the spring, in a single place, but you follow the traveler on his way. How poor and inadequate a description of what you are! You are a spring that itself seeks out the thirsty traveler, the errant wanderer. Who has ever heard the like of any spring! Thus you are unchangeably always and everywhere to be found. And whenever any human being comes to you, of whatever age, at whatever time of the day, in whatever state, if he comes in sincerity he always finds your love equally warm, like the spring's unchanged coolness, oh you who are unchangeable!

With respect to God, the *how* is the *what*. He who does not involve himself with God in the mode of absolute devotion does not become involved with God. In relationship to God one can not involve himself to a certain degree. God is precisely the contradiction to all that is "to a certain degree."

A second-hand relationship to God is just as impossible and just as nonsensical as falling in love at second-hand.

To become involved with God in any other way other than being wounded is impossible.

When children are together all day long, they naturally play with each other. But what happens – suddenly there comes a message that little Peter, Christian, Soren, Hans, or whatever the child is called, must go home. It is the same with us adults. We go and talk with each other about what we want to be in the world, that we want to be this and that, and it seems that we are earnest, almost as earnest as anybody else. But what happens – suddenly there comes a message that we must go home. That is, God calls to us. This, you see, is why the truly religious individual can never engage in the strange sort of earnestness which is so common in the world, the kind that leaves God out. The child cannot be allowed to get stuck in the illusion that his relationship with the other children is the whole thing – for then comes the message that he must go home. The same goes for us.

We do not begin to comprehend God until we realize first that we are comprehended by him.

Whoever does not wish to sink in the wretchedness of the finite is constrained in the most profound sense to struggle with the infinite.

God can imprint himself in a person only when he himself has become nothing. When the ocean is exerting all its power, that is precisely the time when it cannot reflect the image of heaven, and even the slightest motion blurs the image. But when it becomes still and deep, then the image of heaven sinks into its nothingness.

The inward person looks not upon the gifts but upon the Giver. He knows that God not only gives gifts, but gives himself with the gifts. And that alone is what is important.

Oh God, let not joys separate us from you in the forgetfulness of pleasure; nor sorrow set a barrier between you and us. Give what you will – but give only the testimony with your gift, and therein yourself.

It is not because you have a father, or because people in general have fathers, that God is called Father in heaven. Rather, it is because he is your father that all fatherhood in heaven and earth is named.

The simple and humble thing is to love God because you need him. It may seem so lofty a thing to love God because he is so perfect, it may seem so selfish to love him because you need him, yet the latter way is the only way in which you can in truth love God. Woe to him who would make bold to love God without needing him! The one who most deeply recognizes his need of God loves him most truly. You should not presume to love God only for God's sake. No, you should understand that your life's welfare eternally depends on your need, and for this reason and this reason alone you should love him.

The difference that we make between sleeping and waking is only a whimsical distinction, as if we needed God to watch over us as we sleep, whereas we can guard and keep ourselves when we are awake.

Instead of all this preaching about lofty virtues, about faith, hope, and love, about loving God, and so forth, someone ought rather to say: Never get involved with God, and above all never in any really intimate way. Get involved with men and imagine that together with them you are involving yourselves with God, because you name the name of God just as meaninglessly as the physicians scribble embellishments on prescriptions. Never let yourself be alone with God lest you venture too far out, but see to it that your relationship with God is like everybody else's so that you can get someone to assist you right away if God should leave you in the lurch. If you were to talk this way you would talk far more accurately than if you used all those high-flying religious phrases, which over the generations we have so nicely perfected.

Many relate to God so that it may go well with them on earth – consequently to profit from God in an earthly sense. Many also relate to God in order to be saved from sin, in order to find a merciful judge. Is there a difference?

75 | God's Love

The logic of God's love is this: Love relates itself inversely to the greatness and excellence of the object. If I am a nobody, if in my wretchedness I feel more miserable than the most miserable person of all, then it is eternally, no absolutely, certain that God loves me. Christ says: Not a sparrow falls to the earth without his will. Yes, one could suppose that God has so much to look after. But a sparrow – no, no! God is love, and love relates itself inversely to the worthiness of the object. So I offer a lower bid, for in my sin I am less than a sparrow. Yet God is love and for this reason love's logic is more quickly completed. The harder the fall, the greater the love.

You feel yourself abandoned, that no one understands or cares for you, and so you decide: God does not care for me, either. You fool! Shame on you to think this way about God. No, for even the person of whom it can literally be said that he is of all people most abandoned, he is the very one whom God loves. And all the more certainly!

Think what it means to believe that God came into the world, and for your sake too. It almost sounds as though it were the most blasphemous presumption. If it were not God himself who had said it, yes, of all blasphemies it would be the most terrible. This is not an invention to show how important we are to

God. It is to show how infinite God's love is. For it is certainly infinite that he should care for a sparrow, but for the sake of a sinner to let himself be born and die, oh, infinite is his love.

This is all I have known for certain, that God is love. Even if I have been mistaken on this or that point, God is nevertheless love. If I have made a mistake it will be plain enough; so I repent – and God is love. He is love, not he was love, nor, he will be love, oh no, even that future was too slow for me, he is love. Oh, how wonderful. Sometimes, perhaps, my repentance does not come at once, and so there is a future. But God keeps no person waiting, he is love. Like spring-water which keeps the same temperature summer and winter – so is God's love. His love is a spring that never runs dry.

That God is love means that he will do everything to help you to love him, that is to change you into his likeness. He knows well how infinitely painful this change is for you, and so is willing to suffer with you. He suffers more in love than you do, suffers all the heartache of being misunderstood – but he is not changed.

God has only one passion: to love and to be loved. What compels God to create is not amusement. No, no, this is just the opposite of what God wills. To love and to be loved is God's only passion. It almost seems – infinite love! – as though he himself were bound by that passion, in the power of that passion, so that he cannot cease loving, almost as though it were a weakness, whereas it is of course his strength, his omnipotent love, to such a degree is his love above all change.

Oh, marvelous omnipotence of love! But God who creates out of nothing, who almightily takes from nothing and says, "Be," lovingly adjoins, "Be something even in opposition to me." Marvelous love, even his omnipotence is under the sway of love!

Lord, help us to love you much. Increase our love and inflame it. Oh, this is a prayer you will surely hear, you who indeed are love. Compassionate, loving, in love, you are love of such a sort that you yourself woo forth the love that loves you and fosters it to love you more.

Ah, when Christ wandered in Judea he moved many by his miracles. But nailed to the cross he did a still greater miracle, he did the miracle of love, that without doing anything, except to suffer, he moves every one who has a heart.

The greatest danger for a child, where religion is concerned, is not that his father or teacher should be an unbeliever, not even his being a hypocrite. No, the danger lies in their being pious and God-fearing, and in the child being convinced thereof, but that he should nevertheless notice that deep within there lies hidden a terrible unrest. The danger is that the child is provoked to draw a conclusion about God, that God is not infinite love.

Heavenly Father, great and boundless is the expanse of your kingdom. You support the constellations and the pillars of a widening universe; you bear up the weight of a weary world; and you direct the tiniest footstep on the pathways of earth. The grains of sand along the ocean's shore do not approach in number the sum of all the responsibilities that are yours. In spite of your boundless power and limitless sovereignty you give heed to us lowly human beings. You bend down to listen to each one so attentively and so caringly that, amidst all the cacophony and confusion of the daily clamor, each person is assured that you are giving all concern to him alone.

Not only do you pay attention to the one who commands and leads; not only do you listen to the voice of him who prays in intercession for loved ones as if he had a special conduit to your favor. No! You pay attention also to the one who is the most miserable, the most abandoned, the most solitary – whether he moves among the multitude or plods along the trackless desert. And if others have forgotten him and cast him out of their caring, if in the crowd he has lost all identity, if he has ceased, really, to be a human being and has become no more than a number on a list, you know him, oh God. You have not forgotten him. Wherever he is, lost in the desert or just as lost and unnoticed in the crowd; whatever state he is in, whether it be in agonizing pain, or in bondage to terrible and terrifying thoughts, abandoned, so cut off from communication that in the prolonged silence he has forgotten his native tongue – nevertheless you, oh God, have not forgotten him and you hear and comprehend his speechless cry! You know at once how to find the road that leads to him, and rapid as sound and prompt as light you speed to his side.

You loved us first, oh God. Alas, we speak of it as if you loved us first one time only, historically speaking, when in very truth, without ceasing, you love us first all the time. When I awaken in the morning and my soul turns at once toward you, you are first. You have already turned toward me. If I rise at dawn and in the very first second of my awakening my soul turns to you in prayer, you have beat me to it. You have already turned in love toward me. Thus, we speak ingratitude if, unthankful and unaware, we speak of you as having loved us first only one time.

God be praised that it is not because of my worthiness that God loves me. Otherwise, I might at any moment die of fear lest the next moment I cease to be worthy.

While all the other qualities attributed to God are adjectival, love alone is substantive. How could one ever think of saying, "God is loving?"

He who loves God is loved forth by God.

76 | Grace

It was said of Christ that he would reveal the thoughts of many hearts, and this he did. How? Simply by proclaiming grace. He who proclaims the law forces a person into something. People try to hide themselves when faced with the law. But grace, the fact that it is grace, makes them completely unconstrained. Face to face with grace a person really learns to know what lies deepest within. Tell a child to do something – this does not mean the child does it, nor do you really get to know the child's nature. No, but say, "You are free, you may do as you please" – then you find out what lies deepest in the child.

Christianity's intention is that because of grace, now as never before under the law, we shall see what a person can achieve. But instead of this we have used "grace" to prevent acting. Instead of grace being the basis of courage and mobility for action it gets applied in such a way that it even causes an unnatural obstruction. It is applied in such a way that one sinks deeper and deeper so as to require continually more and more grace. We continually run across this kind of thing: Since we are all saved by grace anyway, why should I exert myself. Let's keep clear of any kind of effort because it's all grace anyway. What a mockery! With Christ's grace we can then venture all the more intrepidly. We men, however, do it thus: Even the least little venture is foolish – since there is grace anyway.

No amount of striving can earn salvation. Therefore there is grace. But here there is a danger, the danger that grace may have a stupefying, paralyzing effect. The mystery of grace consists in the fact that the most strenuous human effort is still fool's play, a wasted inconvenience, a ridiculous gesture, if it should be an attempt to earn salvation – and still to push on just like one who soberly and seriously believed that by his efforts he could earn salvation.

If preaching grace is by someone whose life expresses the opposite, then this is taking grace in vain.

Consider a person who is conscious of his guilt and offense. For a long time he goes about in quiet despair and remorsefully broods over it. Then he learns to flee to grace, and he is forgiven everything; everything is infinitely forgiven. But, the moment he shuts the door of grace, as it were, and goes out full of holy resolve to begin a new life, alas, blissfully stirred by the thought that now all is forgiven and he will never get into that situation again, that very same minute, that very same second, he is on the way to new guilt – in the form of "the best he can do."

In that same moment he must return again and knock on the door of grace. He must say: Oh, infinite grace, have mercy on me for being here again so soon and having to plead for grace. Now I understand that in order to have peace and rest, in order not to perish in hopeless despair, in order to be able to breathe, and in order to be able to exist at all, I need grace not only for the past but grace for the future.

The difference between an unbeliever and a Christian is not that the latter is without sin. The difference is how he regards his sin and how he is kept in the striving. When an unbeliever sins – and precisely the more profound and noble he is – there is a dreadful halt in striving. He sinks into depression, despairs over his guilt, and the sin then perhaps gets more and more power over him, so that he hopelessly sinks deeper and deeper. The Christian has a Savior. He takes refuge in "grace." As with a child, his sin is transformed into a fatherly discipline intended to help him go forward – and he perhaps makes the self-assured step forward right now. Bold confidence is not necessarily irresponsibility, but a trusting in grace.

I remember my youth, when it really bored me to copy father's letters. But he only had to say to me, "All right then, I will do them myself." I was immediately willing. Oh, if only he had scolded, alas, there would simply have been a row; but this response was truly moving. In the same way, self-denial is difficult and can embitter a person, if it is imposed by law. But the Savior's look and his words are something very different. He says, "Everything is given to you, it is nothing but grace, only look upon me and upon my suffering which won this grace for you." Yes, that is moving!

You must give yourself to Christ unconditionally. Now if you surrender, you run the risk that he may make things awkward for you – so awkward that you feel almost ready to despair. This is, and must be, the thing about unconditional surrender that makes flesh and blood tremble. But remember that Christ is grace, and it is to grace that you surrender.

As earthly parents, we give to our children, and often, with proud generosity, they will return a portion of that gift to us, really giving back what had belonged to us. We do not, for that reason, reject their gifts or the givers but love them the more. God's gift is like the parent aiding his child in writing a greeting to the parent himself, who receives it as the child's own. The error of the pagan is that he knows *about* his god, and knows that he is not a free giver. The believer, however, *knows* his God and knows that his blessings are free!

Grace has been pushed into an entirely wrong direction; we use it to slough off the requirement of the law. This is meaningless and unchristian! No, God's requirement is and remains the same, unaltered, perhaps even sharpened under grace. The difference is this: under the law my salvation is linked to the condition of fulfilling its requirement. Under grace I am freed from this concern – but God's requirement remains.

The law's requirement is a tightening. The tightening of a bowstring creates motion, but one can tighten a bowstring to the breaking point. This is precisely what the law does. Yet it is not the requirement of the law which breaks, but that which is added – the fact that my eternal salvation depends upon my fulfillment of the requirement. No human being can endure this. Indeed, the more serious he is, the more certain is his despair, and it becomes completely impossible for him to even begin to fulfill the law.

But then comes grace. Naturally, God's grace knows very well what the trouble is, where the shoe pinches. It takes away this concern, the appendage of fulfilling the law, which is precisely what makes the fulfilling of the law impossible. Grace takes away this anxiety and asserts: Only believe – then salvation is assured to you. But not more, not the slightest change of the law's demand. Now you are to begin to fulfill it. But there will be rest and peace for your soul, for your salvation is secured to you as long as you believe.

77 | The Human Condition

Not just in commerce but in the world of ideas too our age is putting on a veritable clearance sale.

A revolutionary age is an age of action; ours is the age of advertisement and publicity.

The confusing thing about us is that we are simultaneously the Pharisee and the publican.

To love God is the only happy love, but on the other hand it is also something terrible. Face to face with God we are without standards and without comparisons; we cannot compare ourselves with God, for here we become nothing, and directly before God, in the presence of God, we dare not compare ourselves with others. Therefore in every person there is a prudent fear of having anything to do with God, because by becoming involved with God he becomes nothing. And so, we desire this relationship at a distance and spend our lives in temporal distractions. All this busyness in life is but a distraction.

We are a composite of the lower and the higher, and from birth on we are almost completely in the power of the lower. The pleasant – and the unpleasant – are what determine us, and it remains just about that way throughout life for most of us.

In a certain sense all of us are running. We are running after money, status, pleasure. We run with gossip, rumors, foul talk, with lies, fiction, and trivialities. We run now to the east and now to the west, panting on our activistic errands. But we are not running on the racetrack.

This is how human nature is related to the divine: the disciples sleep – while Christ suffers.

There is a lot of talk about the danger and faithlessness that exist in the world. But let us never forget that every person has in *himself* the most dangerous traitor of all.

There are altogether too many individuals who live in fear of the one restless disturber that is nevertheless the true rest – eternity.

When a person struggles with the future, he learns that however strong he is otherwise, there is one enemy that is stronger – himself. There is one enemy he cannot conquer by himself, and that is himself.

When people or when a generation live merely for finite ends, life becomes a whirlpool, meaninglessness, and either a despairing arrogance or a despairing anguish. There must be weight – just as the clock or the clock's works need a heavy weight in order to run properly, and the ship needs ballast. Christianity furnishes this weight, this regulating weight, by making it every individual's life-meaning. Christianity puts eternity at stake. Into the middle of all these finite goals Christianity introduces weight, and this weight is intended to regulate temporal life, both its good days and its bad days. And because the weight has vanished – the clock cannot run, the ship steers wildly – human life is a whirlpool.

The result of human progress is that everything becomes thinner and thinner. The result of divine providence is to make everything deeper and more inward.

God created humankind in his own image, and in requital we created God in ours. A person's conception of God is essentially determined by the kind of person he is.

Deep within every human being lies the dread of being alone in the world, forgotten by God, overlooked among the tremendous household of millions upon millions. That fear is kept away by turning to those whom one feels bound to as friends or family; but the dread is nevertheless there and one hardly dares think of what would happen if all the rest were taken away.

Oh God, forgive me for seeking excitement and enjoyment in the allurements of the world which are never truly satisfying. If like the prodigal son, I have gone in search of the wonders of the transient world, forgive me, and receive me back again into your encircling arms of love.

Some birds take off quietly and neatly from the branch on which they are perching and ascend heavenward in their flight, proudly, boldly. Others, like crows, for example, make a big fuss when they are about to fly. They lift one foot and then promptly grab on again, and no flight takes place. In so many ways we are just like this when it comes to achieving movement from understanding to action. A few arrive at the proper understanding of what they should do – and then they hold back.

78 | The Individual

Every call from God is always addressed to one person, the single individual. Precisely in this lies the difficulty and the examination, that the one who is called must stand alone, walk alone, alone with God. Hence, everything that makes its appearance statistically is not from above. If anyone construes this as a call, you can be sure it is from below.

"The single individual" – with this category the cause of Christ stands or falls.

When the individual relates himself to God through the race, through an abstraction, through a third party, Christianity is abolished. And when this happens, the God-man becomes a phantom instead of our example.

Christianity does not join people together. No, it separates them – in order to unite every single individual with God. And when a person has become such that he can belong to God and to God alone, he has died away from that which usually joins people together.

It is impossible to be involved with God without enduring the weight of the pressure of being *I*. Yet thousands live on without having to become I, or they live on as truncated Is, truncated to the third person. They fill their lives with all sorts of things, imagine that they are really involved with God, flatter themselves that they have not ventured farther out because they are so humble. What confusion! The first condition for getting straightened out is to see that this notion about humility is complete rubbish, that one is dragging his feet only because of weakness, thin skin, and cowardice.

The spiritual differs from the religious in being able to endure isolation. The rank of a spiritual person is proportionate to his strength for enduring isolation, whereas we religious people are constantly in need of "the others," the herd. We religious folks die, or despair, if we are not reassured by being in the assembly, of the same opinion as the congregation, and so on. But the Christianity of the New Testament is precisely related to the isolation of the spiritual man.

Every person shrinks from becoming personality, from standing face to face with the others as a personality. We shrink from this because we know that others will take aim at us. We shrink from being revealed. Therefore we live, if not in utter darkness then in the twilight, in hoaxes, in the impersonal. But Christianity, which knows the truth, knows that life means: revelation.

A person's salvation lies precisely in his becoming a person. Why? Because he is so illuminated that he cannot hide from himself – yes, illuminated as if he were transparent. The municipality is already of the opinion that gas-illumination at night helps to prevent crime because light frightens crime away. Consider, then, the piercing illumination of being personality – light everywhere!

Nowadays, one does not become an author through his originality, but by reading. Similarly, one now becomes a human being by aping others. We no longer seem to know, within ourselves, what it means to be human. Rather, through an inference we conclude: we are like the others – therefore we are human. Only God knows whether any one of us is that!

In the animal world "the individual" is always less important than the race. But precisely because we are each created in the image of God the individual is above the race. Of course, this can be wrongly understood and terribly misused. But that is Christianity. And that is where the battle must be fought.

Christianity wants to grant the single individual eternal happiness, a good that is not distributed in bulk but only to one, and to one at a time.

In eternity there is no common plight. In eternity, the individual, yes, you, my listener, and I as individuals will each be asked solely about himself.

God desires to have *I's,* for God desires to be loved.

There are people who handle the ideas they pick up from others so frivolously and disgracefully that they ought to be prosecuted for illegal exchange in lost and found property.

Who is the authentic individual? One whose life, in the fruit of long silence, gains character and whose actions acquire the power to excite and arouse.

It seems to be forgotten that the distinctions of earthly existence are only like an actor's costume or like a travelling cloak. Every individual should therefore watchfully and carefully keep the fastening cords of this outer garment loosely tied, never in tight knots, so that in the moment of transformation the garment can easily be cast off. We all have enough knowledge of theater to be offended at an actor who, when he is supposed to cast off his disguise in the moment of transfiguration, runs out on the stage before getting the chords loose. Alas, in actual life one laces the outer garment of distinction so tightly that the inner glory of equality never, or very rarely, shines through, something it should do and ought to do constantly.

If one would describe the confusion of the modern age, I know of no more descriptive word than: it is dishonest. Young people, even children, are aware of how fraudulent everything is and how everything depends on clinging to their generation, following the inconstant demands of the age. Thus the life of each generation hisses and fizzes uninterruptedly. Although everything is a whirlwind, a signal-shot is heard, the ringing of the bells, signifying to the individual that now, this very second, hurry, throw everything away – reflection, quiet meditation, reassuring thoughts of the eternal – because if you come too late you will not get to go along on the generation's next whirling expedition, which is just pulling out – and then, then, how terrible! Ah, yes, how terrible!

Everything, absolutely everything is calculated to nourish this confusion, the unholy taste of this wild hunt. The means of communication become more and more excellent, but the communications become more and more hurried and more and more confusing. And if anyone dares, either in the name of originality or of God, to resist it – woe unto him! Just as the individual is seized by the whirlwind of impatience to be understood immediately, so this generation domineeringly craves to understand the individual at once.

79 | Inwardness and Subjectivity

The prophet Nathan told David a story. But as happens when it is only a matter of history or doctrine and so forth, David listened quite calmly. But then the prophet gave the story another turn and said: You are the man! This made it personal. Christianity is not the objective; it is just the opposite, the subjective.

The movement that leads Christianity back to Christ is a movement of inwardness. It is as if a lawyer came to an estate and in a certain sense found everything entirely in order – except that the occupants had got the idea that the property belonged to them and not to the benevolent owner.

To believe is not an indifferent relation to something that is true. It is an infinitely decisive relationship. The accent always falls upon the relationship.

All understanding fundamentally depends upon how one is disposed toward something. If a misfortune happens when you are really trusting and full of faith – well, even if it were utterly disastrous – if you are trusting and full of faith, you can accept it in the context of joy. God is letting something happen to you simply because now you have the strength to bear it, now you can use the occasion to learn to know yourself in surmounting it. If you are despondent, broken-hearted, melancholy, then the most insignificant matter is enough to make you suspect of bad luck, the law of fatality, in what happens. Therefore, your whole view of life actually is a confession of the state of your inner being.

Like is understood only by like, whatever is known is known in the mode of the knower. If Christianity is essentially something objective, it behooves the observer to be objective. But if Christianity is essentially subjectivity, it is a mistake if the observer is objective or speculative. Since Christianity requires an infinite interest in the individual subject, it is easy to see that the speculative thinker cannot possibly find what he is seeking.

Whereas objective thinking is indifferent to the thinking subject and his existence, the subjective thinker is essentially interested in his own thinking, is existing in it. Whereas objective thinking invests everything in the result and assists all humankind to cheat by copying and reeling off the results and answers, subjective thinking invests everything in the process of becoming and omits the result. The subjective thinker is continually in the process of becoming. The objective thinker has already arrived.

The subjective thinker is continually striving, is always in the process of becoming. How far the subjective thinker might be along that road, whether a long way or a short, makes no essential difference (it is, after all, just a finitely relative comparison); as long as he is existing, he is in the process of becoming.

Imagine a heavenly body, in the process of constituting itself. It would not first of all determine how great its surface was to be and which other body it was to move. It would first allow the centripetal and centrifugal forces to harmonize its existence, and then let the rest take its course. Similarly, it is useless for a person to constitute himself by first determining the outside and afterwards the fundamentals. One must know oneself before knowing anything else. It is only after a person has thus understood himself inwardly, and has thus seen his way, that life acquires peace and significance.

The solid, sensible thinker goes about Christianity this way: "Just let there be clarity and certainty about the truth of Christianity and I will surely accept it." The trouble, however, is that the truth of Christianity has something in common with the nettle: the solid, sensible thinker only stings himself when he wants to grasp it this way. In fact, he does not grasp it at all; he grasps its objective truth so objectively that he himself remains outside.

Let us take an analogy. Take a married couple. See, their marriage clearly leaves its mark in the external world; it constitutes a phenomenon in existence (on a smaller scale, just as Christianity has left its mark on all of life). But their married love is not a historical phenomenon. The external by itself is insignificant. It has significance to the married couple only through their love. The same is true for Christianity. Is that so original?

The various states of a person's soul ought to be like the letters listed in a dictionary – some are very strongly and copiously developed, others have but a few words listed under them – but the soul itself ought to have a full and complete alphabet.

Philosophy is life's dry nurse who can take care of us – but not suckle us.

Though the system were politely to assign me a guest room in the loft, in order that I might be included, I still prefer to be a thinker who is like a bird on a twig.

80 | Love

The more superior one person is to another whom he loves, the more he will feel tempted, humanly speaking, to draw the other up to himself. Divinely speaking, however, the more he will feel moved to come down to him. This is the logic of love. Strange that people have not seen this in Christianity.

By this we can see that love has overcome the world – that it repays evil with good.

It is still the greatest, the roomiest part of the world, although spatially the smallest, this kingdom of love in which we can all be landholders without the need of one person's property crowding another's. Yes, rather it extends another's holdings. On the other hand, in the kingdom of anger and hate – how small it is in its egotistic isolation and how great the space it demands – the whole world is not spacious enough; this kingdom has no room for others.

You talk about wanting to find comfort in Christ. All right, then try this: at the very moment you yourself are suffering most of all, simply think about comforting others, for this is what he did. The task is not to seek consolation – but to be consolation.

People despair about being lonely and therefore get married. But is this love? I should say it is self-love.

"He who sees his brother in need, yet shuts his heart" – yes, at the same time he shuts God out. Love to God and love to neighbor are like two doors that open simultaneously. It is impossible to open the one without opening the other, and impossible to shut the one without also shutting the other.

The distinguishing characteristic of Christian love is that it contains this apparent contradiction – that to love is duty. And yet it is only this kind of love that discovers the neighbor.

The love that has undergone the transformation of the eternal by becoming duty has won continuity; it is sterling silver.

To be busy, to be divided and scattered, to occupy yourself is far from love. Christian love is whole and collected in its every expression, and yet it is sheer action. Consequently it is just as far from inaction as it is from busyness. It never becomes engrossed in anything beforehand and never gives a promise in place of action. It never draws satisfaction from imagining that it has finished, nor does it ever loiter delighting in itself. It is no secret, private mysterious feeling behind the lattice of the inexplicable, which the poet wants to lure to the window, nor a soul-mood which fondly knows no laws, wants to know none, or wants to have its own law and hearkens only to singing. It is pure action and its every deed is holy, for it is the fulfilling of the law.

Justice avenges itself – love is avenged.

When a fisherman has caught a fish in his net and wishes to keep it alive, what must he do? He must immediately put it in water; otherwise it becomes exhausted and dies after a time. And why must he put it in water? Because water is the fish's element, and everything that is kept alive must be kept in its element. And what about love? Love's element is infinitude, inexhaustibility, immeasurability. If you wish to keep your love, you must take care that it remains in its element. Otherwise, it droops and dies – not after a time, but at once, which itself is a sign of its perfection, that it can live only in its element – the infinite.

When sin in a person is encompassed by love, sin is out of its element. It is like a besieged city with all communications cut off. True, sin may use love as an occasion (for what can't a corrupt person use for corruption!). The sinner can become embittered by love, and rage against it. Yet, in the long run sin cannot hold out against love.

What can take love out of its element? As soon as love concentrates upon itself, as soon as it is an object for itself. Imagine an arrow flying. Imagine that for a second it got a notion of wanting to concentrate on itself, perhaps to see how far it had come, or how high over the earth it skimmed, or how its course was related to that of another arrow. In that very moment the arrow would fall to the earth.

When an artist devises a plan, a sketch of a work, however exact the sketch is, there is always something indeterminate. Only when the work is finished is there definition. Similarly, the law is a sketch; love the fulfillment and complete definition. In love the law is completely defined. There is only one power that can complete the work for which the law is a sketch – that is love. Yet the law and love, just like the sketch and the work, are by one and the same artist, are of one and the same origin. They do not quarrel with each other.

Justice separates and divides; it determines what each one has the right to call his own. Justice judges and punishes anyone who refuses to recognize the distinction between mine and yours. But at times, change intrudes, a revolution, a war, an earthquake, or some such terrible misfortune, and all is disturbed. Justice seeks in vain to protect each one's own; it cannot hold the scales amid confusion. Therefore it throws the scales away – it despairs!

What a terrifying spectacle! And yet, in a certain sense does not love bring about the same confusion, even though in a most life-infusing way? Love is a change, the most remarkable of all. Love is a revolution, the most profound of all but the most blessed! With love, too, there comes confusion. But in this life-giving confusion there is no distinction between mine and yours. Remarkable! There are a *you* and an *I* and yet no *mine* and *yours!* For without you and I there is no love, and with mine and yours there is no love.

This is why love is the fundamental revolution. The deeper the revolution, the more the distinction between mine and yours disappears, and the more perfect is the love. Love's perfection consists essentially in the depth of the revolution. The

deeper the revolution is, the more justice shudders; the deeper
the revolution is, the more perfect is the love.

Love is perhaps best described as an infinite debt: when a person is gripped by love, he feels like he is in infinite debt. Usually
one says that the person who receives love comes into debt by
being loved. Similarly we say that children are in love's debt to
their parents, because their parents have loved them first and
the children's love is only a part-payment on the debt or a re-
payment. This is true, to be sure. Nevertheless, such talk is all
too reminiscent of a bookkeeping relationship – a bill is submitted and it must be paid; love is shown to us, and it must be
repaid with love.

We should not, then, speak about one's coming into debt by
receiving love. No, it is the one who loves who is in debt. Because he is aware of being gripped by love, he perceives this as
being in infinite debt. Remarkable! To be sure, by giving money
one does not come into debt; it is rather the recipient who becomes indebted. But when love gives, the one who loves comes
into infinite debt. What a beautiful, holy modesty love takes
along as a companion!

Consider creation for a moment. With what infinite love God
surrounds the great variety which has life and being! Remember the beauty of the fields! There is no, not any, discrimination
in love – yet what a variety among the flowers! Even the slightest, most insignificant, the most plain-looking, the poor little
flower overlooked even by its closest neighbors, the one you can
hardly find without looking carefully, it is as if this, too, had
said to love: let me be something with its own distinctive, indi-

vidual characteristic, but far more beautiful than what the poor little flower had ever dared hope for. What love! First of all, love makes no distinction. Second, which is like the first, it makes infinite distinctions in loving the differences. Wondrous love!

Perfect love is to love the one who made you unhappy.

Unhappiness is not to love without being loved, but to be loved when one does not love.

Suppose that the victim, whom the merciful Samaritan took care of, died in his hands. Then suppose the Samaritan had to report it to the police, and the police had said: Of course we must keep you under arrest for the time being. What then? His contemporaries would have laughed at him for being so stupid as to let himself get into such a scrape. They would think he was crazy. Behold, these are the wages of mercy.

The true consoler is one who suffers and for whom it becomes a consolation to comfort another who is suffering.

Oh our Loving Father, help us remember that it is not where we breathe, but where we love, that we live.

If we were honest, many of us would want to upbraid Christ for putting a man like Judas in charge of the bag. Was it not "irresponsible" of him, seeing Judas had a tendency to pilfering? But we should rather say, "What faith and love on Christ's part!" For

the best means of saving such a man as Judas is to show unconditional confidence in him. If that does not help him, then what
will?

What is it that makes a person unwavering, more unwavering
than a rock; what is it that makes him soft, softer than wax? It
is love. What is it that cannot be taken but itself takes all? It is
love. What is it that cannot be given but itself gives all? It is love.
What is it that remains when everything falls away? It is love.
What is it that does not cease when the vision ends? It is love.
What is it that sheds light when the dark saying ends? It is love.
What is it that gives blessing to the abundance of the gift? It is
love. What is it that makes the widow's gift an abundance? It is
love. What is it that turns the words of the simple person into
wisdom? It is love. What is it that is never changed even though
everything is changed? It is love; and that alone is love, that
which never becomes something else.

81 | Obedience

When it comes to doing what we know to be God's will, we do not dare to say: I will not! So we say: I cannot. Is this any less rebellious? If it is God's will that you do it, how is it possible that you cannot?

Today's Christianity is a matter of being elevated for an hour once a week just as in the theater. It is now used to hearing everything without having the remotest notion of doing something.

It is a very simple matter. Pick up the New Testament; read it. Can you deny, do you dare deny, that what you read there about forsaking everything, about giving up the world, being mocked and spit upon as your Lord and master was – can you deny, do you dare deny, that this is very easy to understand, indescribably easy, that you do not need a commentary or a single other person in order to understand it? But you say, "Before I do this, however, before I risk such a decisive step, I must first consult with others." Insolent, disobedient one, you are cheeky! You cheat; all you are looking for is a way out, an excuse. For God's sake, spare yourself.

What would a father think if his son, instead of immediately obeying a command that was easy enough to understand, first of all consulted with – another boy – as to whether he should do his father's will or not. Would the father not say: The very fact that you have the nerve to talk to a single one of your comrades about whether or not you should do what I have commanded, that alone is guilt enough to deserve every punishment. What is the meaning of consulting with the other boys – you certainly can come to me.

To leave out the strenuous passages in the New Testament is now the method. We hush them up and then we arrange things on easier and cheaper terms. I think it is better to take them along, to acknowledge that these demands are found in the New Testament – and then make confession of our own weakness.

Of every word Christ spoke pointing toward the cost and suffering of being a Christian, we say this: This does not apply to us; this was spoken expressly to the disciples. We make good, however, of every word of consolation, of every promise; whether Christ spoke to the apostles or not makes no difference.

The question is never one of understanding, comprehending; it is a matter of doing what one understands, and the thing that a person actually ought to do is always easy to understand.

Do what you can for God, and God will do for you what you cannot do. And remember, the only thing is to give yourself completely, your weakness also, for obedience is dearer to God than the fat of rams.

If I follow my orders and things go wrong as a consequence of that, then it is a part of providence. Perhaps it will come to have meaning, although I do not understand it. Suppose Stephen by his death achieved nothing else than to influence Paul – did he achieve nothing? And how often is it not the case that the downfall of the courageous becomes itself an awakening. But the fact is, we want to play providence ourselves.

Oh God, teach me so deeply to understand myself that I may understand how utterly impossible it is to be satisfied with the mere fact that I am master of my own destiny, and that there is no satisfaction and joy and happiness for a person except in obedience.

82 | Passion

To be a true Christian is so agonizing that it would not be endurable if one did not continually need Christ's second coming and expect it as imminent. It is wonderful that in the Danish language the word nourishment is related to near. To the degree that the need is greater, the nourishment is nearer; the nourishment is in the need, and even if it is not the need, it still is the nearest.

Longing is the umbilical cord of the higher life.

How fearfully true are Christianity's metaphors. To cast fire upon the earth. Yes, for what is a Christian? A Christian is a person who is caught on fire.

Spirit is fire, Christianity is fire-setting. And by nature we shrink more from this fire than from any other. The fire Christianity wants to light is not intended to burn up a few houses but to burn up the *human* zest for life – burn it out into spirit. Spirit is fire. From this comes the frequent expression: As gold is purified in fire, so the Christian is purified. But spirit-fire must not be regarded merely as the fire of "tribulations" – that is, something coming from the outside. No, a fire is kindled within the Christian, in this burning comes the purification.

It is incendiarism, this is how Christ himself describes his commission, setting fire to individuals by introducing a passion that makes them at odds with what is naturally understood, an incendiarism that must necessarily cause discord between father and son, daughter and mother, an incendiarism that tears apart "the generations" in order to reach "the individual."

It is not always water that is used to put out a fire. To keep the metaphor, sometimes one uses, for example, featherbeds, blankets, mattresses, and the like to smother a fire. In this sense, if you want Christianity again, fire again, then do all you can to get rid of the featherbeds, blankets, and mattresses, the grossly bulky stuff – and there will be fire.

It is a great question whether those whom God cannot make mad have ever really existed for God.

Authentic religion has to do with passion, with having passion. Sadly, there are thousands who take a little something out of religion, and then dispassionately "have religion."

Herein lies the difficulty with today's religion. It is like trying to push a boat off a shoal where the ground on all sides is a quaking bog, so that when the pole is thrust down it gives way and offers no resistance.

Imagine a jewel that every one desired to possess. It lay far out on a frozen lake where the ice was very thin, watched over by the danger of death, while closer in, the ice was perfectly safe. In a passionate age people would applaud the courage of the one who ventured out, they would tremble for him and with him in the danger of his decisive action, they would grieve over him if he were drowned, they would make a god of him if he secured the prize. But in an age without passion, in a "reasonable" age, it would be otherwise. People would think it was foolish and not even worthwhile to venture so far out. And in this way they would transform daring and enthusiasm into a feat of skill. How so?

The crowds would go out to watch from a safe place, and with the eyes of connoisseurs judge the skater who could skate almost to the very edge (that is, as far as the ice was still safe and the danger had not yet begun) and then turn back. The most accomplished skater would manage to go out to the furthermost point and then perform a still more dangerous-looking run, so as to make the spectators hold their breath and say: "Ye gods! How mad; he is risking his life." But look, and you will see that his skill was so astonishing that he managed to turn back just in time, while the ice was perfectly safe and there was still no danger. As at the theater, the crowd would applaud and acclaim him, surge homeward with the heroic artist in their midst, to honor him with a magnificent banquet. For intelligence has got the upper hand to such an extent that it transforms the real task into an unreal trick and reality into a play.

During the banquet admiration would reach its height. Now the proper relation between the admirer and the object of admiration is one in which the admirer is edified by the thought that he is a man like the hero, humbled by the thought that he is incapable of such great actions, yet morally encouraged to emulate him according to his powers; but where intelligence has got the upper hand the character of admiration is completely altered. Even at the height of the banquet, when the applause was loudest, the admiring guests would all have a shrewd notion that the action of the man who received all the honor was not really so extraordinary and that only by chance was the gathering for him, since after all, with a little practice, every one could have done as much. Briefly, instead of being strengthened in their discernment and encouraged to do good, the guests would more probably go home with an even stronger predisposition to the most dangerous, if also the most respectable, of all diseases: to admire in public what is considered unimportant in private – since everything is made into a joke. And so, stimulated by a gush of admiration, they are all comfortably agreed that they might just as well admire themselves.

Our age is without passion. Everyone knows a great deal, we all know which way we ought to go and all the different ways we can go, but nobody is really willing to move.

The ludicrous aspect of a zealot is that his infinite passion thrusts itself upon the wrong object. The divine aspect of him, however, is that he dares with passion.

If I could only have the experience of meeting a passionate thinker, that is, someone who honestly and honorably expressed in his life what he has understood!

Existing, if this is not to be understood as just any sort of existing, cannot be done without passion. I have often thought about how one might bring a person into passion. So I have considered the possibility of getting him astride a horse and then frightening the horse into the wildest gallop. I think this would be successful. And this is what existing is like if one is to be truly conscious of it and is, if existing is not to be what people usually call existing. Merely existing is like a drunken peasant who lies in the wagon and sleeps and lets the horses shift for themselves. But true existence has to do with the one who drives.

All existence-issues are passionate. To think about them so as to leave out passion is not to think about them at all. It is to forget the point that one indeed is oneself an existing person. To exist is an art. The subjective thinker is esthetic enough for his life to have esthetic content, ethical enough to regulate it, passionate enough in thinking to master it.

Life's earnestness does not consist in the pressure of busyness, but in the will to be, the will to express the eternal in the dailyness of actuality, to will it so that one does not busily abandon it or conceitedly take it in vain as a dream.

However much one generation learns from another, it can never learn from its predecessor the genuinely human factor. In this respect every generation begins afresh. The authentically human factor is passion. But no generation can learn from another how to love, no generation can begin other than at the beginning.

The highest passion in a human being is faith, and here, again, no generation begins other than where its predecessor did. Every generation begins from the beginning, and the succeeding generation comes no further than the previous, provided the latter was true to its task and didn't betray it. Therefore, no generation has the right to say that its task is wearisome, for each generation has its own task.

The first Christians thought that by properly living this life it was possible for one to become an angel and thus step into the place of a fallen angel. Alas, no one knew the number of these fallen angels; admittedly it was not large. But they could not agree on the extent to which God would raise the number in proportion to the original plan. But that it consequently still was possible to become an angel, that this life properly lived was tied to this eternal decision: yes, this was the Christian's deepest concern, this was his highest passion. Therefore the first Christians were willing to renounce everything, willing to suffer everything, willing to be sacrificed. Therefore every minute was infinitely important, and the believer called himself to account for his every deed, for every word he spoke, every thought in his mind, and every look on his countenance. He dared not become guilty of missing the highest passion.

Now we live in such a way, that no one thinks of doing the least bit, the very least, about relating oneself with passion to the decision to become an angel. Becoming an angel appears ridiculous to us now. If anyone were to declare seriously that he was trying to become an angel, we would all laugh. We would scarcely find it as ridiculous if someone assumed that after death one becomes a camel. How far we have come that the highest passion has become the funniest joke.

To be made well with the aid of Christianity is not the difficulty; the difficulty is in becoming sick to some purpose.

It is spirit, it is of passion to ask: Is what is being said possible? Am I able to do it? But it is lack of spirit to ask: Did it actually happen? Has my neighbor actually done it?"

Our God, we are aware that life upon this planet comes to an end for each of us. No one knows the exact hour or day. Moment by moment we come closer to the last breath. May we make each day count as though it were our last. If we have wasted days and weeks, forgive us. Let us have a sense of tremendous urgency to live today with Christian richness so that we can make up for squandered time. We remember him who in thirty precious years lived as though he was abiding eternally in time. In his name we pray.

The person who is neither cold nor hot is an abomination, to God. God is no more served by dud individualities than a marksman is served by a rifle that, in the moment of decision, clicks instead of firing.

83 | Politics and the State

Imagine this. Suppose that a coachman sees an absolutely remarkable and utterly faultless five-year-old horse, an ideal horse, snorting and as full of vigor as any he has seen, and he says: "Well, I cannot bid on this horse, nor can I afford it, and even if I could it is quite unsuitable for my use." But after a dozen years, when that remarkable horse is spavined and spoiled etc., the coachman says, "Now I can bid on it, now I can pay for it, and now I can make enough use of it, from what is left in it, so that I can properly see my way to spending a little for its upkeep."

It is the same with the state and Christianity. Of the radical Christianity which entered into the world, every state is obliged to say, "I cannot buy this religion; not only that, but I will say: God and Father, save us from buying this religion. It would surely be to our ruin." But when after a few centuries Christianity had become spavined and decrepit and on its last legs, spoiled and muddle-headed, then the State said, "See, now I can bid on it; and smart as I am I can see very well that I can use it and profit from it enough so that I can properly see my way to spending a little to polish it up."

That the goal of the state is to improve its citizens – is obviously nonsense. The state is of the evil rather than of the good, a necessary evil, in a certain sense a useful, expedient evil, but not a good. The state is actually human egotism in great dimensions. Just as we speak of a calculation of infinitesimals, so also the state is a calculation of egotisms, but always in such a way that it egotistically appears to be the most prudent thing to enter into and to be in this higher egotism. But this, after all, is anything but the moral abandoning of egotism.

To be improved by living in the state is just as doubtful as being improved in a prison. Perhaps one becomes much shrewder about his egotism, his enlightened egotism, that is, his egotism in relation to other egotisms, but less egotistic he does not become, and what is worse, one is spoiled by regarding this official, civic, authorized egotism as virtue – this, in fact, is how demoralizing civic life is, because it reassures one in being a shrewd egotist.

The state is continually subject to the same sophistry that engrossed the Greek Sophists – namely, that injustice on a vast scale is justice. Yes, politics is nothing but egotism dressed up as justice.

For so many, the state is counted on to develop people morally, to be the proper medium for virtue, the place where one really can become virtuous! But to believe this is like believing that the best place for a watchmaker or an engraver to work is aboard a ship in a heavy sea. Christianity does not believe that the Christian is to remain in the body politic for the purpose of moral improvement – no, in fact it tells him in advance that it will mean suffering.

As soon as the thought of human assistance arises, of not refusing the help of the world, all is essentially lost. The faith in martyrdom as having value in and by itself is thereby abandoned, and Christianity runs downhill until, just as the Rhine ends in mud, it ends in the mud of politics.

On their part the clergy think it very prudent to accept the protection of the state. They understand, all right, that it is considerably more pleasant to be a hired servant of the state than to serve Christianity according to New Testament. But this prudence is not only short-sighted, it is blasphemy.

What Christianity needs is not the suffocating protection of the state; no, it needs fresh air, it needs persecution, and it needs God's protection. The state only works disaster, it wards off persecution and thus is not the medium through which God's protection can be conducted. Above all, save Christianity from the state. By its protection it smothers it to death.

The state thinks it prudent to accommodate Christ's teaching in order to tranquilize people and thus be better able to control them. The state never accommodates Christianity in its truth (as salt in character); it rather has it up to a point, which we "Christians" are also happy to have.

Christianity came into the world through its desire to suffer to the death for the faith; precisely for this reason it was victorious over the world. Its urge to martyrdom was partially marked by its "suffering" intolerance. Now it has lost the desire and the need to suffer, lost martyrdom's acceptance of intolerance, and is well satisfied with being a religion just like any other religion.

Christianity detests the intolerance that wants to put others to death because of their faith. But to be personally willing to be put to death for one's faith – well, let us not overlook this – it, too, is intolerance, it is suffering's acceptance of intolerance. Modern religion is indifferentism and thus does not so much express that Christianity has abandoned the world as that Christianity has abandoned itself, or, more correctly, that Christendom has abandoned Christianity.

84 | Prayer

The earthly minded person thinks and imagines that when he prays, the important thing, the thing he must concentrate upon, is that God should hear what he is praying for. And yet in the true, eternal sense it is just the reverse: the true relation in prayer is not when God hears what is prayed for, but when the person praying continues to pray until he is the one who hears, who hears what God is asking for.

Prayer does not change God, it changes the one who offers it.

Always remember that the task is toward being able to hold fast to the thought of God more and more for a longer time, not the way a dreamer does, idling and flirting, but by clinging to it within your work. God is pure act. A mere dreamy loitering over the thought of him is not true prayer.

If a person does not yield himself completely in prayer, he is not praying, even if he were to stay down on his knees day and night. It is the same here as with a person who is maintaining a connection with a distant friend. If he does not see to it that the letter is addressed properly, it will not be delivered and the connection will not be made, no matter how many letters he writes.

Similarly, let the one who prays see to it that the prayer is proper, a yielding of himself in the inner being, because otherwise he is not praying to God. And let the one who prays be scrupulously attentive to this, since no deception is possible here in relation to the searcher of hearts.

I have often wondered when I thanked God for something whether it was motivated by fear of losing it, or whether my prayer came out of the deep assurance that had conquered the world.

The Apostle Paul says: "Everything created by God is good if it is received with thankfulness." He also says: "Every good and every perfect gift is from above and comes down from the Father of lights." Are these dark and difficult sayings? If you think that you cannot understand these words, have you truly wanted to understand them?

When you have doubts about what comes from God or about what is a good and a perfect gift, do you risk the venture? And when the light sparkle of joy calls you, do you thank God for it? And when you are so strong that you feel you need no help, do you then thank God? And when your allotted portion is little, do you thank God? And when your allotted portion is suffering, do you thank God? And when people wrong you and mistreat you, do you thank God?

We are not saying that in our thankfulness wrong ceases to be wrong – what would be the use of such destructive and foolish talk! It is up to you to decide whether it is wrong; but do you take the wrong and abuse to God and by your thanksgiving receive it from his hand as a good and a perfect gift? Do you do that? Well, then you have worthily understood the Apostle's words. Yes, it is wonderful that a person prays, and many a promise is given to the one who prays without ceasing, but it is more blessed still always to give thanks.

The great actor Seydelmann, on the night he was crowned with a wreath in the opera house "to applause that lasted several minutes," went home and very fervently thanked God for it. Might not the very fervency of his giving thanks show, however, that he did not really thank God? Would not his giving his fervent thanks when booed instead of praised have shown better the sincerity of his thankfulness to God?

Life very much depends upon being alert to catch one's cue.

The important thing is to be honest towards God, until he himself gives the explanation; which, whether it is the one you want or not, is always the best.

Father in heaven, to whom belong boundless wisdom and deepest compassion, you understand us, our going out and our coming in; you know what is in man. But you desire that we understand you. Even as our Master answered not a word to his haughty accusers, thus exposing their fraudulent deceit and revealing his own innocence, so you speak in love and understanding when you speak not a word! For one is speaking when he remains silent in order to show the listener that he is beloved. One is speaking when, as teacher, he listens to the pupil. One is speaking when he demonstrates that profound understanding comes from listening. We may fear that we are lost in the desert of abandonment when we do not hear your voice. But it is only the golden moment of stillness in the intimacy of conversation and communion. When we come imploring, pleading, promising, even threatening, and you greet us with barely a word, you understand us completely, and you speak by answering our needs. Bless, then, the golden moment of silence, for the same paternal love is ours when you are silent as well as when you speak!

It is unbelievable what a person of prayer can achieve if he would but close the doors behind him.

He who prays knows how to make distinctions. Little by little he gives up what is less important, since he does not really dare to come before God with it, demanding this and that. On the contrary, he wants to give all the more emphasis to the request for his one and only wish. Then before God he concentrates his soul on the one wish, and this already has something ennobling about it, is preparation for giving up everything, because only he can give up everything who has but one single wish.

In proportion as one becomes more and more earnest in prayer, one has less and less to say, and in the end one becomes quite silent. Indeed, one becomes quite a hearer. And so it is; to pray is not to hear oneself speak, but it is to be silent, and to remain silent, to wait, until the one who prays hears God.

To pray is a task for the whole soul.

Even if prayer does not accomplish anything here on earth, it nevertheless works in heaven.

Father in heaven! You hold all the good gifts in your gentle hand. Give everyone his allotted share as it is well pleasing to you. And give everyone the assurance that everything comes from you, so that joy will not tear us away from you in the forgetfulness of pleasure, so that sorrow will not separate you from us, but in joy we may go to you and in sorrow remain with you. And when our days are numbered and our outer being is wasted away, grant that death may not come in its own name, cold and terrible, but gentle and friendly, with greetings and news, with witness from you, our heavenly Father!

God possesses all good gifts, and his bounty is greater than human understanding can grasp. This is our comfort, because God answers every prayer; for either he gives what we pray for, or something far better.

85 | Preaching and Proclamation

It is absolutely unethical when one is so busy communicating that he forgets to be what he teaches.

All genuine instruction ends in a kind of silence; for when I live it, it is no longer necessary for my speaking to be audible.

On Sunday it is taught that Christ is everyone's example – and if anyone on Monday were to talk about Christ as his example, people would call this presumption, terrible arrogance, and so on. Consequently, most preaching is nothing more than Sunday jargon.

Christianity cannot be proclaimed by talking – but by acting. Nothing is more dangerous than to have a bunch of high-flying feelings and exalted resolutions go off in the direction of merely eloquent speaking. The whole thing then becomes an intoxication, and the deception is that it becomes a glowing mood and that they say, "He is so sincere!" – alas, yes, in the sense of the mood of the moment.

Preaching by means of action is more like a fast, and therefore the audience does not flock to it. Such preaching is almost boring, and what is boring is that it promptly makes an issue of doing something about it.

It is existence which preaches, not the mouth. What my existing says is my sermon.

If it is assumed that speaking is sufficient for the proclamation of Christianity, then we have transformed the church into a theater. We can then have an actor learn a sermon and splendidly, masterfully deliver it with facial expressions, gesticulations, modulation, tears, and everything a theater-going public might flock to.

The reason why preachers are so eager to preach in a chock-full church is that if they were to say what they have to say in an empty room they would become anxious and afraid, for they would notice that it pertains to themselves.

To preach from the pulpit means to bring charges against oneself.

A speech expert is just as suitable for proclaiming Christianity as a deaf-mute for being a musician.

I wish to discuss proclaiming Christianity without tying a knot in the thread. Suppose that a speaker preaches on the Christian theme of self-denial, renunciation of the world. Superbly, incomparably! He charms, enthralls, sweeps his audience off its feet in a matchless way. A rich man is in the audience; deeply, deeply stirred, really profoundly moved, he goes home and says to his wife: It was absolutely amazing, and I want to show my gratitude by giving the preacher a present – a very expensive fruitbowl. Likewise another deeply moved rich man digs deep, deep into his pocket and gives a gold snuffbox, and the preacher accepts them, gives courteous thanks so as not to offend. This is how one sews without tying a knot in the thread, and this is how the whole mess comes about.

Genuine Christianity holds that "the sermon" comes on Monday, when the preacher sends the gifts back and says: After all, I teach self-denial – ergo, I cannot accept such things; otherwise the next time I speak about self-denial I run the risk of being inspired by the prospect of an elegant carriage.

The person who is going to preach ought to live his Christian ideas in daily life. Then he, too, will have eloquence enough. He will have what is needed to speak extemporaneously without specific preparation. However, it is a fallacious eloquence if someone, without living his thoughts, once in a while sits down and laboriously collects such thoughts, and then works them into a well-composed sermon, which is then committed to memory and delivered superbly, with respect both to voice and diction and to gestures. No, just as in well-equipped houses one need not go downstairs to fetch water but has it up there on tap, under pressure – one merely turns on the faucet – so also is the authentic Christian speaker who, because the essentially Christian is his life, at every moment has eloquence present, immediately available, precisely the true eloquence.

You simple one, even though you are of all people most limited – if your life expresses the little you have understood, you speak more powerfully than all the eloquence of orators, if your life expresses what you hear, your eloquence is more powerful, more true, more persuasive than all the art of orators.

There is incessant preaching in Christendom about what happened after Christ's death, how he triumphed and how his teachings triumphantly conquered the whole world. In short, we hear nothing but sermons that could more appropriately end with "Hurrah" than with "Amen." No, Christ's life here on the earth is the Pattern; I and every Christian are to strive to model our lives in likeness to it, and this should be the primary subject of preaching.

As soon as I take Christianity as a doctrine and then apply my acumen or my profundity or my eloquence or my imagination to presenting it, people think it is fine and I am regarded as an earnest Christian, I am esteemed. As soon as I live out what I say, make it a reality – then it is exactly as if I had blown up the world. People are immediately scandalized.

Take the rich young man – let me preach about his not being perfect, that he could not bring himself to giving everything to the poor, but that the true Christian is always willing to give everything. Let me preach this way, and people are deeply moved and I am esteemed. But if I were a rich young man and went and gave all my possessions to the poor – then people would be scandalized. They would find it a ridiculous exaggeration. Take Mary Magdalene. Let me preach about her deep consciousness of sin, which goes out to the Savior, opening herself up to all kinds of ridicule. I concentrate on moving people to tears, and I the speaker (note – if preaching happens to be my job, for otherwise the affair would appear to be exaggerated) will be regarded as a committed Christian. I will be highly esteemed. If, however, I myself, conscious of being a sinner, if suddenly I actually step forward with a public confession of sin, offense would immediately arise, people will consider it vanity and ridiculous exaggeration. People will almost regard it as their duty to ridicule and laugh at me. They would certainly find every way to play it down.

It is a risk to preach, for as I stand up – whether the church is packed or as good as empty, whether I myself am aware of it or not – I have one listener more than can be seen, an invisible listener, God, whom I certainly cannot see but who truly can see me. This listener pays close attention to whether what I am saying is true, whether it is true in me, that is, he looks to see – and he can do that, because he is everywhere present – in a way that makes it impossible to be on one's guard against him. He looks to see whether my life expresses what I am saying. And although I do not have authority to commit anyone else, I commit myself to every word I say from the pulpit – and God hears. Truly it is a risk to preach!

If Christianity is to be preached in truth to those who are happy, to those who enjoy life, then Christianity is a kind of cruelty. This is why it is far easier to proclaim the consolation of Christianity – to cripples.

I have never heard a single preacher speak about prayer nor have I ever read a sermon by him about prayer without promising myself to demonstrate, as 2 plus 2 equals 4, that the preacher himself hardly ever makes the practice of praying. The preachers are like gymnastics coaches who cannot swim themselves and then instruct people in swimming, even standing on the dock and shouting: Just strike out briskly with your arms – as if one could not strike out all too briskly with his arms, something every swimmer knows.

The punishment I should like the clergy to have is a tenfold increase in salary. I am afraid that neither the world nor the clergy would understand this punishment.

If someone were to give up his position in order to proclaim Christianity gratis, people would revolt.

Order the preachers to keep quiet on Sunday. What is left? Well, then the essential thing is left: lives, the daily existence with which the pastor preaches. But seeing those, will you get the impression that it is Christianity that is being preached?

It is not so much that doctrine has been falsified, but the proclamation. It is like water that in the reservoir is pure but is infected in passing through contaminated pipes – like taking someone to the water reservoir and telling him: "You see, the water is pure," while actually it is contaminated by the medium. Whenever something can be shared only through a medium, the quality of the medium is almost as important as the quality of that which is communicated through the medium. This shows what a dubious thing it is to proclaim Christianity without ever practicing it.

The greatest possible error arises when we reduce the clergy to teachers. Imagine that the police, instead of acting, began to teach about thievery.

Today, if you would talk about preaching Christianity in poverty, affirming that this is the genuine Christian preaching and you literally are a poor devil – my dear fellow, this is no subject for you to talk about, the congregation might in fact believe that it was seriousness, become fearful, feel quite put out and in the highest degree uncomfortable at having poverty come so close to them. No, first procure a fat living, and then when you are about to be promoted to a still fatter one, that is the appropriate time, then you should appear before the congregation to preach and "witness," and you will completely satisfy them. For then your life will furnish guarantees that the whole thing turns out to be a jest, such as serious people might desire once in a while at the theater or in church, in order to gather new strength…to make money.

In the magnificent cathedral the honorable and Right Reverend Geheime-General-Ober-Hof-Pradikant, the elect favorite of the fashionable world, appears before an elect company and preaches with emotion upon the text he himself elected: "God has chosen the base things of this world, and the things that are despised" – and nobody laughs.

Pastor: You must die to the world – that will be ten dollars.

Novice: Well, if I must die to the world, renounce all the things of this world, I certainly understand that I will have to put out more than ten dollars for the sake of the cause, but there is just one question: Who gets the ten dollars?

Pastor: I do, of course; it is my wages. After all, I and my family have to make a living you know. It is a very cheap price, and very soon much more will have to be charged. If you are fair, you yourself will understand that it takes a lot out of a man to proclaim that one must die to the world if the proclamation is made with earnestness and zeal. And that is also why it is very necessary for me and my family to spend the summer in the country in order to recuperate.

The most fatal thing of all is to satisfy a want which is not yet felt, so that without waiting till the want is present, one anticipates it, likely also using stimulants to bring about something which is supposed to be a want, and then satisfies it. And this is shocking! And yet this is what so many clergy do, whereby they really are cheating people out of what constitutes the significance of life, and instead helping them to waste it.

Here is proof that the clergy are cannibals. As in the farmhouses at the slaughtering season provision for the winter is salted away, so the "minister" keeps in brine tubs the martyrs who suffered for the truth. In vain the deceased witness cries out, "Follow me, follow me!" "That's a good joke," replies the preacher, "No, keep your mouth shut and stay where you are. What nonsense to require that I, or anyone else, should follow you. I keep you alive precisely by eating you, and not I alone, but my wife and my children! To suppose that I should follow you, perhaps myself become a sacrifice – instead of making a living off you, or eating you, is ridiculous."

As a career man and job holder the pastor proclaims Christianity. He says: My job is to proclaim Christianity – I am hired simply to preach. And so it is with the pastor's proclamation. The congregation on the other hand excuses itself from doing what the sermon says by declaring: We have so many other things to take care of; such a stringent Christianity can be required only of the pastor, the man of God. And thus we arrive at the result: Christianity – but no Christians.

If the Sunday ordinance were to be strictly observed, the churches first and foremost ought to be locked up on Sunday. After all, being a pastor is a means of living and the church is the pastor's shop; why then, should the pastor be the only business-man permitted to stay open on Sunday?

86 | Purity

Sincerity is not a gift but a duty.

Purity of heart: it is a figure of speech that compares the heart to the sea, and why just to this? Simply for the reason that the depth of the sea determines its purity, and its purity determines its transparency. Since the sea is pure only when it is deep, and is transparent only when it is pure, as soon as it is impure it is no longer deep but only surface water, and as soon as it is only surface water it is not transparent. When, on the contrary, it is deeply and transparently pure, then it is all of one consistency, no matter how long one looks at it. Then its purity is this constancy in depth and transparency.

On this account we compare the heart with the sea, because the purity of the sea lies in its constancy of depth and transparency. No storm may perturb it. No sudden gust of wind may stir its surface, no drowsy fog may sprawl out over it. No doubtful movement may stir within it; no swift-moving cloud may darken it. Rather it must lie calm, transparent to its depths.

If you should see it so, and contemplate the purity of the sea, you would be drawn upwards. As the sea, when it lies calm and deeply transparent, yearns for heaven, so may the pure heart, when it is calm and deeply transparent, yearn for the Good. As the sea is made pure by yearning for heaven alone, so may the heart become pure by yearning only for the Good. As the sea mirrors the elevation of heaven in its pure depths, so may the heart when it is calm and deeply transparent mirror the divine elevation of the Good in its pure depths.

When the sea rages in the storm and the sky is hidden, when sea and sky blend as one in the turmoil, we do not say that the sea is pure, however terrifying this drama is. Not until they are distinguished in peace, when the sky arches high over the sea, which deeply reflects it, not until then do we say that it is pure. Purity is not in the blending-into-one of the raging storm but in the distinction.

In this way, we compare the soul with the sea. When in unity of confusion it arrogantly breaches the distinction between good and evil, it is riled and impure. But when the good, like the fortress of heaven arches high over the soul, which deeply reproduces this oneness, we say it is pure. Distinction between good and evil is purity. Confused unity is duplicity.

When a fog hangs over the sea, of what good is it that the heavens are high and bright; the sea is still not pure. Similarly there is a fog that hangs over willing the good; this fog is willing the good for the sake of reward. Reward never helps a person to will the good in truth.

He who is not himself a unity is never anything wholly and decisively; he only exists as a shell.

What means do you use in order to carry out your occupation? Are they as important to you as the end? If not it will be impossible for you to will only one thing. Eternally speaking, there is only one means and only one end: the means and the end are one and the same. There is only one end: the genuine Good; and only one means: to be willing only to use those means which are genuinely good. The good is precisely the end. One may think that the end is the main thing and that one need not be so particular about the means. Yet this is not so. To gain an end in this fashion is an unholy act of impatience.

Reaching the goal is like hitting the mark with one's shot. But using the means is like taking aim. And certainly the aim is a more reliable indication of the marksman's goal than the spot the shot strikes.

Father in heaven. What are we without you! What is all that we know, vast accumulation though it be, but a chipped fragment if we do not know you! What is all our striving but a half-finished work if we do not know you: the One, who are one thing and who are all! Therefore, give to the intellect, wisdom to comprehend that one thing; to the heart, sincerity to receive this one thing; to the will, purity that wills only one thing. In prosperity may you grant perseverance to will one thing; amid distractions, collectedness to will one thing; in suffering, patience to will one thing.

Oh, you who give both the beginning and the completion, may you early, at the dawn of day, give to the young the resolution to will one thing. As the day wanes, may you give to the old a renewed remembrance of his first resolution, that the first may be like the last, the last like the first, in possession of a life that has willed only one thing.

Take the story about the widow who placed two pennies in the temple-treasury. She had saved for a long time and then had hidden them wrapped in a little cloth in order to bring them when she herself went up to the temple. But a swindler had detected that she possessed this money, had tricked her out of it, and had exchanged the cloth for an identical piece which was utterly empty – something which the widow did not know. Thereupon she went up to the temple, placed, as she intended, the two pennies, that is, nothing, in the temple-treasury. I wonder, would Christ not still have said that "she gave more than all the rich?"

No matter how much all the earth's gold hidden in covetousness may amount to, it is infinitely less than the smallest mite hidden in the contentment of the poor!

When a book has become old and shabby, the binding separates and the pages fall out. Similarly in our time people are disintegrated; their understanding, their imaginations do not bind them in character.

We can flee evil either out of fear for punishment – like slaves, or out of hope for reward – like hirelings, or out of love of God – like children.

87 | Repentance

The fire of repentance and of the accusing conscience is like that Grecian fire which could not be put out with water – so, too, this one can be extinguished only with tears.

Repentance means to lament the sins one has committed and not to commit any more the sins one has lamented.

There is a Savior, not merely so that we can resort to him when we have sinned, receiving forgiveness, but precisely for the purpose of saving us from sinning.

That a person wants to sit and brood and stare at his sin and is unwilling to have faith that it is forgiven is itself a further guilt. It simply ignores what Christ has done.

That Christ makes something big out of something small, as at the feeding of the five thousand, is usually referred to as a miracle. But Christ also works a miracle inversely – makes something big (everything that wants to be something) into something little. He makes it infinitely nothing in humility.

God creates everything out of nothing – and all God is to use he first turns to nothing.

God in heaven, let me rightly feel my nothingness, not to despair over it, but all the more intensely to feel the greatness of your goodness.

God chooses and is closest to the despised, the castoffs of the race, the one single sorry abandoned wretch. He hates this business of the pyramid.

Our hearts often pay far greater toll to sin than do our words or deeds. They invite us to self-excusing. Thoughts invite us, more than words and deeds, to continue in sin; for thought can be concealed, while words and deeds cannot.

It is precisely our consciousness of sin that can lead us nearer to God. For there is hope of conquering the evil, if only, every time sin attacks us, it leads us nearer to God.

How shall God be able in heaven to dry up your tears when you have not yet wept?

To grumble about the world and its unhappiness is always easier than to beat one's breast and groan over oneself.

The all-knowing One does not get to know something about the one who needs confession, rather the one who confesses gets to know something about himself.

Be not afraid of the penitential preacher, who perhaps has terror in his appearance and wrath in his voice, who chides and rebukes and thunders. No, in the inmost depths of every man's heart there dwells his own preacher of repentance. When he has a chance to speak, he does not preach to others. He preaches before you alone. He does not preach in any church before an assembled multitude, he preaches in the secret chamber of the heart. He has nothing else whatever to attend to but to attend to you, and he takes good care to be heard when all around you is silence, when the stillness makes you lonely.

The remedy seems infinitely worse than the sickness. "But if your hand or your foot causes you to sin, cut it off" (Mt. 18:8–9).

Whoever is intent upon confession is as solitary as one who is dying.

Teach me, oh God, not to torture myself and not to make a martyr of myself in suffocating introspection, but to take deep and wholesome breaths of faith!

Oh infinite love, I do desire to be involved with you! If I make a mistake, oh, you who are love, strike me so that I get on the right path again.

Father in heaven, open the fountains of our eyes, let a torrent of tears like a flood obliterate all that which has not found favor in your eyes. But also give us a sign as of old, when you set the rainbow as a gateway of grace in the heavens, that you will no more wipe us out with a flood.

Father in heaven, let your face shine upon me, that I may walk in your ways and not stray more distantly from you, where your voice can no longer reach me. Oh, let your voice inspire faith and let me hear it, even if it overtakes me with its terrors upon my erring paths, where I live as one sick and tainted in spirit, apart and lonely, far from fellowship with you and with neighbor! Lord Jesus Christ, you who came into the world to save the lost – you who left the ninety and nine sheep to seek that one which was lost – seek me, lost as I am upon my erring paths. Good Shepherd, let me hear your voice, let me know it, let me follow it! Holy Spirit, come to me with groanings that cannot be uttered. Pray for me as Abraham did for Sodom, that if there be but one pure thought, one better feeling in me, the time of probation may be prolonged for the barren fig tree. And Holy Spirit, you who give birth to the dead and youth to the aged, renew me also; create in me a new heart.

I seek you alone, you the Omniscient. If I am guilty, enlighten my understanding that I may see my error and my depravity. I do not wish to escape suffering – that is not my prayer – but let me learn never to argue with you. I must conquer, even though the manner of it is infinitely different from what I can imagine.

88 | Sacrifice and Self-Denial

Is a loss a sacrifice? What nonsense! To sacrifice means voluntarily to bring a loss upon oneself. A person is sick, presto! – it is the thorn in the flesh. Life is carried on as in paganism.

The true Christian is one who becomes a sacrifice in order to call attention to the truth that Christ is the only true sacrifice.

Self-denial is a matter of casting off burdens and this might seem to be easy enough. But it is indeed strenuous to have to cast off the very burdens that self-love is eager to carry, yes, so eager that it is even very difficult for self-love to understand that they are burdens.

In eternity you will not be asked how large a fortune you are leaving behind – the survivors ask about that. Nor will you be asked about how many battles you won, about how sagacious you were, how powerful your influence – that, after all, becomes your reputation for posterity. No, eternity will not ask about what worldly goods remain behind you, but about what riches you have gathered in heaven. It will ask you about how often you have conquered your own thought, about what control you have exercised over yourself or whether you have been a slave, about how often you have mastered yourself in self-denial or whether you have never done so, about how often you in self-denial have been willing to make a sacrifice for a good cause or whether you were never willing, about how often you in self-denial have forgiven your enemy, whether seven times or seventy times seven times. It will ask about how often you in self-denial endured insults patiently, about what you have suffered, not for your own sake or for your own selfish interests' sake, but what you in self-denial have suffered for God's sake. Yes, in eternity you will indeed be asked what you left behind.

Take a purely human relationship. If the lover is not able to speak the beloved's language, he or she must learn it, however difficult it may seem to them – otherwise, if they cannot talk together, there cannot be a happy relationship. It is the same with dying to the world in order to be able to love God. God is spirit – only one who has died to the world can speak this language at all. If you do not wish to die to the world, then you cannot love God either. You are talking about entirely different matters than he is.

It is more blessed to give than to receive, but then it is also more blessed to be able to do without than to have to have.

Just as Christ tells the rich young ruler to sell all his goods and give to the poor, so one could also speak of the requirement to give all his rank and dignity to the poor, something we are even more reluctant to give.

The administration of the world is like running an enormous household, like making an immense painting. Yet it is the same for him, the Master, God in heaven, as it is for the cook and the artist. He says: "There must be a little dash of cinnamon now; a little bit of red must be introduced." We have no idea why, we can hardly detect it since the little smidge vanishes in the whole, but God knows why. A little dash of cinnamon! This means: here someone must be sacrificed; he must be added to give the rest a specific taste. These are God's correctives.

Abraham is an eternal pattern of faith. To be a stranger and in exile is the peculiar suffering of faith.

Since God himself has created and sustains this world, one ought to guard against the ascetic fanaticism which hates it and annihilates it. This said, God still wants us to make, once and for all, such a clean break with this world that the spirit really comes into existence. He wants us, even now, to wean ourselves away.

To be nothing is precisely the burr under the saddle of zealousness. To be nothing is precisely what makes delusions impossible; only when a person is nothing can he in truth serve an idea. The point is this. When a person is something, when he possesses the world's advantages he is no longer a burr under the saddle of worldliness. But is this not what it means to sacrifice oneself for the truth?

It is terrifying when God takes out the instruments for the surgery for which no human being has the strength: to take away a person's human zest for life, to slay him – in order that he can live as one who has died to the world and to the flesh. It cannot be otherwise, for in no other way can a human being love God. He must be in such a state of agony that if he were an unbeliever he would at no time hesitate to commit suicide. But in this state he must – live. Only in this state can he love God.

Just as the ship which lightly proceeds at full sail before the wind deeply cuts its heavy path through the ocean, so also the Christian's way is hard if one looks at the laborious work in the depths.

89 | Silence and Solitude

A person rarely amounts to anything, either good or evil, who has never lived in solitude. In solitude there is the Absolute, but also the absolute danger.

It is true that a mirror has the quality of enabling a person to see his image in it, but for this he must stand still.

It is a frightful satire and an epigram on the modern age that the only use it knows for solitude is to make it a punishment, a jail sentence.

God loves silence. Silence in relation to God is strengthening. Absolute silence is like a lever, or like the point outside the world which Archimedes talks about. To talk lightly about God, therefore, is a depletion that weakens. God hates it when we gossip with others about our relationship with him. To do so is sheer vanity, or else it is cowardice and lack of faith, because one does not really rely upon him. Don't be fooled into thinking that when a person has progressed further than others, it is so kind-hearted of him to let others share in his relation to God. This is not only contrary to God's will, it is conceited. Has not God proclaimed that every person, absolutely every person can turn to him?

In observing the present state of affairs and of life in general, from a Christian point of view one would have to say: It is a disease. And if I were a physician and someone asked me "What do you think should be done?" I would answer, "Create silence, bring about silence." God's Word cannot be heard, and if in order to be heard in the hullabaloo it must be shouted deafeningly with noisy means, then it is not God's Word; create silence!

Ah, everything is noisy. Just as a strong drink is said to stir the blood, so everything in our day, even the most insignificant project, even the most empty communication, is designed merely to jolt the senses or to stir up the masses, the crowd, the public, noise! And we humans, we clever fellows, seem to have become sleepless in order to invent ever new means to increase noise, to spread noise and insignificance with the greatest possible ease and on the greatest possible scale. Yes, everything has been turned upside down. The means of communication have been perfected, but what is publicized with such hot haste is rubbish! Oh, create silence!

If you forget to introduce silence into your home, then the most important thing is lacking. Silence – it is not a specific something, nor does it consist simply in the absence of speaking. No, silence is like the subdued lighting in a pleasant room, like the friendliness in a modest living room. It is not something one talks about, but it is there and exercises its beneficent power. Silence is like the tone, the fundamental tone, which is not given prominence and is called the fundamental tone precisely because it lies at the base. And silence brought into a house – that is eternity's art of making a house a home.

What is talkativeness? It is the result of doing away with the vital distinction between talking and keeping silent. Only someone who knows how to remain essentially silent can really talk – and truly act. Silence is the essence of inwardness, of the inner life. Mere gossip mocks real talk, and to express what is yet in thought weakens action by forestalling it. Where mere scope is concerned, talkativeness wins the day, it jabbers on incessantly about everything and nothing. But someone who can really talk, because he knows how to remain silent, will not talk about a variety of things but about one thing only, and he will know when to talk and when to remain silent.

When people's attention is no longer turned inwards, when they are no longer at ease with their own inner lives, but turn to others and think outside themselves, in search of that satisfaction, when nothing important ever happens to gather the threads of life together with the finality of a catastrophe: that is the time for talkativeness. In a passionate age great events give people something to talk about. Talkativeness, on the contrary, also has plenty to talk about, but in quite another sense. In a passionate age, when the event is over, and silence follows, there is still something to remember and to think about while one remains silent. But talkativeness is afraid of silence, for silence always reveals its emptiness.

Only he who can keep silence can really act, for silence is of the heart.

The beginning is found in the art of becoming silent. Human beings differ from the beasts in that they can speak, but in relation to God it is to their ruin that they are so willing to speak.

Talk takes the name of enthusiasm in vain by proclaiming loudly from the housetop what it should work out in silence.

Pausing is not a sluggish repose. Pausing is also movement. It is the inward movement of the heart. To pause is to deepen oneself in inwardness. But to go on and on is to go straight into the abyss of superficiality.

Silence is the measure of the power to act; a person never has more power to act than he has silence. Every person understands very well that to act is something far greater than to talk about it. If, therefore, a person is sure that he can do the thing in question, and if he is resolved that he will do it, he does not talk about it. What a person talks about in connection with a proposed action is precisely what he is most unsure of and unwilling to do.

The one who is truly resolved is silent. It is not as if being resolute were one thing and being silent another. No. To be resolute means to be silent; for silence alone is the measure of power to act.

90 | Sin

Man is not conscious of guilt because he sins, but consciously sins because of his guilt.

Rarely do we ever really try to understand why Christ collided with those around him or why he was crucified. Perhaps we fear getting to know anything of the proof of the existence of evil in the world.

It is so heartbreaking that Christ, who is the teacher of love, is betrayed – with a kiss. Such is the nature of sin.

Sin cannot arise out of a person alone any more than one sex alone can have a baby; thus the Christian teaching about the devil's temptation.

Only through the consciousness of sin is one admitted; to want to enter by any other road is high treason against Christianity.

The consciousness of sin is the essential condition for understanding Christianity. This is the very proof of Christianity's being the highest religion. No other religion has given such a profound and lofty expression of our significance – that we are sinners.

What is sin? It is the pact of an evil conscience with darkness.

What else has a memory like that of a bad conscience?

A person sins out of weakness, then out of despair. In the strict sense the latter alone is the sin. Here, also, is the cross. You doubt that the sin you have committed out of weakness can be forgiven. All is lost, you think, and thus you sin. But the cross can bring you to a halt, if you let it.

What sin cries to heaven? The very one that hides most secretly and most quietly within. What the adulterers, murderers, and thieves do cries out already here on earth.

To be a mere observer is actually sin.

Whenever sin is thought of as a disease, or as an abnormality, it is falsified.

The demonic manifests itself clearly only when it is in contact with the good.

It has been said that it costs a person just as much or even more trouble to go to hell as to enter heaven. Consequently, the way of damnation is also a narrow way. It is so easy to trip the light of desire, but when, after a while, it is desire that dances with the person against his will – that is a ponderous dance! It is so easy to give free rein to the passions, until they have taken the reins and tear a person along at daring speeds. One hardly dares to look where they are taking him!

It is so easy to let a sinful thought sneak into the heart. No seducer was ever so adept as is a sinful thought! It is so easy. It is not as it usually is – that it is the first step that costs – oh no, it costs nothing whatever. It costs nothing at all – until at the end, when you must pay dearly for this first step that cost nothing at all. Very often sin enters into a person as a flatterer; but when the person has become the slave of sin, it is the most terrible slavery – a narrow, an extremely narrow way to damnation!

"Do not fear those who can kill the body." Physically it is indeed true that one can fall by the hand of another. Spiritually the truth is that one can fall only by his own hand. No one can corrupt you except yourself.

Of all the brilliant sins, affected virtues are the worst.

When someone is sick or indisposed, the first thing he does is to see a physician. It is medication he wants. Spiritually it is just the opposite – when a person has sinned, the last thing he wants is the physician and medicine.

The gospel about the Ten Lepers is about how the nine were healed of their leprosy – and then caught, so to speak, an even worse leprosy: their ingratitude and unthankfulness. Herein lies the difference between sickness of the body and sickness of the spirit.

The danger with sickness of the spirit is just that a certain amount of health is required in order to become aware and acknowledge that one is sick.

A person can be both good and evil, but one cannot simultaneously choose to become good and evil.

Oh my God, even when I go wrong, your guidance is over me, lovingly overruling innumerable possibilities, so that even this error becomes beneficial to me.

To sin against God is to punish yourself.

It is not dreadful that I have to suffer punishment when I have acted badly. No, it would be dreadful if I could act badly – and there were no punishment.

It is small things that irritate and so embitter one's life. I can gladly fight against a storm so that my blood almost bursts from my veins; but the wind that blows a grain of dust into my eye can irritate me to such an extent that I stamp with rage.

The opposite of sin is faith. And this is one of the most decisive definitions of all Christianity – that the opposite of sin is not virtue but faith.

91 | Spiritual Trial

How horrible it must have been for the apostles when it seemed as if Christ had deceived them – luring them with attractive prospects – and then reversing the whole thing so dreadfully on the cross.

But it cannot be otherwise in our relationship to God. There has to come a moment (specifically, when all our purely human world of concepts is toppled), when God seems to be a deceiver. Yes, we will have many weak moments when we will long for the good old days, when it will seem to us that we could love God better if our relationship with him were as it once was, when God pulled us along by adapting to our own ideas. But God in his love will not comply.

This is the truth. Really and truly. Anyone who has the faintest idea of what it actually means to die to the world knows that this does not take place without terrible agonies. No wonder, then, we cry out, sometimes even rebel against God, because it seems to us as if God is deceiving us, we who from the beginning became involved with God on the understanding that God would love us according to our idea of love but now see that it is God who wants to be loved and according to God's idea of what love is. But, of course, God is still infinite, infinite love. Just hold fast to this – that it is out of infinite love that God performs this excruciatingly painful operation. Yes, it is painful, yet it is all the more necessary.

Christ's prayer, "Father forgive them for they know not what they do," became a kind of sermon or word which converted the thief. In the same instance the thief's faith was immediately put to the test. For very soon afterward he who had promised him that he should be with Him in paradise sighs and says, "My God, my God, why have you forsaken me?" This was the one upon whom the thief had built his hope!

If a person is actually to be an instrument of God's will, then God must first of all take his will from him. A fearful operation!

If you want to love God in truth, you must show it gladly, adoringly letting yourself be totally shattered by God. Only then can he unconditionally advance his will.

In the case of temptation the right thing to do may be to fight it by avoiding it. In the case of spiritual trial, however, one must go through it. Temptation should be avoided? Try not to see or hear what tempts you? Temptation is best fought by running away? But this does not work with thoughts that try the spirit, for they pursue you. If it is spiritual trial, go straight toward it, trusting in God and Christ. When you are weak, he is strong.

The difference between temptation and spiritual trial is that the temptation to sin is in accord with inclination, the "temptation" of spiritual trial is contrary to inclination. Therefore the opposite tactic must be employed. The person tempted by sin does well to shun the danger, but in relation to spiritual trial this is the very danger, for every time he thinks he is saving himself by shunning the danger, the danger becomes greater the next time. The fleshly person is wise to flee from the sight of sin or the enticement. But for the one not so tempted but who is ridden with anxiety about coming in contact with it (he is under spiritual trial) it is not so wise to shun the sight or the enticement; for spiritual trial wants nothing else than to paralyze him by striking terror into his life and enslaving him in anxiety.

As long as there are many springs from which to draw water, anxiety about possible water failure does not arise. But when there is only one source! And so it is when Christ has become a person's one and only spring that spiritual trials begin. Spiritual trial is the expression of a concentration upon Christ as the only source. This is why most people have no spiritual trials.

It is much easier to suffer on account of one's sin than to suffer because one relates himself to God.

With regard to self-renunciation, who can ever say: I can go no farther, or I cannot go that far out? It ought to become a burr that helps you along by keeping you awake and in the striving.

It is a very special spiritual trial when a person in the strictest sense sins against his will, plagued by the anxiety of sin, when he has, for example, sinful thoughts which he would rather flee, does everything to avoid, but they still come. It is a special kind of spiritual trial to believe that this is something he must submit to, that Christ will come to console him as he bears this cross, plagued as he is by a thorn in the flesh. This kind of spiritual trial is very painful and excruciating. It is an educational torture that is intended to break all self-centered willfulness.

Even when we talk confidentially about God testing us, this talk is meaningless unless God is holding on to us. We know that if God should put to the test our faithfulness to him, we know well that at the moment of testing, he himself must hold on to us, that is, we know that at bottom we are unfaithful, and that every instant it is he who at bottom holds us.

From your hand, oh God, we are willing to receive everything. And even if it seems that your arm is shortened, increase our faith and our trust so that we might still hold on to you. And if at times it seems that you draw your hand away from us, oh, then we know it is only because you close it, that you close it only to save the more abundant blessing in it, that you close it only to open it again and satisfy with blessing everything that lives.

Father in heaven! Well do we know that all seeking has its promise. But we also know that all seeking has its pain, and so too does the seeking that seeks you. Well do we know that to seek does not mean that one must go into the wide world; for the more glorious the thing one seeks, the nearer to him does it lie. And if one seeks you, oh Lord, you are the nearest of all things to him.

92 | Suffering

Force ought never be used; this is the mind of Christ. Instead you ought to endure injustice, witnessing also to the truth until the other party cannot hold out in doing wrong and voluntarily gives up doing it. Suffering can have a paralyzing effect. Just as a hypnotist puts his subject to sleep, and one limb after another loses its vitality, so suffering endurance paralyzes injustice. No evil can ultimately hold out against it.

The use of force is in league with injustice. Perpetuating injustice and in hasty impatience to want to protect oneself through force against injustice are essentially the same thing. At best there is an entirely accidental difference – the suffering party only lacks an opportunity to commit injustice.

They say Christ did not go out into the desert or enter a monastery; he remained in the world: ergo – by saying this they think they have justified unlimited worldliness. But hold on! Undoubtedly Christ did not go out into the desert, did not enter a monastery. He remained in the world – but not, however, to become decorated, a cabinet member, an honorary member of this and that, but to suffer. This was the advantage, and the only advantage he had from remaining in the world.

To suffer patiently is not specifically Christian – but freely to choose the suffering is.

Sorrow is like an arrow in the breast – the more vigorously the deer runs in order to run away from it, the more firmly the arrow becomes embedded in it.

To be an alien, to be in exile, is the mark of Christian suffering.

Is this not really the meaning of Christianity: Have you suffered for the teaching? Then why all the bustle to get human assistance? I must rather take care to prevent it, lest it possibly result in my scoring a success instead of suffering.

You are now thirty years old; you still have perhaps forty years to live, perhaps only ten, perhaps only a day. You can fill up this time with becoming just like the others, nice, amiable people, above all with whatever counts in having advantages in life, with whatever gains you pleasure. Let us assume that you succeed in making this kind of life for yourself, and then you die.

You desire, of course, to be saved. But have you ever pondered this – I wonder if it is really true what the gushing preachers assure us, that "in eternity there is sheer joy and happiness." Do you believe that "every suffering and pain is forgotten"? I do not. The New Testament makes the very specific exception of one suffering: having suffered for the truth. Or do you believe that Christ's suffering, and for that matter, anyone else's who suffered for the truth, is forgotten in eternity? Now don't forget that you are going to live together with these glorious witnesses for eternity, you who avoided suffering, even so much as a little bit, for the truth!

Consequently an eternity in this heavenly company and seventy years at the most, perhaps only ten, perhaps only a day in this earthly company. Was it by judicious calculation, then, that you decided to choose to conform to this earthly company in order not to be conspicuous here – thereby making sure of being conspicuous for all eternity?

Adversities do not make a person weak, they reveal what strength he has.

He who himself does not wish to suffer cannot love him who has.

The intensity of suffering is greatest when you have the power to free yourself from it. I must use my energy to force myself out into the suffering and then use it to endure the suffering.

God punishes the ungodly simply by ignoring them. This is why they have success in the world – the most frightful punishment, because in God's view this world is immersed in evil. But God sends suffering to those whom he loves, as assistance to enable them to become happy by loving him.

Voluntary suffering is suspect at three points. First, I must use my strength to compel myself to go forth into the suffering. Second, I must use my strength to bear it. And third, I must put up with the advice of relatives and sympathizers who insist that I go too far. Such is the way of Christian suffering.

Voluntary suffering provides the double collision which is the mark of everything essentially Christian: to become hated, cursed, detested, to have to suffer. No one ever thinks of persecuting someone because he is in poverty against his will, but no one is as hated as the one who voluntarily renounces that in which people naturally center their lives. Only one who is marked by the voluntary can be entrusted with Christ's command.

To suffer rightly is to have a secret with God!

You do not dare for the sake of suffering, but you dare in order not to betray the truth.

How strange that the most coveted good in the world is independence, yet almost no one covets the only way that truly leads to it: suffering.

Authentic Christian suffering has been abolished, suffering "on account of the Word" (Mt. 13:21), or "for righteousness' sake" (Mt. 5:10), and more. On the other hand, ordinary human sufferings have been dressed up to be Christian sufferings and in turn made out to be like the Pattern – what a masterpiece of upsidedowness! Hence the pastor preaches about Abraham who sacrifices Isaac, and the widower is eloquently portrayed as a kind of Abraham. There is naturally not a trace of sense in this kind of talk, but the widower likes it, gladly gives what he owes, and the congregation sits by idly, since each one expects his turn to come – should one not then be willing to pay for coming to resemble Abraham so easily! So it is also with respect to Christ, and in so doing we have managed to consign to total oblivion what is to be understood by authentic Christian suffering.

It takes moral courage to grieve; it takes spiritual courage to rejoice.

Oh Lord, not only do you know our sorrow better than do we ourselves, but you feel it, too. You understand the burden, the heavy grief that we bear. Make us humble, therefore, so that in our rebellion against life's injustices we do not turn for comfort to those who are like wandering stars, or to those who are like the raging waves of the sea foaming out their own shame. You are our refuge and our strength, and there is none other.

93 | Tribulation and Persecution

Christianity requires simply that we love others with our whole heart; it is not the fault of Christianity that this is rewarded with persecution.

There is an almost mad self-contradiction in Christianity's requirement. It sets a task and exclaims: In the same degree as you succeed in faith, you will come to suffer more and more. You will continually think: "But, Lord God, if I rightly love others – then…" The Christian answer to this must be: Stupid, did not the Savior of the world rightly love others, but was mocked, spit upon, and more? Has it not been this way for all true Christians? If you desire, humanly speaking, pleasant and happy days, then never get seriously involved with Christ.

The consequence of having seen God is madness, not in the sense that one becomes mentally ill, no, but that a kind of madness is set between you and others: people cannot nor will not understand you.

If you are a millionaire and give 100,000 dollars to the poor, you make people happy; if you give it all away, you will collide. Accept a big salary and a distinguished office in order to further

Christianity, and you will perhaps make people happy; renounce everything, every personal advantage, in order to proclaim Christianity, and you will be scorned.

Nothing is more certain. Coming close to God brings catastrophe. Everyone whose life does not bring relative catastrophe has never even once turned as a single individual to God; it is just as impossible as it is to touch the conductors of a generator without getting a shock.

All striving of a more noble character always meets with opposition. If you hold only to God, the attack and contempt and the storm of opposition will help you discover things you otherwise would never discover; they will add new strings to your lyre. Every person is like an instrument which no doubt can be disturbed and damaged by the world's wretchedness – but if you hold on to God, it can help you to an ever new melody.

Everything that helps us along the way we are to go is prosperity; but this is exactly what adversity does. Ergo, it is prosperity.

The pathway of tribulation remains just as long and just as dark right to the end – the pathway that gradually becomes lighter must be a different one. Neither do we know when the change will come nor precisely whether we have reached it or how much nearer we have come (for such things cannot be determined in the dark). But we do believe that the change will come and then with the blessedness of eternity.

When a child in a dark room is waiting for the door to be opened and all the anticipated joy to be restored, at the last second before the door is opened it is still just as dark as at first. The child still does not know how much longer he has to wait. But one thing is sure, the second the door opens the glory will be revealed. The child may have the sad thought that he has been forgotten. But then the child says to himself: How could I ever think that my parents could do a thing like that. So the child sees it through, for he well knows that to call out in fear of having been forgotten would upset everything.

Oh, how hard it is for us to have to stick it out this way, to stake everything on that last moment. We would far prefer to have the glory revealed gradually – that is, we prefer spoiling it for ourselves by receiving a little beforehand.

Christianity has been made so completely devoid of character that there is really nothing to persecute. The chief trouble with Christians, therefore, is that no one wants to kill them any more!

At the hour of death there is only this one consolation, that one has not avoided opposition but has gone through it and persevered.

What Christianity calls self-renunciation involves precisely a double-danger. The purely human conception of self-renunciation is this: give up your selfish desires, longings, and plans – and then you will become appreciated and honored and loved as a righteous person. The Christian conception of self-renunciation, however, is to give up your selfish desires and longings, give up your arbitrary plans and purposes – and then submit to being treated as a criminal, scorned and ridiculed for this very reason. Christian self-renunciation knows in advance that this will happen and chooses it freely. It does not let the Christian get by at half-price.

So many Christians look on the world's opposition as something entirely accidental. But this view is altogether unchristian. Nothing should be promised the young that Christianity cannot deliver, and Christianity cannot deliver something different from what it has promised from the very first: the ingratitude of the world, opposition, mockery, and always to a higher degree the more dedicated a Christian becomes. This is the final difficulty in being a Christian, and when you recommend Christianity there should be silence least of all about this.

This is the paradox of Christianity – namely, that a kingdom which is not of this world still wants to have a visible place, yet without becoming a kingdom of this world. This is why Christian collisions are produced.

It is no good for you to say that the world is immersed in evil, and then slip through it easily. If you do this, your life expresses that it is really a very good world and simply cannot be done without your also being an accomplice in one way or another.

See to it that you take your life's examination, obediently submitting to the final test, to be sacrificed. Don't worry about the ill treatment that will be meted out to you by your contemporaries. No, see to it that you take your examination. If you take it, this is eternally and infinitely decisive. Maybe it will then happen, maybe not, that an individual in the next generation can be inspired by your life to be willing to take his life's examination. There will happen to him what happened to you, and perhaps in thinking of you he will find some encouragement.

94 | Truth

The law is this: If the proclamation is true, it must produce what it proclaims.

The expression, "Truth is naked," may also be interpreted in this way: truly relating to truth means that all the inner and the outer garments of illusion have to be discarded.

The truth is incessantly subject to fraud, particularly on the part of those closest to it. Since truth is never decided by the "what" but by the "how," it is clear that we will always have false editions of the same truth.

The exact opposite of the truth is "the probable." Truth does not consist of an approximation. That which lies nearest to the truth is not, if you please, closest to the truth – no, this is the most dangerous delusion of all, the most dangerous simply because it lies so near to the truth without being the truth.

Let us be honest about it. We are more afraid of the truth than of death.

The truth is a snare: you cannot get it without being caught yourself. In fact, you can never get the truth by catching it yourself but only by its catching you.

Christ says, "I will manifest myself to him who loves me" (1 Jn. 14:21). But this is true always. The thing one loves manifests itself to one; truth manifests itself to whoever loves it. One too easily thinks of the recipient as inactive and that which manifests itself as actively communicating. No, the relationship is that the recipient is the lover and so the thing loved is made manifest to him, for he himself is transformed into the likeness of the thing loved. To become what one loves is the only sure way of understanding. You only understand to the degree in which you become what you love.

If God held all truth enclosed in his right hand, and in his left hand the one and only ever-striving drive for truth, even with the corollary of erring forever and ever, and if he were to say to me: Choose! – I would humbly fall down to him at his left hand and say: Father, give! Pure truth is indeed only for you alone!

Only the truth that builds up is truth for you.

"Authority" does not mean to be a king, but by a firm and conscious resolution to be willing to sacrifice everything, one's very life, for a cause. It means to articulate a cause in such a way that a person is at one with himself, needing nothing and fearing nothing. This infinite recklessness is authority. Those with authority always address themselves to the conscience, not to the understanding. True authority is present when the truth is the cause. The reason the Pharisees spoke without authority, although they were indeed authorized teachers, was precisely because their talk, like their lives, was in the power of endless finite concerns.

In order to swim you must take off all your clothes. In order to aspire to the truth you must undress in a far more inward sense, divest yourself of all your inward clothes, of thoughts, conceptions, selfishness. Only then are you sufficiently naked.

95 | **Venturing and Risk**

It is dangerous business to arrive in eternity with possibilities that you have prevented from becoming actualities. Possibility is a hint from God. A person must follow it. The possibility for the highest is in every soul; you must follow it. If God does not want it, then let him hinder it. You must not hinder it yourself. Trusting in God, I have ventured, but I have failed – there is peace and rest and God's confidence in that. I have not ventured – it is an utterly unhappy thought, a torment for all eternity.

Surely Christianity's intention is that a person use this life to venture out, to do so in such a way that God can get hold of him, and that one gets to see whether or not he actually has faith.

Practicing Christian faith is not very useful and it is highly impractical. Indeed, is there anything more impractical than offering one's life for the truth? Is there anything more foolish than not looking to one's own advantage? Is there anything more ridiculous than making one's life difficult and strenuous and being rewarded with insults? Is there anything more impractical than being labeled – not with titles and honors – but with abuse and ridicule? For a sailor to die at sea where he risked his life in the hope of profit, for the soldier to fall in battle where he risked his life in the hope of becoming a general – that is more like it, that is practical – but to die for the truth!

A person can distress the spirit by venturing too much. Yet there is comfort in knowing that discipline will surely come and will help him if he honestly humbles himself under it. But a person can also distress the spirit by venturing too little. Alas, but this comes home to him only after a long time, perhaps after many years when he is living in the security he sought by avoiding danger. Now he must experience the truth that he was untrue to himself. Perhaps it does not come until old age, perhaps not until eternity. In any case, the thing to do about venturing too little is to admit humbly before God that you are coddling yourself.

Unless you do this, you will begin to imagine that what you are doing is mighty clever – alas, for then you are lost forever. At that very moment the eternal flickers out, your relationship with God closes up, the truth in you dies, and you become untrue. If, on the other hand, you make the humble admission – perhaps you are sick and therefore despondent, perhaps you are too hard on yourself in judging yourself – you at least preserve your relationship to God. Your admission will keep you awake and alert, and will not permit you to become happy in a dearly purchased security, distanced from danger. Perhaps tomorrow, perhaps in a year, faith and confident boldness will rise up in you and you will once again be able to venture.

We delude ourselves into thinking that to refrain from venturing is modesty, and that it must please God as humility. No, no! Not to venture means to make a fool of God – because all he is waiting for is that you go forth.

During the first period of a person's life the greatest danger is to not take the risk. When once the risk has been taken then the greatest danger is to risk too much. By not risking you turn aside and serve trivialities. By risking too much, you turn aside to the fantastic, and perhaps to presumption.

To venture the truth is what gives human life and the human situation pith and meaning. To venture is the fountainhead of inspiration. Calculating is the sworn enemy of enthusiasm, the mirage whereby the earthly person drags out time and keeps the eternal away, whereby one cheats God, himself, and his generation.

The servant in the gospel who hid his talent in the earth was wise and farsighted. Yet his master rejected him. Imagine a different scenario where a servant comes and says, "Lord, I wanted so much to gain something from the talent you entrusted me, so I took a risk – I suppose too much of a risk, because I have gained nothing and lost my one talent." Now, which servant will find forgiveness?

A bold venture is not a high-flown phase, not an exclamatory outburst, but arduous work. A bold venture, no matter how rash, is not a boisterous proclamation but a quiet dedication that receives nothing in advance but stakes everything.

We all know what it is to play warfare in mock battle. It means to mimic everything, just as it is in war. The troops are drawn up, they march into the field, seriousness is evident in every eye, but also courage and enthusiasm, the orderlies rush back and forth intrepidly, the commander's voice is heard, the signals, the battle cry, the volley of shooting, the thunder of cannon – everything exactly as in war, lacking only one thing: the danger.

So it is with playing Christianity, that is, imitating by way of Christian preaching in such a way that everything, absolutely everything is included in as alluring a form as possible. Only one thing is lacking – the danger.

Imagine a mighty spirit who promised to a certain people his protection, but upon the condition that they should make their appearance at a definite place where it was dangerous to go. Suppose that these folks waited to make their appearance, and instead went home to their living rooms and talked to one another in enthusiastic terms about how this spirit had promised them his potent protection. No one would be able to harm them. Is not this ridiculous?

So it is with today's Christianity. Christ taught something perfectly definite by believing; to believe is to venture out as decisively as it is possible, breaking with everything one naturally loves. But to him who believes, assistance against all danger is also promised. But today we play at believing, play at being Christians. We remain at home in the old grooves of finitude – and then we go and twaddle with one another, or let the preachers twaddle to us, about all the promises that are found in Christ. Is this not ridiculous?

Preserve me, Lord, from the deceit of thinking that by being prudent and looking after my own interests I am necessarily using my talents aright. He who takes risks for your sake may appear to lose, but he is accepted by you. He who risks nothing appears to gain by his prudence, but he is rejected by you. But let me not think that by avoiding risk I am better than the other. Grant me to see that this is an illusion, and save me from such a snare.

96 | Witness

There was a time when one could almost be afraid to call himself a disciple of Christ, because it meant so much. Now one can do it with complete ease, because it means nothing at all.

You can be Christian only in opposition, can confess Christ only in opposition. There is always danger bound up with confessing Christ.

When a fisherman wants to make a good catch he has to know where the fish are – but the fish swim against the current – consequently he has to go to that side.

Christianity is also a revolt, that is, as soon as it is set forth in all its truth people will revolt against it.

You can always accomplish something by giving witness to joy.

Act just once in such a manner that your action expresses that you fear God alone – you will in some measure or another, instantly cause a scandal.

What is a witness? A witness is a person who directly demonstrates the truth of what he proclaims – directly, yes, in part by its being truth in him and blessedness, in part by volunteering his life and saying: Now, see if you can force me to deny this truth.

Let this propensity to preach that there is joy in suffering insult be met with insults, and then we will see what becomes of the speaker. The essentially Christian makes witnesses, and so good night to eloquence.

A witness to the truth is a person who in poverty witnesses to the truth. For him there is never promotion, except in an inverse sense, downward, step by step.

When Christianity came into the world the task was simply to preach. Among "Christian nations," however, the situation is different. What we have before us is not Christianity but a prodigious illusion, the people are not pagans but live in the blissful conceit that they are Christians. So if in this situation Christianity is to be introduced, first of all the illusion must be debunked. But since this vain conceit, this illusion, is to the effect that we are all Christians, it looks indeed as if introducing Christianity amounts to taking Christianity away. Nevertheless this is precisely what must be done, for the illusion must go.

Anyone who knows even a little bit about bird-life knows that there is a kind of understanding between wild geese and tame geese, regardless of how different they are. When the flight of the wild geese is heard in the air and there are tame geese down on the ground, the tame geese are instantly aware of it and to a certain degree they understand what it means. This is why they also start up, beat their wings, cry out and fly along the ground a bit in awkward, confused disorder – and then it is over.

There was once a wild goose. In the autumn, about the time for migration, it became aware of some tame geese. It became enamored by them, thought it a shame to fly away from them, and hoped to win them over so that they would decide to go along with it on the flight. To that end it became involved with them in every possible way. It tried to entice them to rise a little higher and then again a little higher in their flight, that they might, if possible, accompany it in the flight, saved from the wretched, mediocre life of waddling around on the earth as respectable, tame geese.

At first, the tame geese thought it very entertaining and liked the wild goose. But soon they became very tired of it, drove it away with sharp words, censured it as a visionary fool devoid of experience and wisdom. Alas, unfortunately the wild goose had become so involved with the tame geese that they had gradually gained power over it, their opinion meant something to it – and gradually the wild goose became a tame goose.

In a certain sense there was something admirable about what the wild goose wanted. Nevertheless, it was a mistake, for – this is the law – a tame goose never becomes a wild goose, but a wild goose can certainly become a tame goose. If what the wild goose tried to do is to be commended in any way, then it must above all watch out for one thing – that it hold on to itself. As soon as it notices that the tame geese have any kind of power over it, then away, away in migratory flight.

Christianity is not exactly like this. True, a Christian who is under the Spirit is as different from the ordinary man as the wild goose is from the tame goose. But Christianity teaches conversion and what a person can become in life. Consequently there is always hope that a tame goose might become a wild goose. Therefore, Christians must remain with them, these tame geese, but only with one thing in mind – wanting to win them for the transformation. But for heaven's sake watch out for one thing. As soon as you see that the tame geese begin to have power over you, away, away in migratory flight, so that it does not all end with your becoming like a tame goose, blissfully sunk in wretched mediocrity.

It happened that a fire broke out backstage in a theatre. The clown came out to inform the public. They thought it was just a jest and applauded. He repeated his warning, they shouted even louder. So I think the world will come to an end amid general applause from all the wits, who believe that it is a joke.

I wonder if a person handing another person an extremely sharp, polished, two-edged instrument would hand it over with the air, gestures, and expression of one delivering a bouquet of flowers? Would not this be madness? What does one do, then? Convinced of the excellence of the dangerous instrument, one recommends it unreservedly, to be sure, but in such a way that in a certain sense one warns against it. So it is with Christianity.

Just as in a large shipment of herring the outermost layer gets crushed and ruined, just as the outermost fruit gets bruised and damaged by the crate, so in every generation there are a few who stand farthest out and suffer from the crate, who alone guard those who are in the middle.

Most people are really only sample copies. Of them it may be said: They derive benefit out of living, but the world has no benefit out of their having lived.

Being a Christian is, without a doubt, neither more nor less than being a martyr. Every Christian, that is, every true Christian, is a martyr. But I hear one of those shabby pastors say (by shabby I mean one who accepts a nice salary, prestige with recognition, and such – in order to betray Christianity): "But, of course, we cannot all be martyrs." To this God would reply: "Stupid man, do you think I don't know how I have arranged the world." The point is this – becoming a Christian is an examination given by God. In every age it must continually be equally difficult to become Christian.

Just as all the nerves converge in the fingertips, so the entire nervous system of Christian faith converges in the reality of martyrdom. If this is reversed, you have what we are now stuck in – a nice world where reforming means coming out unscathed and on top.

No doubt there is an infinite difference between a tyrant and a martyr; yet they have one thing in common: the power to constrain. The tyrant constrains by force; the martyr, unconditionally obedient to God, constrains by suffering. The tyrant dies, and his rule is over; the martyr dies, and his rule begins.

Suffering for the truth is the only possible awakening. An appalling, all-engulfing web of knowledge and sophistication such as now envelops the generation cannot be exploded by words; greater powers are needed. And martyrs are the only ones who can do it.

In our human speech we often say of a child that he looks like an angel. Christianly speaking, a dying person does. To die is to be born again. When the world shuts itself against a witness, heaven opens for him. Stephen, the first Christian martyr, bears witness to this fact. They saw his face as if it had been the face of an angel. Someone will say: "Angels? Nobody has ever seen angels. That is something for children." Answer: "Stuff and nonsense! Hold your tongue! See to it that you become like Stephen, that your face is an angel's face – then we will have an angel to look at."

Today's martyrs will not bleed, as formerly, because they are Christians – yes, it is almost insane! They will be put to death because they are *not* "Christians." Frightful drama! And how alone the martyr will stand!

*

97 | Works

It is not our effort that brings atonement. No, joy over being reconciled, over the fact that atonement has already been made, produces an honest striving. It is not good works that make a good person but the good person who does good works. And one becomes good by faith alone. Consequently, faith first of all. It is by faith that one does truly good works.

The very fact that I am saved by faith and that nothing at all is demanded from me should in itself cause me to strive.

God cannot stand good works in the sense of earning merit. Yet good works are required. They shall be and yet shall not be. They are necessary and yet one ought humbly to ignore their significance or at least forget that they are supposed to be of any significance. Good works are like a child giving his parents a present, purchased, however, with what the child has received from his parents. All the pretentiousness which otherwise is associated with giving a present disappears when the child understands that he has received from his parents the gift which he gives to them.

Imagine a girl in love: for a time she will find it sufficient to express her love in words, but there will come a moment when this will no longer satisfy her, when she will long to embrace her beloved. So also with the believer in relation to God – expressing his gratitude in words. He will finally reach a point where he must say: I cannot stand it, this no longer satisfies my need. You must, oh God, permit me a far stronger expression for my gratitude – works.

In every human being there is an inclination either to want to be proud when it comes to works or, when faith and grace are emphasized, to want to be free from works as far as possible. Christianity's requirement is that your life should express works as strenuously as possible. Then one thing more is required – that you humble yourself and confess: I am saved nevertheless by grace. Luther wished to take meritoriousness away from works. In typical fashion, we have not only taken meritoriousness away, but also the works.

True ethical enthusiasm consists in willing to the uttermost of one's capability, but also, uplifted in divine jest, in never thinking that one thereby achieves something.

If a person of talent is actually to become spirit, he must first of all acquire a distaste for all the satisfactions the talent has to offer. He should be like the apprentice in the pastry trade who has permission from the start to eat as many cakes and cookies as he wants – in order to acquire a distaste for cakes and cookies.

A human being is only an instrument and never knows when the moment will come when he will be put aside. If he himself does not at times evoke this thought, he is a hireling, an unfaithful servant, who is trying to free himself and to cheat the Lord of the uncertainty in which he comprehends his own nothingness. Even the highest mission in the spiritual world is only an errand.

Father in heaven, awaken conscience within us. Teach us to open our spiritual ears to your voice and to pay attention to what you say, so that your will may sound purely and clearly for us as it does in heaven, unadulterated by worldly cunning, undeadened by the voice of passions. Keep us vigilant in fear and trembling to work out our salvation. But also – when the law speaks loudest, when its demands terrify us, when it thunders from Sinai – let there be a soft voice which whispers to us that we are your children, so that we may cry out with joy: Abba, Father.

98 | Worship

God is worshipped not by moods but by action. But this, too, has the problem of so easily turning into pettiness and temptation in the form of self-righteousness. Only the childlike heart that wholly loves God can do this rightly.

God is spirit and thus finds no additional pleasure in our hymn singing any more than in the smell of incense. What is most pleasing to him is that we genuinely need him.

One cannot serve God as one serves another Majesty who, humanly speaking, has a cause. Action is indeed true worship, but it is true worship only when it is freed from all busyness, as if God had a cause. To give up everything – not because God must make use of you as an instrument, no, by no means – to give up everything! This is what it means to worship and serve God.

Christ has desired only one kind of gratitude: the praise that comes from the transformed individual.

Beware, lest your jubilating thanks to Christ is not loving him but loving yourself.

It is no good for us to bow and scrape before God in words and phrases and in such activities as building churches and binding Bibles in velvet. God has a particular language for addressing him – the language of action, the transformation of the mind, the course of one's life.

The only art Christians should practice is worship. Not with words and chatter – no, with action in unconditional obedience.

God is a spirit; consequently worship of God should be in spirit and in truth. The customary Sunday service these days, however, is rather strongly designed for a sensate effect. Even more so, on the great festival days of the Church, on precisely these days the worship service moves even farther from the spiritual. Trumpets and every possible appeal to the senses are used – this is because it is one of the great festival days of the Church. What nonsense, what an anticlimax!

In the world the theater is worship – in Christendom the churches are. Is there a difference?

We are able to tell from a person's behavior that he is in love. Likewise, we are able to tell when someone is in the power of a great thought. How then should we not be able to tell that someone is in the presence of God?

You can worship only by becoming weak. Woe to the presumptuous person who in his proud strength is audacious enough to worship God! The true God can be worshipped only in spirit and in truth – but precisely this is the truth, that you are entirely weak. In fact, you are nothing.

Imagine that geese could talk – and that they had planned things in such a way that they, too, had their divine worship services. Every Sunday they gathered together and a goose preached. The gist of the sermon was as follows: What a high destiny geese have, to what a high goal the creator – and every time this word was mentioned the geese curtsied and the ganders bowed their heads – had appointed geese. With the help of their wings they could fly away to distant regions, blessed regions, where they really had their homes, for here they were but alien sojourners.

It was this way every Sunday. Afterwards, the assembly dispersed and each one waddled home to his family. And so to church again next Sunday, and then home again – and that was the end of it. They flourished and grew fat, became plump and delicate, were eaten on St. Martin's Eve – and that was the end of it.

Yes, that was the end of it. Although the Sunday discourse was so very lofty, on Monday the geese would discuss with each other what had happened to the goose who had wanted really to use his wings according to the high goal set before it – what happened to it, what horrors it had to endure. Of course the geese would not talk about it on Sunday; that, after all, was not appropriate. Such talk would make a fool of God and of themselves.

Still, there were a few individual geese among them who looked poorly and grew thin. The other geese said among themselves: There you see what happens when you take seriously this business of wanting to fly. Because they harbor the idea of wanting to fly, they get thin, and do not prosper, do not have God's grace as we have it, and become plump, fat, and delicate. For by the grace of God one becomes plump, fat, and delicate.

So it is with our Christian worship services. We, too, have wings, we have imagination, intended to help us actually rise aloft. But we play, allow our imagination to amuse itself in an hour of Sunday daydreaming. In reality, however, we stay right where we are – and on Monday regard it as a proof that God's grace gets us plump, fat, delicate. That is, we accumulate money, get to be a somebody in the world, beget children, become successful, and so forth. And those who actually get involved with God and who therefore suffer and have torments, troubles, and grief, of these we say: Here is proof that they do not have the grace of God.

The preacher says: It is good to be here in God's house. Would that we could remain here, but we must go out again into the confusion of life! Lies and nonsense! The most difficult thing of all would be to remain day after day inside of God's house.

Oh God, even though I am very little before you, this little – this being nothing before thee – is for me infinitely much. All else is to me worth nothing, absolutely nothing!

At the altar what counts above everything else is to hear his voice. It is true that a sermon should also bear witness to God, proclaiming his word, and his teaching, but for all that a sermon is not his voice. If you do not hear his voice, you have come in vain to the altar. Even if the Lord's minister speaks every word precisely as it was handed down from the fathers; even if you hear precisely every word, if you do not hear his voice, you have come in vain to the altar. Even though you are seriously resolved to take the preacher's word to heart and to order your life accordingly – if you do not hear his voice, you have come in vain to the altar. It must be his voice you hear. For at the altar there can be no talk about him; there he himself is personally present, it is he that speaks – if not, then you are not at the altar.

Jesus says, "When you are offering your gift at the altar, and there remember that your enemy has something against you, go and be reconciled to your enemy, and then come and offer your gift." Ah, what sacrifice do you think is dearest to him, the sacrifice you offer by being reconciled with your enemy, that is, by sacrificing your anger to God – or the gift you could offer upon the altar? The sacrifice of reconciliation is dearest to God and to Christ, and it is there that the altar is.

True worship of God consists in doing God's will. But this sort of worship is not to our taste. Generation after generation, people have busied themselves with a worship that consists in having one's own will, but doing it in such a way that the name of God is brought into conjunction with it. For example, a person is inclined to want to support himself by engaging in activities that involve killing people. Now he sees from Scripture that this is not permissible, that God's will is, "You shall not kill." "All right," he thinks, "but that sort of teaching doesn't really suit me, but neither do I want to be an ungodly man." So what does he do? He gets hold of a minister who in God's name blesses the sword. What a clever trick!

Learn first how to be alone, and you will doubtless also learn the true worship of God, which is to think highly of God and humbly of yourself. Not as if you ought to make yourself humbler than your neighbor, as if that would lend you dignity; for remember that you are before God. Not to make yourself more humble than your enemy, as if that would make you better; for remember that you are before God. But true worship is to think humbly of yourself.

Index of Parables and Stories

Sources

Abbreviations for Sources

AC   *Kierkegaard's Attack Upon "Christendom" 1854–1855*, trans., with introduction, Walter Lowrie. Princeton University Press, 1944.

CA   *The Concept of Anxiety*, trans. Reidar Thomte in collaboration with Albert B. Anderson. Princeton University Press, 1980.

CD   *Christian Discourses*, trans. Walter Lowrie. London: Oxford University Press, 1952.

CUP *Concluding Unscientific Postscript*, ed. and trans. Howard V. Hong and Edna H. Hong. Princeton University Press, 1989.

E/O *Either/Or*, trans. Walter Lowrie, 2 vols. New York: Doubleday & Company, Inc., 1959.

EUD *Eighteen Upbuilding Discourses*, ed. and trans. Howard V. Hong and Edna H. Hong. Princeton University Press, 1990.

FT   *Fear and Trembling*. Trans. Alastair Hannay. London: Penguin Books, 1985.

J   *The Journals of Søren Kierkegaard*, ed. & trans. Alexander Dru (Oxford University Press: London, 1938).

JP   *Søren Kierkegaard's Journals and Papers*, ed. and trans. Howard V. Hong and Edna H. Hong. 7 volumes.

M   *Meditations from Kierkegaard*, by T.H. Croxall. London: James Nisbet and Company, LTD, 1955.

P   *Parables of Kierkegaard*, edited by Thomas C. Oden. Princeton University Press, 1978.

PA   *The Present Age*, trans. Alexander Dru and Walter Lowrie. London: Oxford University Press, 1949.

PC   *Practice in Christianity*, trans. Howard V. Hong and Edna H. Hong. Princeton University Press, 1991.

PF   *Philosophical Fragments* and *Johannes Climacus*, trans. Howard V. Hong and Edna H. Hong. Princeton University Press, 1985.

PH   *Purity of Heart is to Will One Thing*, trans. & intro. Douglas V. Steere. Harper Torchbooks. The Cloister Library. New York: Harper & Row, 1956.

PK   *The Prayers of Kierkegaard,* edited by Perry D. LeFevere. Chicago: University of Chicago Press, 1956.

S   *Selections from the Writings of Søren Kierkegaard,* by Thomas S. Kepler. Nashville: The Upper Room, 1952.

S/J   *For Self-Examination* and *Judge for Yourself,* trans. Howard V. Hong and Edna H. Hong. Princeton University Press, 1990.

SD   *The Sickness Unto Death,* trans. & introduction by Alastair Hannay. London: Penguin Books, 1989.

SK   Søren Kierkegaard: The Mystique of Prayer and Pray-er, trans. By Lois S. Bowers and edited by George K. Bowers. CSS Publishing Company, Inc., 1994

SLW   *Stages on Life's Way,* trans. by Walter Lowrie. London: Oxford University Press, 1940.

TA   *Two Ages: The Age of Revolution and the Present Age: A Literary Review,* trans. Howard V. Hong and Edna H. Hong. Princeton University Press, 1978.

TD   *Two Discourses of God and Man,* Søren Kierkegaard. Minneapolis: Burgess Publishing Company.

UD   *Upbuilding Discourse in Various Spirits,* ed. and trans. Howard V. Hong and Edna H. Hong. Princeton University Press, 1993.

WL   *Works of Love: Some Christian Reflections in the Form of Discourses,* trans. Howard and Edna Hong, preface R. Gregor Smith. Harper Torchbooks, The Cloister Library. New York: Harper & Row, 1962.

Sources

1. Dare to Decide: EUD, 347–375

2. Either/Or: UD, 203–208

3. Under the Spell of Good Intentions: WL, 91–95

4. The Greatest Danger: JP-III, 120,121; 178–179; JP-IV, 319–320

5. The Task: JP-II, 397–433; JP-III, 334–352; PH, 185

6. Against the Crowd: JP-III, 305–311

7. Suspending the Ethical: FT, 83–98

8. To Need God Is Perfection: EUD, 297–326

JP-III, 357; JP-IV, 232; JP-IV, 338–339; JP-IV, 478; J, 347; JP-I, 219–221; AC, 74–76; AC, 168; JP-I, 386–388; JP-I 244; JP-I 179; JP-III, 214–215; JP-I, 208–211

63. The Cross: JP-I, 148; J, 57; J, 63; J, 300; M, 65; M, 46; JP-I, 246; J, 78; JP-I, 124; JP-I, 127; J, 361

64. The Crowd: JP-II, 296; JP-II, 297; JP-II, 306–310; JP-II, 373; JP-II, 375–376; JP-II, 420–422; JP-II, 438; JP-III, 168; JP-III, 297–298; JP-III, 318; JP-III, 323–324; JP-III 325; JP-III, 333; JP-III, 338–339; JP-III, 339; JP-III, 350–351; JP-III, 488; JP-IV, 139; JP-IV, 141; JP-IV, 522–523; JP-IV, 160–161; JP-IV, 147–148; JP-III, 320–321; JP-IV, 540–541

65. Decisiveness: J, 20; J, 268; J, 366; EUD, 363; EUD, 349–350; EUD, 349; PH, 40; PH, 113; UD, 330; M, 31–32; PH, 199; CUP, vol. 1, 226; JP-I 174–175; JP-I 177; JP-IV, 508–509; JP-IV, 241; JP-I, 312; AC, X; P, 16; SLW, 114; AC, 81–82; JP-III, 550; EUD, 335; E/O, vol. II, 171–173

66. Doctrine and Theology: JP-I, 168; JP-I, 190–191; JP-I, 463; JP-III, 360; JP-III, 656; JP-I, 44; JP-III, 723–4; SK, 22; JP-III, 635; JP-IV, 21; JP-IV, 462; J, 9; JP-III, 639

67. Doubt and Skepticism: JP-I, 201; JP-I 359; JP-III, 346–347; JP-II, 368; JP-I, 359; JP-I, 99; JP-II, 536; JP-III, 533; JP-VI, 243–244; S/J, 70; CUP, 23–24; JP-I, 133–134; JP-II, 13–14; M, 113–114

68. The Eternal: JP-I, 131; JP-I, 447; JP-I, 448; JP-IV, 477; AC, 100; FT, 49; SD, 225, P, 37–38; JP-I, 415; JP-IV, 476–477; PH, 139; CUP, 173–177; CD, 212; AC, 248–249

69. Existence and the Existential: JP-I, 450; J, 57; JP-I, 452–453; JP-I, 460; JP-I, 467; JP-II, 420–422; JP-II, 537–538; JP-IV, 39; JP-IV, 275; J, 15–16; J, 219; JP-II, 164–166; WL, 88; CUP, 370; CUP, 380; CUP, 393; CUP, 454; CUP, 162–163; CUP, 348; CUP, 560; JP-IV, 347; JP-IV, 287–288; PA, 10; CUP, 281–282; CUP, 394; TD, 28

70. Faith and Reason: JP-III, 719–720; JP-III, 717; PC, 95–96; JP-IV, 513–514; JP-III, 663–664; JP-I, 366; FT, 20; JP-II, 25; JP-II, 335–336; JP-II, 534; JP-III, 665–666; JP-II, 89; JP-II, 21–22; JP-II, 315; JP-III, 196; JP-III, 198–199; JP-III, 591; J, 91; S/J, 18; UD, 218; EUD, 12; EUD, 19; PC, 141; JP-II, 408–409; JP-IV, 602; FT, 37; FT, 58–66; FT, 58–66; PC, 62–63

71. Following Jesus: JP-I, 123; JP-II, 317; JP-II, 322–323; JP-II, 350; JP-I, 162; JP-I, 420; JP-II, 323–324; JP-II, 335; JP-II, 338; JP-II, 340; JP-II, 367; JP-II, 471; CUP, 465; JP-III, 404; JP-VI, 558–559; JP-VI, 560; UD, 225–229; PC, 249; PC, 233; UD, 217; UD, 222; JP-IV, 570–571

72. Forgiveness: M, 65–66; JP-I, 24–25; JP-II, 45–46; JP-II, 45; JP-II, 46; JP-II, 46; JP-II, 49; JP-II, 50–52; JP-II, 52, JP-II, 53; JP-II, 126–127; WL, 273–278; JP-III, 63–64; JP-III, 70; UD, 246; UD, 247; EUD, 433; CD, 385; CD, 385–386; JP-II, 88; JP-II, 512; M, 130; CD, 297; J, 217;

73. Freedom: JP-II, 61–62; JP-II, 68; JP-II, 69; JP-II, 68–69; JP-II, 74; JP-II, 70–72; J, 454; J, 474; CA, 108; CA, 203; AC, 290; S/J 67; UD, 327; M, 164; JP-II, 58; CD, 187

74. God: JP-II, 113; JP-II, 114–116; JP-II, 118; JP-II, 138–139; JP-II, 117–118; JP-II, 155–156; JP-II, 304; JP-IV, 36; EUD, 393; S, 13–14; JP-II, 123; JP-II, 145; JP-II, 153; JP-IV, 293; SK, 11; CA, 160; EUD, 299; M, 147–148; M, 148; M, 147–148; CD, 197; SK, 49; JP-II, 101–102; JP-IV, 297–299

75. God's Love: JP-II, 132–133; J, 238; J, 394; J, 529; J, 535; CD, 132; CD, 379; CD, 288; J, 374–375; SK, 39–40; SK, 55; M, 61–62; J, 72; JP-VI, 40

76. Grace: JP-II, 175–176; JP-II, 176–177; JP-II, 134–137; JP-II, 334; JP-II, 359–350; JP-IV, 114; J, 482; M, 155–156; SK, 46; JP-II, 166

77. The Human Condition: FT, 41; PA, 6; JP-I, 393; JP-II, 110–111; JP-IV, 312–314; JP-IV, 334–335; JP-IV, 383–384; WL, 39; CA, 152; EUD, 18; JP-I, 437–438; J, 250; SLW, 217; J, 220; S, 14–15; JP-III, 716

78. The Individual: JP-I, 100; JP-II, 401–402; JP-II, 282; JP-II, 425; JP-II, 437; AC, 162–163; JP-III, 487–488; JP-III, 488–489; JP-III, 631; J, 370; CUP, 123 & 129–130; PH, 211; JP-IV, 248; JP-II, 280; JP-III, 361; WL 86–88; JP-I, 260–293

79. Inwardness and Subjectivity: JP-IV, 359–360; JP-I, 157–158; JP-IV, 346; JP-IV, 354; CUP, 52–53 & 57; CUP, 73; CUP, 91–92 J, 17; CUP, 46–47; CUP, 54; JP-IV, 36; JP-III, 50; JP-III, 517;

80. Love: JP-I, 128; JP-I, 394; JP-I, 394–395; JP-II, 316–317; JP-III, 40–41; JP-III, 47; JP-I, 413; WL, 47; WL, 105–106; JP-III, 46; WL, 175; WL, 273–278; WL, 175–177; WL, 110–111; WL, 248–249; WL, 172–173; WL, 252; JP-VI, 313; CUP, vol. I, 396; JP-III, 267; JP-IV, 395; S, 12; M, 52; UD, 55–57

81. Obedience: JP-II, 74–75; JP-I, 315; JP-III, 267–268; JP-III, 277; JP-III, 283; JP-III, 273–274; EUD, 369; JP-III, 680; M, 163

82. Passion: JP-I, 340; JP-IV, 282; JP-IV, 251–252; JP-VI, 549–550; J, 342; AC, 185–186; PA, 8–11; PA, 60; CUP, 35–36; JP-III, 699–700; CUP, 311–312; CUP, 350–351; PC, 190; FT, 145–146; JP-I, 380–381; JP-II, 18; CUP, 322; S, 19; CUP, 230

83. Politics and the State: JP-IV, 194–195; JP-III, 200; JP-III, 200; JP-III, 200; JP-IV, 200; JP-IV, 189; JP-IV, 203; AC, 139–140; JP-IV, 203; JP-IV, 479

84. Prayer: J, 154; PH, 51; JP-II, 403–405; EUD, 383; JP-III, 547; EUD, 43; CUP, 446; JP-IV, 274; J, 124; SK, 37–38; J, 250; EUD, 394; CD, 323; EUD, 427; EUD, 442; EUD, 79; M, 150

85. Preaching and Proclamation: JP-I, 275–276; JP-I, 285–287; JP-II, 371–372; JP-III, 601; JP-III, 602; JP-III, 607; JP-III, 606; JP-III, 607; JP-III, 617; JP-III, 620–622; S/J, 10–11; PC, 107; JP-I, 204–205; PC, 234–235; JP-VI, 189; JP-I, 309; JP-III, 221–222; JP-III, 586; JP-III, 601; JP-III, 619–620; JP-IV, 177; AC, 172–173; AC, 181; JP-III, 452–453; AC, 139–141; AC, 268–270; JP-III, 453; JP-I, 154

86. Purity: TD, 31; JP-IV, 288; PH, 176–177; JP-IV, 288–289; PH, 184; PH, 201–202; PH, 203; PH, 31–32; WL, 294; PH, 60; JP-III 346; JP-I, 215

87. Repentance: JP-III, 761; JP-III, 761; JP-IV, 258; JP-IV, 116; JP-III, 199; JP-II, 455; JP-III, 550; JP-IV, 194; M, 138–139; M, 151; PH, 152; WL, 155; PH, 50–51; CD, 201; PC, 110; TD, 18; SK, 50; JP-VI, 452; JP-III, 549–550; M, 134; M, 139

88. Sacrifice and Self-Denial: JP-I, 154; JP-IV, 4; UD, 223; UD, 224; JP-I, 219; JP-VI, 457–458; JP-IV, 157; JP-I, 331–332; M, 39; JP-II, 119–120; JP-II, 281; JP-III, 59–60; UD, 218

89. Silence and Solitude: JP-II, 408; PH, 108; JP-IV, 225; J, 538; S/J, 47–48; S/J, 49–50; PA, 49; M, 59; CD, 323; PH, 62; PH, 218; PA, 82; PA, 82–85

90. Sin: JP-IV, 101; JP-I, 129–130; JP-I, 130; JP-IV, 101; PC, 68; JP-I, 179; JP-IV, 106; JP-IV, 106; JP-IV, 108; JP-IV, 118; JP-IV, 350; CA, 15; CA, 119; S/J, 66; M, 159–160; JP-I, 405; JP-IV, 119; JP-IV, 238; JP-IV, 238–239; CUP, 420; M, 49; JP-III, 111; JP-III, 684; J, 37; SD, 82

91. Spiritual Trial: JP-II, 125–126; M, 60–61; JP-II, 454; JP-II, 455; JP-IV, 110; CA, 174; JP-IV, 257; JP-IV, 315; JP-IV, 34; CA, 174–175; CD, 293; EUD, 31; M, 37–38

92. Suffering: JP-II, 41; JP-II, 41–42; JP-III, 212; JP-IV, 376; JP-IV, 388; JP-IV, 394; JP-IV, 426–427; JP-IV, 427–428; JP-IV, 465; JP-IV, 460; JP-IV, 378; JP-IV, 417; M, 47; JP-IV, 550; JP-VI, 436; J, 473; UD, 252; PC, 108; JP-II, 493; SK, 34

93. Tribulation and Persecution: JP-I, 194–195; JP-I, 198–199; JP-II, 306–310; JP-II, 328; JP-II, 444–446; JP-IV, 373–374; JP-II, 498; JP-IV, 375; SK, 23; WL, 93; WL, 188; WL, 187 & 191; JP-I, 249; JP-IV, 591–592;

94. Truth: JP-III, 609; JP-IV, 364–365; JP-IV, 496; JP-IV, 502–503; JP-IV, 503; JP-IV, 503; J, 274; CUP, 106; CUP, 252–253; JP-I, 73; J, 542–543

95. Venturing and Risk: JP-III, 535–536; JP-III, 538–540; JP-III, 542; JP-IV, 535; JP-IV, 543–544; J, 381; EUD, 382; M, 123–124; CUP, 149; AC, 180; AC, 191; M, 124

96. Witness: JP-I, 163; JP-I, 250–251; JP-II, 498; JP-II, 602; JP-II, 494; JP-II, 703; JP-IV, 558–559; JP-IV, 561; AC, 7; AC, 97; JP-III, 389–390; E/O, vol. I, 30; WL, 191; JP-III, 150; JP-I, 474–475; JP-I, 190; JP-III, 97–99; JP-III, 158–159; JP-III, 159–160; M, 30; JP-I, 208

97. Works: JP-I, 428–429; JP-II, 19; JP-II, 10; JP-IV, 335; S/J, 16–17; CUP, 135; JP-IV, 253; EUD, 282; JP-III, 548

98. Worship: JP-I, 9; JP-II, 127; JP-II, 152–253; JP-II, 190–191; JP-III, 51–52; JP-IV, 525; JP-IV, 526; JP-IV, 602–603; JP-VI, 6; J, 358–359; CD, 137; JP-III, 390–392; JP-III, 583; M, 55; CD, 276–281; CD< 276–281; AC, 219; TD, 30

Kierkegaard's Writings:
An Annotated Bibliography

Christian Discourses: The Crisis and a Crisis in the Life of an Actress, ed. and trans. Howard V. Hong and Edna H. Hong. Princeton University Press, 1992. A collection of discourses on anxiety, suffering, and temptation.

The Concept of Anxiety, trans. Reidar Thomte in collaboration with Albert B. Anderson. Princeton University Press, 1980. A tough-going book that deals psychologically with the human condition and sin in terms of anxiety.

Concluding Unscientific Postscript, ed. and trans. Howard V. Hong and Edna H. Hong. Princeton University Press, 1989. An attack on Hegel with an in-depth treatment on the themes of subjectivity, truth, paradox, faith, and how Christianity differs from the religious sphere in general. Difficult and more philosophical.

Eighteen Upbuilding Discourses, ed. and trans. Howard V. Hong and Edna H. Hong. Princeton University Press, 1990. Kierkegaard's early religious discourses on love, God's goodness, the expectancy of faith, and related themes.

Either/Or, abridged & trans. By Alastair Hannay. London: Penguin Books, 1992. A comparison between the aesthetic and ethical life with the recognition that neither are satisfactory. Literary in nature and an example of Kierkegaard's indirect method.

Fear and Trembling. Trans. Alastair Hannay. London: Penguin Books, 1985. A reflection on Abraham as an example of faith and how the religious sphere of existence transcends the ethical. Shorter and very readable.

For Self-Examination and *Judge for Yourself*, trans. Howard V. Hong and Edna H. Hong. Princeton University Press, 1990. A collection of discourses that contain some of Kierkegaard's best-known parables and stories.

Søren Kierkegaard's Journals and Papers, ed. and trans. Howard V. Hong and Edna H. Hong. 7 volumes. Princeton University Press, 1967–1978. Topically and alphabetically arranged, this is the most complete collection in English of Kierkegaard's journal writings. Very readable.

Kierkegaard's Attack Upon "Christendom" 1854-1855, trans., with introduction, Walter Lowrie. Princeton University Press, 1944. A collection of short essays in which Kierkegaard directly attacks the Danish Church and Christendom in general. Spirited and impassioned.

Papers and Journals: A Selection (Penguin Classics), trans. Alastair Hannay. Reprint edition. London: Penguin Books, 1996. A shorter but very readable selection of Kierkegaard's journal writings. Highly recommended.

Philosophical Fragments and *Johannes Climacus*, trans. Howard V. Hong and Edna H. Hong. Princeton University Press, 1985. An argument against the idea of "innate truth" and the Christian solution of the incarnation – the eternal entering time. Difficult but extremely significant.

The Point of View of My Work as an Author: A Report to History and Related Writings, trans. Walter Lowrie, newly edited with a preface by Benjamin Nelson: Harper & Row, 1962. Outlines the meaning of Kierkegaard's method as an author and the relationship between his various works.

Practice in Christianity, trans. Howard V. Hong and Edna H. Hong. Princeton University Press, 1991. A more direct attack against established Christianity with special emphases on faith, in contrast to reason, and on following Christ, not just admiring him.

Purity of Heart is to Will One Thing, trans. & intro. Douglas V. Steere. Harper Torchbooks. The Cloister Library. New York: Harper & Row, 1956. A marvelous meditation on purity of heart with special attention given to excuses and evasions.

The Sickness Unto Death, trans. & intro. by Alastair Hannay. London: Penguin Books, 1989. A profound exploration of the human condition and of sin in terms of despair. Not an easy read, but extremely illuminating.

Stages on Life's Way: Studies by Various Persons, trans. Howard V. Hong and Edna H. Hong. Princeton University Press, 1989. Similar to *Either/Or*, but with a full length discussion on religious sphere of existence. An example of Kierkegaard's indirect method.

Two Ages: The Age of Revolution and the Present Age: A Literary Review, trans. Howard V. Hong and Edna H. Hong. Princeton University Press, 1978. A prophetic discussion on the herd mentality of the modern era.

Upbuilding Discourse in Various Spirits, ed. and trans. Howard V. Hong and Edna H. Hong. Princeton University Press, 1993. One of the best places to start in trying to understand the heart of Kierkegaard. Includes themes such as purity of heart, the lilies of the field, and the school of suffering.

Works of Love: Some Christian Reflections in the Form of Discourses, trans. Howard and Edna Hong, preface R. Gregor Smith. Harper Torchbooks, The Cloister Library. New York: Harper & Row, 1962. Addresses the nature of Christian love. Very readable.

Other Titles from Plough

The Gospel in Dostoyevsky
Fyodor Dostoyevsky

Walk in the Light
and Twenty-Three Tales
Leo Tolstoy

The Early Christians
In Their Own Words
Eberhard Arnold

InnerLand
A Guide into the Heart of the Gospel
Eberhard Arnold

The Violence of Love
Oscar Romero

Seeking Peace
Notes & Conversations Along the Way
Johann Christoph Arnold

Action in Waiting
Christoph Blumhardt

To order or request a free catalog, call
1-800-521-8011 / 724-329-1100 (US)
or 0800 269 048 / +44 (0) 1580 88 33 44 (UK)